The German Car Industry
My Part in its Victory

Nat.

The German Car Industry
My Part in its Victory

E30's E28i, W124s, 911's and all sorts of other German machinery. I know you will appreciate it.

James Ruppert

James.

F◉RESIGHT
PUBLICATIONS

First published in 2011 by Foresight Publications, part of Action Automotive Limited.

More information at
www.jamesruppert.com • www.bangernomics.com • www.foresightpublications.com

A CIP catalogue record for this book is available from the British Library

ISBN 978-09559529-3-7

Contents

Foreword

by Kenny Everett (1944–1995)

The funniest man ever on radio, TV, and a serial BMW owner

Here are a few words from Kenny Everett which now seem very appropriate. He bought all his BMWs from Park Lane, but not from me, it was another salesman with a very similar name. Back in the late '80s I had become a car journalist and writer. After doing quite well with *Dealing with Car Dealers*, how appropriate, I was asked to write a series of books for Haynes Publications (the Manual people). These were meant to focus on a particular marque (Jaguar, Vauxhall and BMW), but in a light, approachable and amusing manner. So a bit of history, lots of pictures, funny stories, fascinating facts and ideally with an introduction by a famous person.

That's where Kenny came in. If you don't know anything about him he was not just the best DJ, he was the funniest bloke in 1980s with the best TV programme, *The Kenny Everett Video Show*.

I had been told that he was an absolutely top bloke and very much in 'Cuddly Ken' character whenever he came to the showroom. I approached him entirely independently through Capital Radio. I walked up to the Euston Tower headquarters of the station and left a note along with a yellow plastic Beetle-shaped digital watch that I thought might amuse him and a promise to give £100 to the charity of his choice. Very graciously he agreed and wrote this brilliant letter.

Dear James,

Herewith...

If Jesus Christ suddenly appeared in my living room and said "Dear Ken, Lay down all your worldly goods and follow me" I'd say "Gosh, I'd love to, but can't I keep my BMW?" I think he'd dissaprove, even though I'd be able to follow him a lot faster in my 325i.

It's been about twenty years since I bought my first car, which I got from Jack Barclay of Barclay Square. It's probably the poshest car showroom in London's West End, brimming with Rolls Royces and Ferrari's. I must have been a great embarrassment to them, as I ordered them to get me a Fiat 850. It was a sweet little tin thing with a washing machine motor for an engine and I loved it dearly. But two years later, my life took a great upward turn as, flushed with cash from my wages as a Radio One DJ, I purchased my first BMW. Life suddenly became worth living. I've had nine other BM's since, and nothing on Earth would induce me to change brands.

They are to me, the most perfect object ever made. Superb craftsmanship, brilliantly engineered, incredibly reliable and remarkably understated.

If Jesus Christ ever did decide to arrive in my living room, He'd probably arrive in a BMW!

Hope this'll do, All the best,

Introduction – Life in the Park Lane

A fellow salesman drove to the entrance of Cooper Park Lane's underground car park in Reeves Mews W1 in a part exchange Lancia Delta and screeched to a halt. He wound down the window and tugged at the dashboard. It moved towards him and dropped onto his lap and he said, "Is it any wonder people buy BMWs?"

With that, the yellow barrier went up and the Lancia disappeared down into the darkness of the lower levels of the garage. For me it still is the most profound rhetorical question ever posed, but then I don't get out much. At the time some people certainly did question why car buyers would pay so much and seemingly get so little for their money. What no radio? Floor mats extra? Well those were the profitable little items which made car salesmen and their employers considerably richer. German cars were so very good they didn't need to throw in loads of extras to get customers interested. Buyers were prepared to invest in the upmarket image that the German cars conveyed and the level of quality and finish that had long since ceased to be an important ingredient of British built cars.

German cars were not just beautifully finished and unlikely to break down, they were very different from what was being offered by any other manufacturer in any other country. At the end of each chapter I have attempted to round up the closest rivals to what was being offered at the time and make facetious comments. Technologically German cars led the way when it came to handling, innovation and safety. Despite the traditionally British speciality in making sports cars, something shared with certain Italian marques, it was the Germans who took fast cars to a whole new, well built and occasionally insane level.

The point of this book is to explain just how the German car industry got to the 1980s and what they did once they got there. It's all about the cars more than chairman, investments, shares, takeovers and company politics. Rather than get bogged down in too many sales figures hopefully I will convey how one model led to another and what its effect was. There will be some numbers relating to mphs and bhps and usually the bigger they are the faster it went. Oh yes, and also some smaller numbers are better too, so 0–60 mph times come into it, even if as a measure of true performance this hardly tells the whole story. It will have to do. Another popular figure during the '80s was Cd. Not the hugely popular shiny silver music storage and delivery device that replaced the bleak black plastic disc. No this was all to do with aerodyanmics. Cd stands for drag coefficient and the lower the number the lower the wind resistance making the car faster and also more fuel-efficient. Don't worry, all this will become a lot clearer.

This is also slightly a story about how I came to be selling BMWs and what I saw and did to bring about the victory of the German car industry. But just in case you find the personal stuff too personal, indulgent and boring I have helpfully put it in *italic print*. Having said that, I know that some readers of *The British Car Industry Our Part in its Downfall* actually preferred the personal stuff and skipped past all the car industry nonsense to find out what my Dad bought next, or where the next breakdown happened. So I hope that helps. Just in case you wondered how that will all work here's a whole chunk of personal paragraph nonsense.

So what exactly qualified me to become a car salesman? Nothing at all. It was just me having a crack at all the most despised careers in the world. So far I have managed to chalk up stints in banking, lawyering, advertising and journalism, whilst carefully avoiding estate agency and politics.

Back in the late '70s after sixth form college I had a gap year, which I filled in the more traditional manner which meant a real job rather than poncing around the world subsidised by over-indulgent parents. So I took the underground train to the City every day and clocked on at Johnson Matthey Bankers in their bullion department. Although technically I was an apprentice banker, it wasn't all baffling abstract concepts such as derivatives, hedges and leveraged buyouts. Instead I dealt with real understandable precious metals, Krugerrands, gold bars and Sovereigns. So it had a more tangible Italian Job *dimension. It allowed me to daydream at just how the Mafia would go about pinching their gold stuff back in green, white and red Fiat Pandas, perfect for the narrow City streets. However, Gli Inglesi Di Lavoro never did get made, so I remained a banker, until that is I became a lawyer.*

My parents' generation had a hard time. From mass unemployment in the 1930s to world war, not forgetting conscription and rationing, it was tough life. Working class people were lucky to have a trade to fall back on and for the Rupperts it was either an East London cigarette factory or the docks. Not surprisingly they wanted their children to not just work hard, but preferably to work smart in a much softer environment. No hobnail boots, overalls and cloth caps, but a suit and a proper profession, ideally as a doctor, lawyer, or accountant. I had already royally mucked up my chances by failing my 11 plus and ending up in Secondary Modern. There was nothing wrong with doing metal work, but it wouldn't exactly fast track me to brain surgery at medical school.

Banking it was then. I really should have stuck it out, but I still believed well into my twenties that if I didn't quite measure up to George Best on the football field, there were always my Jimi Hendrix-like guitar skills to fall back on. Then again I could always try something else which is how I found myself back at school. If only I'd realised how boring and pointless it was going to be training to be a lawyer. Unfortunately I had Hendrix's head for the finer points of the Unfair Contract Terms Act 1973 and George Best's feet for the complex issues surrounding Constructive Trusts and Proprietary Estoppel. At least I could put LL.B. Hons after my name, so it wasn't a complete waste of time, but it also wasn't much help when it came to selling cars

Dad failed to see the positive implications of this sudden career change. Mum was happy, if I was happy. However, I didn't realise that I was embarking on an adventure that would influence the direction I would take for the rest of my life.

So I have taken this opportunity to write down some of what happened and wrap it all up in another book with a title that pays homage, or perhaps rips off, yet another Spike Milligan memoir. This has been written because one day my grandchildren, as part of a school project, may just want to ask their Poppa exactly what he did in the 1980s. For some it may have been manning barricades as miners and policeman fought hand to hand around the Nottinghamshire coalfields. Then again, others simply applied industrial amounts of eyeliner and hairspray and then proceeded to prance around to Spandau Ballet's 'Through the Barricades'. I was with the bunch who reckoned that greed was good and enjoyed some '80s Electro Funk on the Blaupunkt radio/cassette whilst on my way to take a Sloane Ranger for a test drive before getting a non-returnable deposit on a Henna Red 323i.

I didn't mind being called 'Jimmy Spandau' by the other salesmen, on account of my hair being rather lively on top. Actually I was rather closer in spirit and ability to Kirk Brandon, the guitarist out of Spear of Destiny. I also didn't mind that if in the heavy West End traffic around Marble Arch or crossing over Oxford Street I might feel a gentle nudge from the rear. That was just one of my sales rivals reminding me where they were in the traffic and so long as it was behind, I certainly didn't mind. Of course they could always suggest that I wasn't in complete control because if ever I drove with any of them I would find my BMW slowing down on account of them applying the handbrake or flicking the gear lever into neutral. I also knew that when I was walking towards the underground car park I could always rely on any one of them to execute a huge attention seeking handbrake turn to leave them perfectly positioned in front of the entrance.

There are no names mentioned as although I am still in touch with several of my old car sales mates, I thought it might complicate matters to get too personal. However, I've included some sales figures to cover my time in the '80s car business which proves just how profitable it was. No company secrets are being revealed (the stats are over 25 years old) and it is just my own figures and no one else's. If you check back to the beginning of this chapter you will find a graphic that details just how many and what types of cars I sold (zero by the way). It is essentially a year in the life of a West End car salesman. Just to confirm that it wasn't a numbers game but a profit one there is no mention of turnover. Also there is the demonstrator car I ran at the time, so pay attention to the picture, which will change, and the details mentioned in the text. Just for fun in this chapter there is a drawing of the MOT failed Austin Cooper I owned when I first applied for the job. Actually the picture makes it look a whole lot better and far more solid than it really was, but that's artistic licence for you.

I am only sorry now that I didn't take loads of pictures of the cars I sold, the people I sold to and some of things I found in the back of part-exchanged vehicles. There is a record of all my used car sales, but no model breakdown unfortunately. Used sales were a bonus but not regarded as a priority as the showroom was not set up for it because there was no storage or display space. Used cars were treated as a unit and not broken down into models by the company, or by me. I just wanted to get on with the business of selling cars and finished in second place overall for used sales in my first year.

Quite clearly then this book isn't a serious model by model critique with sectional pictures of every vehicle mentioned, plus year on year sales figures and technical specs. Now there may be more detail on BMWs compared to the other marques but that's because I'm biased. It may have helped if I'd sold Porsche, Mercedes and Audis in the '80s but I didn't and it doesn't actually matter. I would like to point out that I do like, though not love, Germany very much. I've been there more times than any other country. It's clean, tidy and the people speak very good English. Better than us mostly. When it came to building cars they were better than anyone, especially in the '80s.

Now, the 1980s was a fascinating time socially, politically and musically because it was the last decade to have any consistently decent pop music in it. Mostly though the 1980s is when German cars didn't just come good, they were undoubtedly the best cars on the planet. Their industry had been building up to it since the late 1940s. They consolidated throughout the 1950s innovated in the 1960s, got their products right in the 1970s and arguably the marketing spot on in the 1980s. The reason why buyers may still want an Audi, BMW, Mercedes, Porsche or a Volkswagen in the future is because of what happened in the 1980s. That's when the German car came of age and I was lucky enough to be there.

This is sort of how it happened.

Oh yes and just in case you wondered, I will mention the war.

On the cassette deck ...

 There will be brief reviews of the cassettes that I owned and played in '80s German cars at the time. These have not be edited to save me embarrassment as my quality control dipped a bit when I did go a bit mainstream with some of my selections. Having been a hardcore muso ever since I didn't buy K-Tel's 20 Golden Greats and came home with 'Killer' by Alice Cooper, my excuse would be that I was trying to identify with my customers. Because if I understood their musical tastes better (Sade), then I would find it easier to make a sale. It seemed to work and I still have the cassettes to prove it. The '80s is wrongly regarded as the CD era; well for cars, the technology of the bright silver disc did not really become more commonplace until the later '80s and '90s. Until then it was all press play, forward and rewind, but at least we listened to the whole album rather than jumping between tracks. Those were the musical, autoreverse, days.

Thanks to everyone (except Dick) I worked with at Park Lane 1983 to 1985 which includes Dee, but not Olivia who hopefully will never have to. Matthew Tumbridge at *Used Car Expert* for reading the early drafts and regretting being born 20 years too late to enjoy it all.

Pictures: Front cover, me in 1985 outside the Park Lane showroom. One of many taken by Dee Gill as she then was for the rear cover of my first book. *Dealing with Car Dealers*. Not used then, very useful now. Rear cover recreates part of my untidy desk at Park Lane with genuine '80s emphemera.

Acknowledgements: I did look at all the books I wrote during the 1980s and that includes the *BMW Driver's Book*, the *Jaguar Driver's Book* and the *Vauxhall Driver's Book*, all very much out of print now. I also re-read my own *VW Golf: The Complete Story*. James Taylor's superb Collector's Guides: *Mercedes-Benz since 1945*, *Volume 2 The 1960s*, *Volume 3 The 1970s*, *Volume 4 The 1980s*.

BMW 5 Series: The Complete Story also by James Taylor. The *Collector's Guides* to the Porsche 924 and 911, and two volumes of the Porsche 911 and derivatives by Michael Cotton. Also Chris Rees' *BMW M-Series Collector's Guide* is very good too. *Car Wars* by Jonathan Mantle is wonderful with some superb anecdotes. All the *A to Z of Cars* series form the 1920s onwards. Graham Robson's books on BMWs and everything he's written on Fords and Austins and really there are hundreds. I have also referred to all the editions of *Car* and *Supercar Classics* magazines I wrote for between 1987 and 2006. Plus my extensive collections of *Autocar*, *Motor*, *Car Mechanics*, *Custom Car*, *Bike*. All pictures are copyright the manufacturers, or suppliers or TV companies or me. I did have access to both BMW's archives and Volkswagen's when I wrote books in the '80s and '90s, plus it was very useful to have a Dad who did work at Motor Shows from the 1960s on and got me all sorts of pictures and brochures. However, if you suspect that any images belong to any other copyright holders please get in contact.

Dedicated to almost everyone (no, not you Dick) who worked at Park Lane in the 1980s and without whom most of this would not have been possible. Oh and car salesmen and women everywhere.

Just in case you wondered, James Ruppert wrote for *Car Magazine*, still writes for the world's oldest car magazine *Autocar*, the *Independent on Sunday* and over the years has written about cars for *The Sunday Times*, the *Evening Standard*, *Tatler*, *Woman's Own* and *MSN Cars*. Oh yes, he's also on the web at MSN Cars, was a founder of 4Car, runs the award winning Bangernomics.com website and blogs away at Autocar.co.uk. On telly, he's been on *Ride On*, *Driven* and produced *Deals on Wheels* for Channel 4. He's also presented ITV 2's *Dealer's Choice* and been on BBC2's *Celebrity Relics*. He's also appeared on loads of radio shows and once made James Naughtie laugh (rather than swear) on Radio 4's *The Today Programme*.

1 Don't mention the Wars

Germans invent the Car Industry, it gets blown up, then they have to invent it all over again. A very brief history of the German firms that made their industry great.

January • New Car Profit: £0 • Used Car Profit: £0 • Total £0

"You'll be walking home tonight."

That's not what you want to hear when your job is selling cars. To be fair I had just resigned, but I wasn't off to flog motors anywhere else. I was just happy to work my notice, earn a month's worth of commission and ideally drive my, sorry the company's BMW 5 Series a bit longer whilst I decided what to do next. The sales director had other ideas. Dick by name and a dick by nature, he was determined to make an example and turf me out of the showroom. I was effectively dishonourably discharged, but instead of snapping my sword in half, Dick stamped on my Parker pen and Casio calculator. Rather than rip off my epaulettes he trimmed my bright blue silk tie to the knot with scissors. Then the Glass's Trade Price Guide was torn from my trembling hands.

Actually none of that happened, but apart from telling me to walk home, which was all too true, and then smirking, it was a disappointingly downbeat end to what had been a very exciting job. My career in the motor trade was over, not quite two years after it had begun. I was walking away from what is the best proper job I've ever had. I would have to start all over again, a bit like the German car industry.

Now I wasn't around in 1945, but then neither was the German car industry. If you haven't read *The British Car Industry: Our Part In Its Downfall*, then you won't know that Volkswagen hadn't actually built a Beetle for all the people who saved up stamps in the 1930s to buy them and it was only when the British Army arrived that production actually started. So I'd recommend you go away and read that critically acclaimed book for a more detailed insight into how the British car industry failed to realise the significance of building a basic but tough car that could be exported and manufactured all around the world. A modest but highly organised Major in the Royal Engineers, Ivan Hirst, clearly saw the potential; no one else, least of all Sir Billy Rootes, did. He led a British delegation to look at VW and turned up his nose at what he thought was a ridiculous vehicle. If upstarts Volkswagen weren't given much hope of survival, what about the true automotive aristocracy such as Mercedes, BMW and Auto Union?

King of the car markers has always been Mercedes-Benz. Their history is rich and complex and the holding company's name, Daimler-Benz AG, is an amalgamation of the two firms that created the motorcar and indeed the whole industry. So as not to confuse stupid people like me, throughout this book I will mostly refer to them simply as Mercedes.

It's 1886 and the car is officially born. On the left is the Benz 'Patent Motor Wagen' and on the right is Daimler's, who installed his engine into a carriage instead of attaching a horse.

Karl Benz was the first to recognise that there was a business in replacing a horse with an engine and set up a production facility to prove it. The 'Motor Wagen' was his big idea and he rolled out the first car, a three-wheeler in 1886. Meanwhile Gottlieb Daimler had been working intensely on internal combustion engines producing the first unit to run on petrol in 1883 followed two years later by a personal transportation machine with one in the middle. Benz was clearly tempting ridicule (especially if he'd called it the Benz Robin) if his vehicle went wrong, but incredibly Daimler bravely went with one wheel less than Benz's car. Yes here was the world's first motorcycle and the very last time that Daimler ever built a bike. With his chief designer Wilhelm Maybach they went on to build cars in the horseless carriage style, until that is a Mr Jellinek made some suggestions.

Already acting as a sort of upmarket sales executive, Emil Jellinek was selling Daimlers to his equally wealthy friends. In 1901 he persuaded its chief designer, Wilhelm Maybach to build what was probably the first sports car, but more important than that it was also the blueprint for the modern motorcar. Instead of simply being a cart with the horse missing it had a pressed steel, rather than a wooden, frame. Up front was an elegant radiator that had a honeycomb finish rather than crude pipes and a gear change using a metal gate so drivers would always slot it into the right place. There were engine innovations too and it was widely copied by all the other upstart motorcar makers, except significantly old Benz who much preferred steering his horseless carriage around.

From left to right: Gottlieb Daimler, Karl Benz and Mercedes Jellinek. That's how you build a brand, take two brilliant engineers and front their work with a posh girl's name.

This car was entered into a series races under the pseudonym Mercedes, after Jellinek's eldest daughter. Obviously it won the lot. So with Jellinek on board the company went racing with stunning success. Whilst others claimed the right to use the Daimler name in certain countries such as France and Austria and the USA, Jellinek found that his eldest daughter's name came in handy so the Mercedes car brand was born.

Daimler expanded rapidly and anything else that needed an engine including aircraft, airships, railcars, boats, lorries and buses were all badged Daimler. The cars though were Mercedes, which consistently won Grand Prix races until the

First World War stopped all that. The war may have kept the factories busy but afterwards Germany slipped into a serious economic decline and in a country where there were 86 motor manufacturers, mergers were inevitable. The most high profile one was the coming together of Mercedes and Benz. As other companies cut prices and quality to survive Mercedes-Benz decided to move in the other direction and stick by their principles. That's why the Mercedes three-pointed star was encircled by the Benz laurel wreath, to remind them of their long held traditions.

Mercedes-Benz built better cars than ever and became even more successful at racing, which soon became state sponsored. (See more on this in Chapter 11 Master Race). Apparently Hitler was a motor racing fan and the National Socialist Party was behind an annual prize for the best German racing car. In 1934 large subsidies were being given to Mercedes-Benz and Auto Union. Grand Prix groupie Hitler may not have realised it but there is a certain irony in that one of the major architects of Mercedes-Benz had a father who was a Rabbi in Leipzieg. Just as there were Jewish backers involved behind Ferdinand Porsche who was engineering Auto Unions. Clearly the pure 'master race' was something of a myth.

When war on the track turned into World War Mercedes-Benz built aero engines that were not as good as the Rolls Royce ones (and neither were the pilots), hence the result of the Battle of Britain. That's the whole 1939–45 thing dealt with then.

In the aftermath of the conflict three-quarters of the factories had been destroyed and nothing actually worked in terms of communications or power; the company nonetheless mustered enough energy to issue the following statement, "Daimler-Benz has ceased to exist."

They were wrong, or at least they were being rather melodramatic in an attempt to deflect attention elsewhere while they regrouped. Like many other ruined factories in Germany they began by repairing vehicles and moved on from there. The biggest help to recovery was currency reform in 1948, which led a year later to some new old vehicles. Diesel engines were revived and their excellent economy came in handy when resources were so scarce. In this way Mercedes-Benz began their enduring relationship with the taxi drivers of the world by making cars that were strong, well finished, durable and had easy clean wipe down seats. Mercedes were not just back; it was as if they had never really been away. BMW though would have a much tougher time, not least because they were one of the smaller scale manufacturers. Although the moniker BMW did not come into being until the mid 1920s it is possible to trace their ancestors back to the dawn of motoring in 1896 and the rather less charismatic name of Wartburg. It was the name of a castle above the town of Eisenach in eastern Germany. Wartburg is a singularly ugly name and they made less than pretty munitions wagons and bicycles, moving on to cars in 1898. These were rebadged as French Decauville cars in the horseless carriage style. Like other early vehicle builders they went racing with a fair amount of success and built Dixi branded models to their own design. However, the company was taken over by Gothaer Waggonfabrik AG, who did pretty much what their name suggested and that included making railway coaches, but also military aircraft. They should have stuck to the railways because making aircraft after the First World War was a difficult business to be in. Impossible actually as Germany wasn't allowed to have an air force. Sales slumped and it was left to one of the investors, Jacob Shapiro, to sort it out. He liked what he saw was happening in England and got in touch directly with Sir Herbert Austin about the smallest car in his range, the Seven.

BMW had to start somewhere and that was with a tiny British car. A rebadged Austin 7, BMW did engineer some changes and even put the tools on a little tray in the boot.

So mass production came to Germany in 1927 with the Austin Seven, though the first hundred came from Blighty in right-hand drive with Dixi radiators, which was the point at which BMW came into the picture. They liked the Dixi and the Eisenach works so much that they bought the company.

BMW was incorporated in 1916 and initially built aircraft engines under contract and then went on to design power units of its own, hence the badge that has caused countless company car park arguments and envious backbiting. The famous roundel design represents the rotating blades of an aircraft which are then frozen, painted blue and white (the state colours of Bavaria) and topped off with the company's initials. It now adorns millions of bonnets and boot lids, but back in the early days they made engines for all sorts of industrial and commercial applications. One was used by a sister company in a motorcycle and BMW being BMW (the Bayerische Motoren Werke) reckoned that they could do far better. Their R32 in 1922 was a giant leap forward in motorcycle design because instead of using a crude chain to take power to the rear wheels, they used a rather more elegant solid metal shaft. BMWs proved themselves in competition and grew steadily. So when they took over the Dixi Automobil Werke in 1928 they also acquired the licence to build the Austin Seven and with it take a large slice of the German small car market.

BMW were not impressed by the level of engineering in the Austin Seven, redesigning significant parts before pulling out of the agreement to build the car. Sixty years later BMW were just as nonplussed when they took over Rover (which included the Austin marque), being very embarrassed by the dated Austin Metro. They were compelled to cancel what was effectively a coffin on wheels according to crash test results.

So BMW had high standards and they continued to take racing seriously, for both bikes and cars. Steadily BMWs became bigger, more powerful and quite beautiful, and the company was slowly irritating Mercedes until the war got in the way. Well actually it was boom time with the Munich and Berlin plants making aero engines whilst Eisenach made military vehicles. However, powering the Focke Wulf Fw 190 and also producing jet engines was not going to help matters when the war finished. The allies wanted their cut as war reparations and in *The British Car Industry: Our Part In Its Downfall* I detailed just how BMW designs helped kick-start production of both Bristol and Jaguar cars. In all, more than 15 countries took some piece of BMW, though by far the biggest part was lost behind the Iron Curtain.

With the Eisenach factory in Russian hands it was the first to reproduce pre-war BMWs. And although the right to use the BMW name reverted to the West all the East Germans did was call the cars EMWs (Eisenach Motoren Werke) and paint the blue part of the roundel Commie red. Eventually though they went back to the Wartburg name and produced cars that were ugly, slow and smelly and not remotely BMW like at all. Indeed, it did seem for a while that there would never be a BMW badge on anything remotely car like ever again.

BMW had to restart somewhere. This time it was a tiny Italian car, the Isetta.

In the west BMW did not have much going for it apart from the determin-ation of ex-workers to do something. At the Munich plant they managed to find lots of aluminium lying around and put it to half decent use initially making pots and pans. Sadly there is no information as to whether they cooked any faster than rival kitchen implements, or could be described as the 'ultimate kitchen utensils'. However, BMW followed up kitchenware with bicycles and inevitably motorcy-cles. That was good, but again they were being distracted by what Mercedes were up to and decided that they would rather build big impressive cars than the cheap small ones that buyers actually wanted. This was especially true as motorbike buyers were now sick and tired of getting cold and damp and a sidecar just wouldn't do, they wanted a proper car. What they actually got was a Bubble on wheels.

BMW had now reached their lowest point as they looked to Italy for inspir-ation. Not Ferrari, or Fiat, but a company called Iso and their tiny Isetta which had two wheels at the front and curiously two more wheels positioned almost right next to each other at the back. Say hello to the bubble car phenomenon that briefly bankrolled BMW until they came up with a better idea, so for the time being BMW were treading bubbly water.

Then there was Auto Union. The four rings of their badge symbolised the German automotive brands of Audi, Horch, DKW and Wanderer, which were combined under the umbrella of Auto Union in 1932. In the beginning there was August Horch who was one of the early pioneers of motoring. Before setting up business on his own, he worked for Carl Benz in Mannheim for three years as head of automobile production. August Horch & Cie was founded on November 14, 1899 in Cologne and built its first car in 1901. In 1904, the company relocated to Zwickau. However, in 1909 August Horch was forced out of the company he had founded, and set up a new enterprise also in Zwickau in 1909.

Unable to use Horch again, he translated his name, which means, "hark!" "listen!", into Latin, hence Audi. It commenced operations under the name Audi Automobilwerke GmbH, Zwickau, in 1910. He built a range of high quality models that excelled in motor sport. However, a post-war rethink by Audi's Technical Director coincided with Horch's departure in 1920. The cars were well built, but expensive and complicated to build. In 1928 AUDI Werke AG was acquired by JS Rasmussen, the head of the DKW Empire famous for its motorcycles. Essentially Audi was dumbed down to develop simpler and cheaper cars. Indeed, Rasmussen gave a brief to designers to build a small car powered by a DKW motorcycle engine, front wheel drive and a wooden body – to be developed in just six weeks. Amazingly the brief was completed and the car went on to sell over 250,000, making the DKW Front Germany's most popular car at the time.

A whole load of badges that added up to Auto Union and later Audi.

Going for the mass market was the right thing to do as demand for cars in Europe increased rapidly. It was in this environment that Auto Union AG was created. In 1932 Audi, Horch and DKW joined forces to create the Auto Union. An agreement was also reached with Wanderer, for the takeover of its automobile division. Germany's second largest motor vehicle manufacturing group had been created. Auto Union expanded fourfold in size between 1932 and 1938. By 1938 Auto Union had 25% of the German car market, and DKW had become the world's largest manufacturer of motorcycles.

A crucial element of the Auto Union legend was their participation in, and it has to be said, domination of, motor sport. Each of the marques, which had come together under the Auto Union banner, had previously enjoyed some degree of competition success. Operating under the same Nazi sponsored racing programme as Mercedes-Benz they were able to build an enormously powerful 16-cylinder Auto Union racer – the world's first successful mid-engined racing car design.

At the opposite end of the of the Auto Union company spectrum was DKW and their small light cars which were responsible for about 80% of Auto Union's volume, and had 19% of the German car market in their own right. However the truly radical wind-tunnel tested and consequently streamlined DKW F9 and scheduled for a 1940 launch, would have been a serious challenger to the Volkswagen's 'People's Car'. Like the Beetle the DKW F9 never got to make much of an impact because the war got in the way.

Auto Union's involvement in hostilities led directly to the company being dissolved in 1945 and rather tellingly several works managers were executed. Some directors and executives did survive and made their way to Munich. The nearby town of Ingolstadt was the ideal location for a large parts store. Preparations were made to restart production, and the Bavarian State Bank agreed to make a loan. In 1949, the 'new' Auto Union GmbH was established meaning that the company had been completely transplanted from East to West Germany, and significantly it was the only automobile manufacturer to be successfully reborn in this way.

DKW rebuilt itself with a so-called rapid delivery van and the Meisterklasse F89 P saloon which looked a bit like a Beetle.

The first product of the new company, befitting the 'back to basics' nature of the post-war German economy, was the DKW F89 L delivery van. The all-new Auto Union was substantially different to the old company as the up market Horch and middle market Wanderer were no more and the distinctive Audi brand was in a deep slumber. Yes the public face of Auto Union was effectively the friendly mass market DKW. They even got to launch their own Beetle as blueprints of the pre-war car had been cleverly smuggled from East Germany and parts were recreated, and the first cars came off the line in July 1950. There may have been no sign of the Audi marque just yet, although the Auto Union nameplate and the four rings logo made a comeback in 1957, but the only way had to be up.

As well as the German car companies, there were also a couple of American ones, not that one of the biggest started out as remotely transatlantic. Adam Opel was born in Russelsheim near Frankfurt in 1837. After training as a mechanic he went into the sewing machine business with great success. Then because his sons enjoyed cycling, as any decent dad would, he set up a company to build Opel bikes. When he died in 1895 both those products dominated their markets, so presumably he was a relatively happy man when he passed away. His family, though, refused to stand still. They could see the next big thing, and that was motoring. To this end they bought the rights to build a car called a Lutzmann with a spectacular lack of success. However, becoming the sole agent in Germany for the established French marque Darraq changed their fortunes. Opel dropped out of the sewing and cycling business and concentrated on cars and then went on to build trucks, trailers and aircraft engines. However after the First World War the French occupied Russelsheim and although things were bleak for a while they mass-produced a tree frog.

Laubfrosch, as it was called in German, was a small green car based on a Citroen that sold in large numbers and helped the company grow again. Opel linked up with General Motors who had an assembly plant in Berlin, which led to the Americans eventually buying a majority share. They introduced the concept of building a car as a complete body chassis unit with the Olympia, named in honour of the following year's Olympic Games which, because of Jesse Owens and the British 4 x 100 relay team, didn't go according to Hitler's master plan. Meanwhile the Opel Kadett sold by the showroom load, then came the war when General Motors gave up control to a general in the German army building trucks and engines. Well that's the official story anyway.

Ford were also in Germany building cars under their own badge, first with the Model T in 1925 and in a purpose built factory later relocated to Cologne. The odd thing is that for both General Motors and Ford, it was pretty much business as usual throughout the war.

Opel built the insensitively named Blitz lorry with Daimler-Benz, which kept the German army operational throughout the hostilities. Opel also helped make the engines for the Junkers 88 bomber which itself played quite a large role in the Blitz on London. Ford subsidiaries also built lorries that were half tank, half lorry which carried troops and supplies. According to British Intelligence these trucks constituted "the backbone of the German Army's transport system". Incredibly General Motor's president Alfred Sloan and his vice-presidents remained on the board of General Motors-Opel throughout the Second World War.

At the end of hostilities both General Motors and Ford asked the American government for compensation. In 1967 General Motors received $33m in tax exemptions for 'troubles and destructions', during the war. By contrast Ford got a million dollars in tax relief for the damage done to its truck plant in Cologne. So it was very much business as usual for the Americans, whilst the real German Car Industry still had to prove itself.

So did I.

The German Car Industry vs The British Car Industry (the 1940s)

Morris Minor, a sort of British Beetle.

Despite its car industry being bombed almost as flat at the German one, Britain had a lot of shadow factories, which were new and ready to start building cars. Economically it was as exhausted and as much as a basket case as the German one and would be saddled with debt for generations to come. By contrast Germany was to be on the receiving end of Marshall Plan aid. Everyone was initially relying on old models but the innovation was still coming from Germany as the exciting new Jaguar XK120 and the new range of Bristol cars (based on pre-war BMWs) proved. The British Beetle was of course the Morris Minor, which wasn't marketed at all really; consequently it sold just over 2 million, whereas the Beetle managed more than 20 million. Go figure.

The German Car Industry vs The French Car Industry

Renault 4CV which would be the French Beetle.

One of the first things that the French Car Industry did was to recruit Ferdinand Porsche to work on a new Renault before he was denounced and imprisoned for war crimes. That was a fate that also befell Louis Renault who was arrested in 1944 as a collaborator. Renault was nationalised in 1945 as the Régie Nationale des Usines Renault. Pre-war 8CV Juvaquarte and 4CV were the basic vehicles that helped the French get mobile again.

Peugeot built commercial vehicles for military use and were able despite bomb damage to their factory to resume car production almost immediately with their old 202. Again basic cars were the order of the day. Indeed, that is what kept Citroen in business as the prototype 2CV which had been hidden away during the war, officially so it would not fall into enemy hands. Actually if the Germans had seen it surely they would have killed themselves laughing? Anyway the French peasantry didn't find it amusing just very useful, getting them across a rutted field and to the market without breaking any eggs, or traumatising livestock.

The German Car Industry vs The Italian Car Industry

And the Fiat 600 would be Italy's baby Beetle.

Fiat seemed to recover very rapidly after the Second World War and by 1949 were making a substantial 75,000 cars a year. There were no new models, just revamped pre-war Topolinos. They were also the beneficiaries of Marshall Plan aid and a brand new engine in the 1400 spearheaded the revival although it was smaller cars, the 600 and 500, which defined the marque.

The German Car Industry vs The Swedish Car Industry

Sweden's 93 was pretty much Scandinavia's aerodynamic Beetle.

Sweden had been neutral in the Second World War and their industry consisted of Volvo. They built large, fairly solid American style cars for Swedes. They did start to downsize in 1944 and their PV444 would eventually be the first Swedish car to sell in substantial numbers outside of Scandinavia. From 1950 they also had some competition in the slippery shape of aircraft manufacturer SAAB. They had started testing during the war and ended up using a DKW type two-stroke engine to power their first cars.

The German Car Industry vs The American Car Industry

America never did Beetles, they just bought them. This is a Ford Custom Coupe.

Here was the world's biggest car industry with millions of cars spewing from Detroit. Ford, General Motors and Chrysler were the behemoths making mainly big cars with big engines. They kept on making cars until 1942 when they entered the war. What they didn't make were small cars, which is where Volkswagen could come in. Although American cars were large, over engineered and chock-full of novelties like electric windows. Mercedes certainly thought that they could do big, but also combined with sophistication and quality. The American Car Industry looked invulnerable and it was. However, the Germans were learning fast.

The German Car Industry vs The Japanese Car Industry

Nissan DS-4 Thrift, ferociously ugly and not that much like Beetle at all. More London FX Taxi gone very wrong.

Rather like the German car industry, flattened but located a lot further East, the big difference was that they had no high profile, well-established companies. Nissan had a opportunity to bounce back in 1953 with their version of the Austin A40. Toyota was the quickest to recover and like Mercedes also built trucks, buses and all manner of commercial vehicles. At the time though they looked no more likely to dominate the car industry than the Belgians.

In the Cassette Deck ...

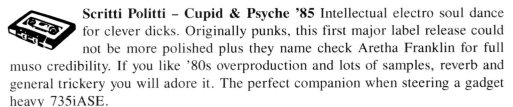

Scritti Politti – Cupid & Psyche '85 Intellectual electro soul dance for clever dicks. Originally punks, this first major label release could not be more polished plus they name check Aretha Franklin for full muso credibility. If you like '80s overproduction and lots of samples, reverb and general trickery you will adore it. The perfect companion when steering a gadget heavy 735iASE.

2 A Domestic Appliance with a Very Long Lead

Say hello to the new People's Car, it's just like a Beetle, but with straight lines. Plus Volkswagen kill off the traditional British sports car thank God...

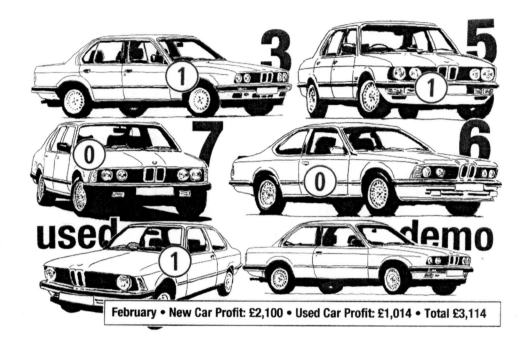

February • New Car Profit: £2,100 • Used Car Profit: £1,014 • Total £3,114

I saw the advertisement for a car sales executive in The Times *and the big appeal for me was the fact that along with the five-figure on target earnings was the promise of a free car. In return all I had to do was sell a few and how hard could that be? Oh yes and the free car was a BMW. For someone who had adjusted badly to student life, especially the lack of ready cash and with only an untaxed and out of MOT Mini Cooper to his name, it was all too hard to resist. Especially as I didn't just like cars, I loved them and all my earliest memories were motoring related. Whether it was pushing a Corgi car through simulated snow, flour supplied by my patient Mum, or sitting in the back of Uncle Charlie's Austin Mini Seven as he swore at my sister while she learnt to drive.*

Living right next to the A12 the main arterial road heading westwards was a major factor in my automotive obsession. Well I say A12, the bit before it got to us which was excitingly dual carriageway was called Eastern Avenue, whereas our more upmarket, but crowded single lane bit was Cambridge Park.

Thereafter it changed into the choking confines of Leytonstone High Road. Despite being lead poisoned by the rush hour tailbacks, the stationary nature of the traffic meant that I could study first hand all the different makes, shapes and models that constituted the Great British car park in the '60s and '70s. I knew what every car was including the less than British ones. The Brits were easy, what got you bonus points in the I-Spy books and in the playground was the foreigners.

In the '60s there was a curious outbreak of Renault Dauphines. A French car with a rear engine, so no grille up front, just two bulging headlamps and a rounded shape, so yes it really did look like a frog to me. I also remember the odd Fiat, mostly the tiny 500 and then there were the Germans. Mercedes all looked the same and it was impossible to differentiate between models as they were all four door saloons with a cliff face chrome radiator topped off with the three-pointed star which my school chums and I, all weaned on a diet of black and white war films, were convinced was a gun sight. Most German cars though were Beetles. Rounded cuddly and soft and identical to most normal kiddies, but not me. I wasn't normal because I knew that the early ones had split rear screens, it was oval screens from 1953 and rectangular from 1958 and even bigger from 1965. Yes there were lots of model year differences for a small strange boy to enjoy. As for the more obscure Germans, their version of the Hillman Imp, the small, square rear engined NSU Prinz would turn up on Cambridge Park Road occasionally, but Porsches almost never.

Similarly BMWs were hardly around at all, except for the comedy one, BMW Isetta. This bubble car would always bring a massive smile to my face, but I still took each sighting seriously enough to double check it was a BMW. Most normal car watchers would simply see a bubble and certainly it was possible to confuse your Isettas with your Heinkels. The Heinkel was an alternative Bubble from Germany which when assembled in the UK was badged as a Trojan. An irrelevance to most adults and just about all children of my age, but important to me.

So I always knew my cars, plus I had one of those large plastic steering wheels with a rubber sucker on the back. Once dampened it could be pressed firmly to the back of my Dad's seat in our Vauxhall Wyvern. There was even an indicator on one side and a gear change on the other side of the column just like the Vauxhall. Yes I always was a brilliant back seat driver, but most important of all I knew my German cars in general and Chitty Chitty Bang Bang in particular.

Showroom condition, zero mileage, one careful owner Chitty. Kept in a dehumidified plastic bag at all times and moved between several secure European locations.

In 1968 my mum took me to the Gants Hill Odeon to see the film. Like most Odeons it was an interesting Art Deco design, but it was much, much bigger than a regular picture house. It may well have had its own post code, not least because it occupied a complete triangular island sandwiched between the A12, Perth Road on the other side and Lonsdale Crescent running behind it. On that day the car park contained something more special than the Ford Cortinas and Hillman Minxes that usually occupied the spaces. It was Chitty. Well one of the Chitties anyway. According to the Cars of the Stars Museum in Keswick, six cars were used in the film. Don't know which one I saw, but it wasn't the racing Chitty seen in the early part of the film or dilapidated Chitty a bit after, but it may well have been the Hovercraft Chitty, which didn't have an engine.

You have to see the film to understand the different stages of Chitty and I sat through two and half hours with my mum wondering why there was so much singing in it and not nearly enough car chase action. It very much glossed over the racing career of Count Louis Zborowski who built four racing cars with aeroplane engines. As I was later to discover the film didn't actually have much to do with the original cars. The Count's cars did fly, but not in the air, only around the Brooklands circuit.

I found out that that the original Chitty Chitty Bang Bang (possibly named after a first world war song) was built in England with German parts, much like present day Rolls Royce cars. The first chassis was from a Mercedes and the engine a Maybach six-cylinder and went racing in 1921. The last Chitty had a huge 27-litre V12 Liberty engine with a Benz gearbox. The Count was racing for

Mercedes at Monza when he was killed and Chitty was sold by the estate to Welsh racer John Godfrey Parry-Thomas. He obviously decided that Chitty Chitty Bang Bang was a bit of a mouthful so instead he called her 'Babs' and used her to set the world land speed record in 1926 by reaching 171.02 miles per hour. Tragically he was killed a year later at Pendine Sands and Babs was buried on the beach. The Chitty/Babs story didn't end there because the car was dug up in 1969 and rebuilt over the next fifteen years.

Sometimes you don't need flying cars, Benny Hill as The Toymaker, the made up country of Vulgaria, and a woman called Truly Scrumptious to make a decent tale. I blame a combination of author Ian Fleming and screenwriter Roald Dahl. However, I wasn't mentally scarred by the Child Catcher, or Benny Hill's performance (that would happen in The Italian Job*) but I did want a Corgi Toys Chitty. Any young boy would, but not just because you could pull the handbrake and the wings would flick out, I loved it because it was fast. The large wheels ran smoothly, were not upset by the potholes in the playground, whilst the weight and low centre of gravity meant it was always stable. When there was a race at school it would win, easily. That's why I wanted one. Launched in November 1968 it would be the perfect Christmas gift, and that's why I got two.*

I wasn't a greedy eight year old, but I was lucky and anyway this was a business decision. My Uncle Charlie was a very smart man. Army tough, short tempered, Heavy Goods Vehicle qualified, with a rollup wedged in the corner of his mouth, he was a proper bloke who worked hard and had brilliant ideas that he seldom put into practice. When he got wind of my plan to get a Corgi Chitty Chitty Bang Bang Uncle Charles suggested getting one for play and another as an investment. He reckoned that it would become a collector's item provided it stayed in the original box and remained untouched. It sounded a bit mad to me and I thought it might provide a good source of spares in the future, but Uncle Charles was right. Into the 1970s there was a mania for limited edition prints and collecting all sorts of things that generations had previously thought of as rubbish. Toys used to be rubbish because children played with them. I never played with one Chitty and it stayed in its box, so here is one of the few recorded cases of a used car actually appreciating in value. On that basis and thanks mainly to my Uncle Charlie, surely I'd be a brilliant car dealer, trader or salesman? If I wasn't deluding myself that I knew what a great car was based on a Corgi toy, I did at least know that the very best car my Dad had bought, apart from the Audi 100LS, was a Volkswagen Golf.

I may be going a bit too early here by claiming that the greatest car ever made was the Volkswagen Golf, but it is hard to come to any other conclusion. Now the Beetle end of the VW story was covered extensively in *The British Car Industry: Our Part In Its Downfall* (yet another good reason to buy), but what happened next is equally fascinating.

In 1960 the Beetle honeymoon seemed to be over. Although Volkswagen had become a public company – with the West German government, the state of Lower Saxony and the workers each holding shares – it did not stop the Hanover factory going on strike. It may have lasted only 24 hours, but it was an unsettling experience. Then in 1961 all the Germans who before the war had bought savings stamps to put towards purchasing the KdF (Strength through Joy Wagen) decided to sue. Not because the name was so stupid, but because they failed to collect what had become known by the much more friendly name 'Beetle'. Volkswagen offered the disappointed either DM100 cash or DM600 off a new Beetle. To cap it all there were whispers that the Beetle had run its course and was a dying model.

Certainly the one model policy adopted by Major Hirst was enough to get the company moving and had been dead right. Crucially his successor Heinrich Nordhoff set about most important business of all which was exporting Beetles. He stuck by the motto 'change only to improve', which in the coming age of almost instant obsolescence for any consumer product would sound rather old fashioned. He did allow some variations on the Beetle theme such as the light commercial Kombi, which became the legendary camper van beloved of continent crossing Aussies. A pretty coupé, the Karmann-Ghia, was a welcome break from the Beetle shape, but underneath they were all Beetles. Certainly the changes to the Beetle over the years were subtle such as the pull heating knob being replaced by a rotary one in 1953, or the leatherette head lining ten years later and all that rear window nonsense I knew as a child. There were more significant upgrades and cumulatively until the end of German production there was some 78,000 modifications. However the fundamental shortcomings like restricted interior space, lacklustre performance and dicey handling were never properly addressed. Instead there were variations on the Beetle theme like the Type 3 launched in 1961.

Volkswagen 411 yet another variation on the Beetle theme. Not very loveable.

Unlike the Beetle it actually looked like a contemporary car with a three-box shape. At the front there was no engine of course, but in the middle a lot more space for passengers and even four doors, whilst at the back lived the engine. So there was space for luggage and people and a larger engine, which made it quicker than a Beetle, but everyone kept buying the Beetle. Although it sold a not inconsiderable 1.8 million it was a failure compared to its dad. So Volkswagen then decided to make an even bigger Type 3 and call it the Type 4 in 1968 but at this point we are straying towards what Audi would do next and you can read about that in a future chapter.

Obviously Volkswagen didn't just need something bigger and more practical, it had to be stylish too and within the company they had been thinking along some pleasingly radical lines. The EA266 doesn't sound very sexy, though the styling was reasonably fresh, but it was a radical new shape that consisted of two boxes. One at the front where the engine should be and another behind it for passengers and luggage. Being a Volkswagen though the engine was not only a noisy one from a Beetle, it was also positioned right at the back which would not help handling or mean there was enough room for the shopping. It needed work. One clue as to where to go next came from a manufacturer they had recently acquired.

NSU had designed an incredibly rectangular three-box saloon called the K70. Putting a VW badge on it in 1970 created a number of firsts. It was their first water-cooled engined car, the Beetle was air-cooled, it was their first front-engined car and also the first car they had built with front wheel drive.

Volkswagen prove with the K70 that they can do right angles and put the engine at the right end and use air to keep it cool. Well actually it was all NSU's idea.

Sadly sales were a very poor second to all those firsts, as over five years just 211,100 were sold. No other parts of this car were used on any other Volkswagen but it did at least prove that they were capable of breaking the Beetle shaped mould. The K70 layout pointed a way forward, but Volkswagen realised that they needed to sharpen up their act when it came to styling. With that in mind Volkswagen President Kurt Lotz took himself and a notepad to the Turin Motor Show in 1969. He had a good look around and even, in what must have been moments of complete madness, asked the opinion of journalists as to what were the most striking prototypes and design studies, jotting down the ones he liked the best. Reducing it down to a shortlist of six, he found that four of them had been designed by Giorgetto Giugiaro.

The Passat, clearly the first proper modern Volkswagen which looks like a great big Golf.

Having worked for some of Italy's best coachbuilders and styled Ferraris, Maseratis and Alfa Romeos, Giugiaro branched out on his own and founded his own company. So Lotz pitched up on the Italdesign stand and reportedly said "Do what you want, but do it fast." The commission was to design a mid size model like the Type 4 and Giugiaro delivered a detailed proposal within six months. It actually scared Volkswagen management a bit so they sent Giugiaro away with a brief to turn an Audi 80 into a Volkswagen. It was a bit of compromise as the front was Audi 80 with the rear end of that original scary proposal grafted on; here was the Passat and a whole family of models that came as a saloon, hatchback and estate. It was proof that Volkswagen could finally build a car which looked as though it belonged to the later half of the twentieth century. It may have been cutting edge for Volkswagen being front wheel drive and water-cooled, but the Passat was also just a little bit dull and Giugiaro knew this. So when Volkswagen asked him to design a new small car, again in no time at all, he wanted full control and without even submitting any drawing or sketch for approval, he got the green light.

In fact Giugiaro also got the landing light with the Volkswagen private plane at his disposal so that he could commute between Turin and VW headquarters and get on with the job of styling their most important car of the decade. Although it was a scaled down and much prettier Passat, the fact that it was to be exported to America meant that some design compromises were essential to comply with their regulations. As a result the windscreen was made more upright, the front end was lengthened along with the bonnet that was also flattened at the same time. Usually designers would want to embellish the flat surfaces to make them less brutal, but there simply was not time. Also to save money the front lights were changed from fancy rectangular ones to off the shelf round ones. Giugiaro may not have been happy at the time, but he has subsequently admitted that the round headlamp and rectangular grille are the most distinctive features of the Golf. A last minute rethink also saw the indicators being moved from each end of the grille to being incorporated into the bumpers. The front end was perfect, but then so was the rear.

The tailgate had been a feature of Volkswagen's earliest prototypes and although Giugiaro claimed to be having fun by the time he reached the back, it seems clear that he realised the original door was flimsy and needed to be properly defined. His new design actually wrapped the tailgate around the side of the car. At a stroke the production process was simplified and it was a design detail that would be copied the world over.

Engine at the front and luggage at the back with its own little door, perfect.

A small square car with an extra door at the rear may now seem quite a boring but back in 1974 it was something of a shock. Most designers were horrified at the sheer brutality of it and at Ford their design chief Uwe Bahsen would later claim that the Golf represented the 'origami school of car design'.

He added, "It is possible to produce a folded cardboard model of a Mark 1 Golf." He did actually mean this as a compliment because this demonstrated how designers approach the problem of car bodywork differently. His theory was that Italian designers operated from a unique perspective as they had no central design school and were more influenced by architecture. That makes the Golf a little house on wheels, which was just how many buyers treated it. But this wasn't just a useful box on wheels that was easy to park because you could see each corner.

The Golf was light and structurally rigid. New computer stressing techniques helped the designers to take full advantage of the front wheel drive layout. This meant that lots of weight could be saved because all the engine, suspension and braking stresses could be contained up front in a strong bulkhead, that's the area below the windscreen. So the Golf only weighed 1700lb (772kg), which helped fuel consumption considerably. However, at the heart of the car's practicality was the transversely mounted engine. Like the Mini, simply turning the engine around so it ran across the engine bay freed up lots of space inside. Also with the gearbox out of the way and there being no need for a transmission tunnel to run towards the rear of the car the boot could be bigger.

What could possibly go wrong? Well quite a lot actually. A brand new car is just waiting to go wrong and Volkswagen had put the Golf together in a huge hurry. Luckily they had a plan. Giugiaro had designed a coupe called the Scirocco that fitted on top of all the Golf's running gear. This was unveiled in 1974 and would be built in small numbers by coachbuilders Karmann. So if they came across any teething troubles, it would be possible to overcome them quickly and quietly while operating at the low volume end of the market. Clever.

And why was it called Golf? Certainly some seat fabrics used in Volks-wagens over the years suggested that someone in the company had donated their questionable plaid trouser fashion sense after playing a round of golf. Actually it has everything to do with matters meteorological. The name is based on the Gulf Stream, which is responsible for Western Europe's moderate climate. In German, gulf is spelt 'golf'. This makes sense when you consider the other windy cars, which were in the early Volkswagen line up. Scirocco is a hot wind, Passat a warm one, and Jetta is just that, a jet of air. In later years, Volkswagen did try to clear up any confusion over the spelling and the obvious fact that Golf is a game involving little white balls and bad fashion. Indeed, the Golf GTI and its golf ball topped gear stick (who says the Germans have no sense of humour?) had reinforced the sport theme. The official explanation, which has lost something in the translation, went like this "Golf is the game and the name suits. Golf stands for endurance, perfect technique and – drive." Not bad dress sense then.

In the UK the Golf did not have much competition. Most rivals were bigger, more expensive, or you had to choose the smallest estate in a particular range to get anywhere near the same practicality. However, the Fiat 127 from 1972 was available as a mould breaking three-door hatch. Good as it was, and probably the first real supermini which sold over 3.7m, compared to the Golf it was small and not nearly as well built.

Not quite as successful and smaller, but with the same two box layout the British Leyland owned Innocenti also from Italy brought out the Mini 90 in the same year. Otherwise the nearest British made equivalent was the Austin Maxi. It had the same general layout with front wheel drive and the engine turned round so that inside the bigger car could famously be made into a double bed. It was never properly explained why that was a good thing unless you were a serial adulterer, a cash strapped rep who could not afford a bed and breakfast or caravanner who needed extra accommodation. Getting back to the point. Any similarity between a Maxi and a Golf ended right there because the build quality of the British car was so poor and mechanically it was flawed.

The French had a couple of hatches with the largely forgotten Peugeot 104 and the rather more successful Renault 5. Vauxhall did have the Chevette, which was based on the Opel Kadett and came out in 1975 as a good basic and reliable hatchback. Meanwhile, Ford's Fiesta was still two years away but they had the Escort and at a stretch the estate version. You could also make a slight case for the Hillman Imp, which was small and had a lift up rear window, although there was the cube-like Husky estate.

For the big manufacturers that was it. If you wanted a rear door it had to be an estate or something sporty and expensive like a BMW 2002 Touring or an MGB GT. Volkswagen in the UK did not see any of those cars as the real rivals. We know this because in 1979 a legendary TV advertisement saw a Golf dropped from a great height (well above the camera line anyway) next to a Datsun and then driven off by a Japanese gentlemen. Except it isn't. The Japanese gentleman is played by the legendary Bert Kwok (Kato in the Pink Panther films) who is Chinese, but was born in Manchester. Anyway, he was pretending to be Japanese to make the point that this was best selling imported car in Japan. If that's not too confusing.

At that time Volkswagen could not just more than match the Japanese for build quality, durability and low level dropability, their Golf was a far better designed and much more interesting proposition than a Datsun Cherry or Toyota Corolla. Most important of all, the German car was far more fun to drive. There are complicated technical reasons why, involving the suspension design, which may cause you to drift off to sleep, so I won't go there. Suffice to say that the low speed ride was smooth, it didn't roll too much when cornering, the grip was good and overall the handling was safe and sporty. These were qualities that did not go unnoticed by those who wanted to go faster. Luckily those who wanted to go faster actually worked at Volkswagen.

An original GTI. Actually this was one of VW's pre-production jobs which still had small bumpers and a fat typeface badge.

The only reason we have the letters G, T and I (all uppercase please note) is because a small group of engineers decided to put hundreds of hours of unpaid overtime into producing a quicker Golf. Whereas these sorts of decisions usually happened in marketing departments when clever people with glasses and a clipboard have discovered that there are potential customers for a particularly sparkly paint job. Doctor Friedrich Goes was the leading engineer in this out of hours project who knew his way around the Volkswagen and Audi parts stores. That meant an Audi engine, wider wheels and a stiffened, lowered and beefed up suspension made it all happen. Meanwhile, a spare set of Recaro sports seats kept the excited driver and passenger in place. Provisionally called the Sport Golf, senior management were not that impressed and suggested that it be parked out of sight and forgotten about.

At the time Volkswagen were far more concerned with shifting their standard Golf to a mass market so as to save the whole company from sliding into bankruptcy, which was a real possibility at the time. The sales department did look at the Sport Golf, but could not see the potential. After all, Volkswagen was best known for making Beetles, noisy and slow perhaps, but they rarely broke down, which is what their customers liked. To suddenly suggest that they would buy a sporting car, which did not have an established sporting pedigree like Alfa Romeo, Porsche or Jaguar, or even Ford for that matter, seemed like madness.

However there were precedents for turning a shopping car into a sporting car, most notably the Mini Cooper. Right from the off it had been clear that Mini could handle much more power without lots of modifications. It seems that both the Volkswagen engineers and the sales department were coming to a similar conclusion. Like the Mini, the Golf was a cleverly packaged, classless, ground breaking design that revolutionised the way that cars would be designed. At the time though Golf engineers did not yet know they had an iconoclastic vehicle on their hands. Even so the Sport Golf was officially sanctioned in 1975, just a year after the ordinary Golf had entered production. Fortunately most of the development work, courtesy of Friedrich Goes, had already been done.

Fifteen durability models did the rigorous testing and were sent north to Scandinavia for winter trials and south to Africa for the hotter climate. Internally there was plenty of debate over how the new model should be equipped. At the time many favoured a stripped out, no-frills, no-nonsense car aimed purely at the young enthusiast. However, they could not ignore the older and more affluent driver who might say they wanted a stripped out racer, but really they wanted a bit of padding and soundproofing and probably an 8-Track music system. To that end they decided on a more generous than usual specification, according to German standards anyway. Then something strange happened; when the car was launched it was actually fairly spartan, just as the engineers originally envisaged. It was car company accountants who had finally done something truly positive by cutting the budgets. It seems that the enthusiastic driving public got the small fast hatchback they deserved. The one that wasn't yet called a hot hatch, but why was it called GTI?

Apparently the origins of the best-known performance car acronym are lost in Volkswagen myth and legend. Certainly Gran Turismo was always accepted as a designation for some of the world's finest specialist sports cars, like the Aston Martin DB4 GT Zagato. Over the years though those two letters were also applied to some of the world's least good GTs, such as the Hillman Hunter and Morris Marina GT. Yes they were appropriated by marketing departments and glued onto any dull model that needed a sales boost. So obviously Volkswagen were aware that the letters had been debased and sought to distinguish their new sports model by adding an 'I' for fuel injection.

However, it has been suggested that the German for fuel injection is Einspritzung, so the designation GTE should have been used as on its subsequent rival, the Vauxhall Astra GTE. The trouble was that Audi had already used GTE on their 80 model so it was decided to use the I for injection. BMW had done that with their CSi fuel injected coupes. Volkswagen set themselves apart from them by using a capital I. If you are really interested though and want to set a question for a pub quiz, it was called a GTi in South Africa.

Approval was given for a limited production run of 5,000 which was the minimum number required to qualify the car for competition purposes. That modest target was soon exceeded and soon production was running at 5,000 a month. The GTI had arrived in an autoverse that was devoid of real competition. British buyers were particularly keen because in 1976 after that long sweltering hot summer the only way to get your hands on one of these fuel injected cars was to place a special order at your local Volkswagen dealer and even then it would be left hand drive only.

There is a detailed specification that I could bore you with, but all you really need to know is that the engine came from an Audi 80 GT, but it had been reworked so that it produced a lot more power. The 1.6 engine produced a fairly modest 110 bhp, would get to 112 mph and reach 60 mph in just over 9 seconds. That may sound quite tame now but it was as quick as 'proper' sports cars like MGB GTs.

Apart from the engine the other modifications that set the GTI apart were an oil cooler, oil temperature gauge and tachometer. There was a larger clutch and uprated shock absorbers on the suspension. There were larger tyres and rims of course and bigger brakes, but perhaps the most endearing aspect of the new Golf was its understated looks. Indeed the GTI kept the go faster trimmings to a minimum. Apart from the subtly lower ride height, spoked sports wheels, chunkier spoiler, plastic wheel arch surrounds, side rubbing strip and discreet badging. Actually there were few clues that this Golf was anything special.

So what was the GTI up against? Probably the best guide was *Motor* magazine which in December 1976 judged the principal rivals as being the Ford Escort RS2000, Triumph Dolomite Sprint, Renault 17TS, Colt Galant GTO and Alfa Romeo Alfetta 1.8. These were certainly a strange bunch. The Renault did have a rear door and front wheel drive, yet it was little more than a good old fashioned fastback coupé, with only average performance and rather odd styling. Ford's RS2000 was proof that a mainstream brand could crossover to performance car greatness. Not as practical as the Golf, it was fast and agile and the wedge nose was distinctive. It had a starring role in *The Professionals* TV Show as Doyle's runabout. The Dolly Sprint was a thing of real beauty (and also popped up in early episodes of *The Professionals*). However, it looked dated and had reliability issues, but had a genuine racing pedigree. As fast as a Golf but rather more expensive the Colt Galant was a real rarity, but every bit as well built as the Golf, with a big 2.0 litre engine. Then there was performance car royalty in the shape of the Alfa Romeo Alfetta. An achingly beautiful coupé, it was what everyone expected a sports car to be. The engine made a wonderful sound and it handled beautifully and few minded that it might fall apart, rust or break down at some point in the near future.

But what did *Motor* think of the GTI? "If done well – and the GTI has been done very well indeed – the result is not only suitable for competition, but also a taut high performance car entirely acceptable to the ordinary driver with sporting tastes." They liked the handling, but not as much as the Alfetta. However, they thought that for its size the accommodation was excellent and went overboard about the quietness and overall refinement. The always observant *Motor* journalists also noticed that the gear lever top was shaped like a golf ball, 'but coloured black'.

Incredibly, British buyers were not put off by the prospect of driving from the passenger seat. Specialist companies such as GTI Engineering produced high quality right hand drive conversions. It wasn't until July 1979 that keen buyers could actually buy a GTI with a steering wheel on the right side of the cabin.

To capitalise on the GTI's success there was a version for the buyer who couldn't afford a real GTI, or just could not manage the insurance. Volkswagen's most enduring and popular special edition was the Driver. Essentially this was a GTI without any of the performance implications, a sheep in a rather wolfish overcoat. Obviously concocted by the marketing department it mixed and matched the Golf specification and used as a starting point a 3 door Golf with a 1.3 engine and 4-speed gearbox. To this they added GTI side stripes, black rear light cluster panels and wider wheels and tyres. Inside the GL dashboard was augmented with a natty centre console, which included a clock and voltmeter, so the occupants knew both the time and charge left in the battery. Useful. Sports steering wheel and seats certainly looked and felt the part, whilst a passenger side storage shelf and door pockets were welcome practical additions. As well as the black velour carpets the whole GTI effect was topped off with that Golf shaped gear knob. All the customer had to do was choose between red, orange and green paintwork. In Europe though there was the added incentive to go diesel with the GTD.

A few years later Volkswagen were brave enough to take the faux GTI formula in further. In 1983 when the original Golf was just months from replacement, they were in the usual predicament of selling their last few cars so had to make them extra attractive to potential buyers. The Driver was based on the humble three door C, but looked even more like the world's hottest hatchback. It adopted the distinctive four-headlamp grille of the GTI, while the black wheel arches, side stripes and passenger door mirror completed the bodywork transformation. Meanwhile sports seats, a tachometer, digital clock and centre console were sufficient to make a genuine GTI driver double take.

Not a GTI. This is what a Golf GX looked like.

The GTI jollity did not end there because Volkswagen took the 1.5 GL and turned it into a GX which was a Driver for the more family orientated owner as it had five doors. On the outside there was the distinctive four headlamp grille, wider wheels with less than sporty chrome hubcaps, plus there were chrome embellishments around the grille, windows and body trim. Like the Driver, sports front seats, centre console, tachometer, lockable glove box and full carpeting no less.

Rear end of a Campaign GTI.

The Mark 1 Golf ceased production in the summer of 1983 and the some six million had found homes throughout the world and the customers were not disappointed. The Golf had created a brand new type of small practical family car. Cars were now described as 'Golf' class. It had taught all manufacturers a lesson, one that the Japanese certainly learnt from as they appreciated the value of good build quality, a versatile hatchback body and a common front wheel drive platform that could accommodate a whole range of related models. Nissan, Mitsubishi and Honda all reportedly bought brand new Golfs so that they could learn more about this new type of car. Certainly a glance at the Honda Accord and Prelude range introduced in 1976 indicated that they were taking lots of design and product planning lessons on board.

So Volkswagen had well and truly replaced the Beetle and the company was now in the early 1980s and poised to update their second most successful model. Unfortunately Giugiaro was not going to be around to do it. Indeed, Volkswagen's revival can be credited almost solely to Giugiaro who within months had revamped the company's entire range. The three seminal models had been the revolutionary Golf, the capable Passat and the beautiful Scirocco, designed by one man with one vision. In particular the Golf had no discernable input from a marketing department, the board of directors or customer clinics that would dilute the original concept. Kurt Lotz who had talent spotted Giugiaro wanted him on board for future projects. His successor disagreed.

Volkswagen now had a big problem. How do you replace the Golf? Volkswagen had never changed any model for the sake of it, the Beetle being the most extreme example. Nevertheless the company always developed their cars carefully and for the better. Volkswagen though could not afford to keep the handbrake on. The automotive world was changing rapidly with probably the biggest threat coming from Japan where model life cycles were getting shorter. It wasn't enough that cars had changed, they had to be seen to change. Volkswagen had created the Golf class and every other manufacturer wanted a large chunk of it. There was no way that there would be such a quantum leap from Beetle to Golf, but that was not necessary. The head of the design department stated that 'The Golf must remain a Golf' which must have lost an awful lot in translation. Presumably the intention was to deliver more of the same in a slightly larger package.

Work on the Mark 2 Golf started way back in March 1977 when Volkswagen commissioned freelance stylists as well in house teams. Two years later they chose an internal proposal and had running prototypes by 1980. They built 49 prototypes for general testing, plus another 38 body shells for specific tests. Crash testing took care of 15 and a further 22 were sent on long distance road trials. Then half the initial pre-production run of 300 were sent to Volkswagen's proving ground. More than 3.7 million miles were covered by prototypes and tests. This probably explains why the Mark 2 was reliable straight out of the showroom.

Reliability through mechanical integrity was the easy bit, because the last thing that Volkswagen wanted to do was frighten off loyal customers by changing the way it looked, too much. So when it came to the styling it was a lot more of the same. Herbert Schafer who uttered the immortal "The Golf must remain a Golf" did qualify this with "Therefore the new Golf will inherit the unmistakable look of the Golf 1 with its typical shape." So for the styling they stuck with the huge rear pillar, which got wider and became even more of a blind spot. There was a reason for this, customers wanted more interior space and statistically they were getting bigger anyway, so the Golf grew up accordingly. The Golf purist may have been horrified, but the car was now 170mm (almost 7 inches) longer and 55mm (just over 2 inches) wider. In passenger terms at the front drivers had 92mm (3.5 inches) of extra elbow-room whilst at the rear it was a massive 120mm (almost 5 inches), combined with 75mm (3 inches) more legroom.

Golf Mark 2 as seen in your local supermarket car park.

Consequently the Golf piled on the pounds and kilos, so its weight went up from 1850lb (840kg) to 2026lb (920kg). That would have been disastrous normally, but the fatter body actually slid through the air far more aerodynamically. Clever touches such as integrating the roof gutter into the roof panel, flush door glass and the softer more rounded bodywork made it more aerodynamic. Also that body was not just slippery it was more solidly built than before. Volkswagen constructed a massive two level assembly plant to cope with estimated demand, which was also heavily automated, which meant robots. Other innovations included dipping pre-heated body shells into liquid wax for maximum protection against corrosion. That's why you see Mark 2 Golfs with wax weeping from the rear tailgate shut panel. And even if you don't it is also the reason why it is possible to see Golf Mark 2s still being used as cars, whereas the only Austin Maestros left belong to fanatical Maestro Owners' Club members, are chicken sheds, or have been recycled into a Nissan hubcap.

Apart from boring things like improved ventilation, there wasn't a huge amount of mechanical difference between old Golf and new. This was due in part to the company policy of test bedding components late in the life of the current models which meant a 1982 Golf was, in essence, mechanically identical to the apparently all-new Golf of 1984. So that's how the second generation set out to rule the world. The Golf Mark 2 carried on from where the old one left off, except that it did not rust quite so easily. It was a much more grown up hatchback that had not lost its charm and most important of all, there was still a sexy, desirable one wearing the GTI badge.

Now a weight gain programme is not usually a good thing for a sporting car. Despite being heavier, the new GTI had Cd (drag coefficient) friendly aerodynamics down from 0.42 on the old car to a more respectable 0.34, so speed and acceleration hardly suffered compared to the 1.8 Mark 1. Officially the top speed was 119 mph and 60 mph arrived in 8.3 seconds.

Announced in February 1984, modifications for the GTI were as the standard cars, although there were disc brakes all round. The 1.8 litre unit was a carry over from the Mark 1. In fact, this was effectively a Campaign specification GTI with lots of extras loaded on as standard including Pirelli alloys, steel sliding sunroof and metallic paint. On the outside the four lamp grille and red inserts on the bumpers. By the end of the year though all those roof and alloy paint freebies were made options, but the asking price was still £7,867.

Mark 2 Golf running on steel wheels.

A year after the new GTI was launched the five door versions were introduced to the UK market for the first time. Pirelli alloys were standard. Also, by September of that year hydraulic tappets meant that adjustment was no longer part of the service schedule. Indicators were added to the wings, and at the front the spoiler became a bit deeper.

September 1986 could simply have been the month when the GTI got the benefit of seat height adjusters and new style alloys, but this is the point when things became more serious with the launch of the 16-valve. If you didn't open the bonnet the only clue that this model had eight more valves than the standard GTI was a small but bright badge bearing the legend 16V. A closer look and the skilled use of a tape measure would also have revealed that the car sat almost half an inch (10mm) closer to the ground. Under the wheel arches were 10 per cent stiffer at the front and 20 per cent stiffer at the rear springs, plus modified shock absorbers and anti-roll bars. Running on 6 inch rims the tyres were slightly wider whilst the front ventilated discs were larger which was also helped out by beefier brake pistons with ducts out of the front spoiler to keep everything cool.

Under the bonnet was the 16-valve first seen in the Scirocco. After the quick performance fix of bolting on turbos in the early 1980s, by far the more sophisticated and effective way of boosting power and engine efficiency was to increase the number of valves. It had a top speed of 129 mph and would get to 60 mph in 8 seconds dead. So it was slightly quicker although for mid range response the old 8-valve was still worth buying.

August 1987 is when the Golf became more UK friendly, as the front door quarter lights disappeared repositioning the door mirrors further forward so that you could actually see out of them. Oh yes, and the windscreen wipers parked on the driver's side of the screen so you could actually see out. Interestingly a digital instrumental pack was an option on the 16-valve but there were few takers with no improvement over the standard very clear instrument layout. Back then no one really wanted to look at some odd Atari/Sinclair ZX readout even if it was in full colour. However, the on-board MFA computer, standard on the GTI, was brilliant and gave just the right amount of display and critical information. Pumping the button on the end of the stalk was simple. For many just the average speed and journey time information was utterly absorbing. Fuel consumption was also worth knowing of course, although the value of the oil temperature readout was debatable. However, on board computing with the brilliantly simple system never got much better than this.

A five door 16-valve GTI from January made it family friendly whilst the 8-valve finally became easy to park thanks to power steering being made standard. The old GTI just made it into the 1990s and the 8-valve was effectively upgraded to 16-valve specification with rainbow seat trim, BBS alloy wheels, electric front windows, smoked rear light lenses and standard metallic paint. It was still the hot hatchback that everybody wanted. The millionth GTI was a Mark 2 and was built on 6 December 1990.

Clearly the GTI had become a replacement for the traditional sports car, which by comparison with the Golf wasn't as practical, flexible or reliable. The younger buyers didn't just want a car that was quick, they needed room for their mates and flat pack furniture from the newly opened IKEA furniture warehouses. Not only that, they would not have time or inclination to repair it and were unlikely to tolerate breakdowns. So it is hardly surprising that the hot hatch market took off with the Golf firmly in the lead. Indeed, Volkswagen also entered what nobody ever referred to as the superhot hatch market, but they will from now on.

It all started with the Synchro. Not exactly hot, or even superhot, it was a technically interesting car that glued itself to the road with a sophisticated and permanent four-wheel drive system. Powered by a 90 bhp 1781cc engine, it was trimmed in a fairly GTI like manner. With a large front spoiler, black wheel arch trims and sills on the outside, inside there was a four spoke steering wheel, padded dashboard and a centre console. They followed it up in '87 though with a proper GT version, which had ABS brakes. Despite weighing 100kg more compared with the standard front wheel drive GTI, performance was pretty much the same.

The really rather pumped up Golf Rallye.

Although the Synchro looked like a standard Golf, there was no mistaking the Rallye for what it was, a bulging package of road legal rally car. Designed specifically for VW's competition department and built in Belgium, the four wheel drive and supercharged car was announced in 1988 and was clearly designed to go racing, except it didn't. Well not initially anyway. Like so many other cars from the era, a change in the rules that outlawed Group B rallying, meant that Volkswagen had built 5,000 (to qualify for racing) seemingly for nothing. Never mind, the Golf fan club was bigger and richer than ever. First of all Volkswagen made it comfortable inside with half leather sports seats and a leather trimmed steering wheel, along with the head restraints and door trim. Most also had a sunroof, central locking, electric windows and electric heated door mirrors. There was a large choice of extras including air conditioning, Recaro sports seats and rear head restraints.

Outside the Rallye was a pumped up Golf with a styling very much of its time with blistered wheel arches, remoulded front and rear bumpers, with an apron that formed a visual link to the side skirts. Most obviously different was the narrow front grille and rectangular headlamps. Darth Vader's helmet is not just a good name for a punk band, it is also sort of what the Rallye looked like except that it sat on fairly average looking 6J x 15 inch spoked alloy wheels which took away some of the Death Star drama.

Well actually most of the drama was underneath the bonnet with a reworked engine, which had a reduced displacement down to 1763cc in order to qualify for the prevailing 2.5 litre motor sport class (you had to multiply the capacity by 1.4). Technically it had a compression ratio of 8:1 and a maximum supercharged boost pressure of 0.65 bar so the engine produced 160 bhp. Oddly this didn't make it hugely quicker than a standard GTI taking 7.6 seconds to 60 mph and onwards to a top speed of 130 mph. If you wondered what a supercharger did, well first of all it was called a G-Lader in Germany because the housing looked like the seventh letter of the alphabet. It was driven from the engine by a ribbed belt. Inside that G were two interlocking snail shaped scrolls. A central oscillating lobe swept pockets of air along the spiral gallery towards the centre from where the hot compressed air was challenged through the intercooler (a tiny radiator) and into the cylinders. Whoosh!

A Passat 5-speed gearbox was a big help in being able to cope with the extra stresses and the suspension was based on the 16-valve GTI but the damping rates for the springs and shocks were higher along with stronger anti-roll bars. However if all that four-wheel drive technology and questionable bodywork addenda made some Golf fans feel queasy there was a more subtle alternative. Volkswagen used the research from the Rallye project to launch a whole range of G-lader models, from the Golf G60, to the Passat Synchro, Corrado G60 and Polo G40.

Golf G60, like a GTI but with a supercharger spinning away under the bonnet.

Mechanically the G60 was different to the Rallye with the standard 1781cc GTI engine, which produced 160 bhp, it translated into a top speed of 134 mph, and would get to 62 mph in 8.3 seconds. Offered as a 3 or 5 door, apart from the badgework the G60 was pure GTI. However it was closer to the ground by 20mm at the front and 10mm at the rear with revised damper settings, Teflon coated suspension struts and thicker anti-roll bars. Oh yes and it remained resolutely left hand drive and was never officially imported to the UK.

Then again, those who even baulked at the over elaborate GTI inspired decoration on a G60 and preferred a Golf to look like it belonged to an almost retired district nurse would have their prayers answered in 1990. That's when Volkswagen launched the Limited. Indeed, Limited by name and limited in production reality, as just 70 were made. By comparison the majority of Ferraris are as common as muck.

The Limited was a bit special despite the two headlamp grille from a base L and the understated but fairly menacing metallic black paintwork. Under that dark bonnet was an engine that wasn't just supercharged it also had a 16-valve head and produced 210 bhp so that 60 mph arrived in 7.0 seconds. The cross spoke alloys were one concession to flamboyance, but there are no Rallye blistered arches. That's because the inner arches had been modified to take the much wider rims, which is clever and proves that this was a hand built car put together in Volkswagen's Motorsport department in Hannover. They seemingly made the Limited because, according to Motorsport Manager Klaus-Peter Rosorious, they wanted to prove it was possible to make a subtle, luxurious, yet compact, high performance hatchback. One with standard leather seats too.

So Volkswagen could do very exclusive and of course they were responsible for the death of the affordable small sports car. Well actually no. In July 1992 when the last Scirocco rolled off the Karmann production line almost 800,000 had been sold over a seventeen-year period. It was quite simply the biggest selling European coupé ever built.

Scirocco, basically a prettier Golf.

As we've already seen the Scirocco beat the Golf to production and was unveiled at the 1974 Geneva Motor Show. Designer Giugiaro always had a problem with the Golf, for him it was too small. Even so he pointed out that such a short wheelbase would make the perfect basis for a 2 + 2 coupé, so he styled the EA 398, or 1970 prototype otherwise known as the Karmann Cheetah which eventually became the Scirocco.

There were four models available from base and L, powered by either a 1093cc producing 50 bhp, or a 70 bhp 1471cc. Reclining seats, two speed wipers, electric windscreen washers and a clock were standard equipment. The higher specification LS and TS models came with the 1.5 engine in an 85 bhp state of tune. Sciroccos got hotter in '76 when the fuel injected 1.6 from the Golf GTI was fitted to two new models: a GTI and more highly trimmed GLI. Carburettor versions of these were also available in some markets badged as GT and GL. At the same time out went the conventional twin windscreen wipers replaced by a single arm. Also, the ventilation system was improved with a three-speed blower.

From there we can get to blow waves and even hair driers as many commentators did unfairly regard the Scirocco as a bit of a hairdresser's car, being light on performance and real sports car substance. 'A Golf in a frock' was as bad as the insults got, but considering the Golf was so good, some sexy Scirocco outer garments certainly helped. The Scirocco was for buyers who did want something different and the appeal to younger drivers was clear.

Actually Volkswagen engineers seriously considered a proper blow job by installing a turbocharger to boost the performance of all their GTI models. Tests began in 1981 with the 1.6 engine, but it was found that uncomfortable amounts of heat were generated, whilst fuel consumption proved to be poor. They tried again in 1983 with a US specification 1.7-litre engine, which produced an impressive 178 bhp resulting in 138 mph top speed. However, development of the 16-valve head blew away the turbo.

Scirocco 16-valve rear end.

For 1981 in came the larger Scirocco 2 with a brand new body. The drag factor went down from 0.42 to 0.38, whilst the repositioning of rear spoiler reduced rear end lift by a massive 60%. In 1984 the Storm badge meant there was a Zender bodykit, 6J x 14in alloy wheels and 185/60VR-14 tyres. Cosmetically buyers could choose from metallic blue or brown, with blue or beige interior plus leather covered steering wheel rim, gaiter and gear knob. GTX models, which arrived at the same time to replace the GTi, also aped the Storm style with the Zender bodykit and similar interior trimmings. In addition, alloy wheels, sunroof, central locking, trip computer and tinted glass completed the standard specification.

Best model of the lot was the 16-valve in June 1985. All of a sudden 130 mph and 0–60 mph in 7.6 secs became possible. Other upgrades included a larger exhaust, stronger drive shafts and a larger fuel tank, with rear discs and ventilated fronts, plus an extra brace on the front wishbones, stiffer springs, anti roll bars and revised shock settings. Then in 1988 the range was revamped for the UK market and rationalised down to three models, a 1.6 GT, 1.8 GTX and in the middle a 1.8 carburettor fed Scala. On the 16-valve front there were two versions already fitted to the Golf and Jetta models. There was the standard 139 bhp version and a catalyst equipped 16-valve unit producing 129 bhp.

The Scirocco died in July 1992, the last examples being badged as Scalas and GT IIs, with colour keyed paint work, revised interiors and offered with 95 bhp, or 129 bhp versions of the 1.8 engine. Britain loved the Scirocco and would miss it dearly, but even the small, affordable coupé market was now under threat. At least there was the Corrado to get excited about.

Corrado, a less practical but brutally pretty Golf.

The Corrado came to the UK in May 1989. Although Golf based, it weighed 400lbs more, which hardly helped the acceleration figures, only the top speed improved because of the superior aerodynamics. It also shared front MacPherson strut and wishbone suspension with the GTI. However, at the back

was a revised torsion beam system first used on the new style Passat which effectively added an element of rear wheel steer. The Passat also donated its five-
speed gearbox combined with a 3.45:1 final drive ratio. This was connected to
a supercharged 1.8 which produced 160 bhp and was badged a G60. It was left
hand drive only until April 1991. Alternatively a special model solely for the UK
and Italian markets was the 16V. Power steering was standard but there were
variations when it came to brakes. ABS was standard on the G60, which had
28cm front discs whilst the 16V made do with 25.6 cm diameter ones. 6.5 x 15in
BBS cross spoke alloys with 195/50VR-15 tyres were the order of the day on the
G60 whilst the 16V made do with 6Js and 185/55VR-15 tyres. Within a year
electric windows, central locking, height adjustable steering column and a
radio/cassette was part of the package along with leather covered steering wheel,
gear knob, gear lever and handbrake gaiters.

For 1992 an exterior facelift amounted to a new four bar grille and a bigger
fuel tank. Inside, the radio/cassette was of the pull out variety, intermittent screen
wipe had an adjustable delay and a torch key illuminated the way. Most improvements came the 16V's way. In the engine department it received the new 1984cc
engine from the Golf 3. Catalyst equipped with K-Motronic fuel injection and
output remained at 136 bhp, although the pulling power was significantly
improved. ABS was now standard along with 6J x 15 Estoril alloy wheels. Taking
on the lower reaches of the Porsche line up in 1992 was the V6 model. The
2,861cc engine produced 190 bhp, powered to 60 mph in just 6.4 secs and the
top speed was 145 mph.

For '93 there were more interior changes as the electric window switches
were repositioned and there were major changes to indicator stalks, air vents
and new rotary heater controls. The finishing touch was neat red instrument
needles. After that, the biggest news was chrome rather than body colour
badging in late 1993. In 1994 an entry level Corrado powered by the 8 valve
2.0 litre model was launched. Electric windows, mirrors, green tinted glass,
alloy wheels, rear wash/wipe, front fog lamps and sports seats were all part
of the package.

The last Corrados to leave the production line in 1995 were 500 right hand
drive VR6 'Storm' models in Mystic blue, or Classic green with leather interior
and the obviously quite lonely Solitude alloys. Apart from the 'Storm' badges the
only specification upgrades were front seat heating and an upgraded Sony
radio/CD player.

As good as the Corrado clearly was Volkswagen were not going to replace
it so perhaps the Golf GTI and all those other copy hot hatches had finally killed
the coupé. Certainly in Europe it was dying off although Japan hadn't given up
on them. What Volkswagen had done though was breathe new life into the
convertible and massively expand the marketplace. Because if you wanted a soft-
top, back in the '70s the choice was hardly inspiring. A prehistoric MGB meant

compulsory flat-capped headgear and routine B road breakdown. Alternatively a cutting edge X1/9 was wonderful but impractical, and rampant rot meant that it was likely to implode. The way forward was the slashed hatchback policy adopted by Karmann in 1979. A Golf was already roomy, reliable and stylish and with the roof missing the sky was the limit.

Introduced back in 1979 at the Geneva Motor Show the convertible was a bit of a heavy old clodhopper. That's because there were major reinforcements to make up for the lack of proper roof. The most obvious manifestation of reinforcement was Karmann's substantial roll bar, which in addition provided anchorage points for the seat belts and guide channels for the door glass and rear windows. At the front an additional crossbeam beefed up the area behind the dashboard and the suspension turrets were also reinforced. Further back, the sills were strengthened between the wheel arches, leading to a back box section cross beam mounted behind the rear seats and onto a boxed boot structure. Not surprisingly, the weight went up by 300lbs over the standard car hence the tardy 0–60 mph time for the GTI version of 9.8 seconds.

American specification (it's the teeth and hair that give it away) Mark 1 Golf Convertible.

Over the years convertible modifications ran parallel with the hatchback's (the GTI badge was finally adopted in 1985), but the one constant was the Mark 1 bodyshell. In 1988 there was a clumsy attempt to soften up the bodywork by adding new smoother moulded bumpers, integrated front spoiler, rear apron and incorporating sill and wheel arch extensions. If you don't want the pram hood purity of the older model (essential for the proper boot that VW demanded), then the later the better. Equipment levels certainly increased in 1990 as the GTI got an electro-hydraulically operated hood.

In 1991 at the suggestion of the UK importers the design department came up with two models to replace the GTI, which demonstrated the huge importance of this market to VW. The resulting 'Sportline' had power steering, Recaro sports seats in black and red trim, red needled instruments, 6J x 15" alloys and either red or black paint work combined with a black hood. If buyers did not fancy black or red, then the 'Rivage' model offered Classic Blue metallic paintwork, Mauritius Blue cloth and an Indigo Blue hood. The Rivage Leather arrived in October of that year with beige leather interior, seats, door handles, handbrake grip and gear lever gaiter with the alternative choice of Classic Green Pearl Metallic and a black hood. Under the bonnet was multi-point fuel injection and a catalytic converter at the back. It outlived the other two models, which were discontinued in July '92. After the Rivage Leather went in July '93, the old Clipper got a 95 bhp version of the 1.8i engine and soldiered on until January 1994.

Chunkier late '80s GTI Convertible. Euro spec, (bad teeth, receding hair not pictured).

Although the Mk1 body style was a constant, the seemingly variable factor was the name of the model, which veered from convertible to cabriolet. Certainly it is the special editions that monopolised the cabriolet name. Initially there were all black, followed by all white special editions, the latter proving incredibly popular and by 1986 it accounted for almost a third of sales in the UK.

VW took the highly popular mix and match colour scheme theme and in 1987 turned it into the Quartet range available on the now officially designated 1.6 Cabriolet and 1.8 GTI Convertible. There were four exterior colours on offer, Alpine White, Paprika Red, Helios Blue and Sapphire Grey, with colour keyed bumpers, wheel arches and door mirrors, with four upholstery options and four hood finishes. Phew! Sixty-four permutations in all. By 1989 the Quartet colour options doubled to eight exterior colours, with three hood colours and a new range of upholstery trim, which included part leather seats. These Quartets were rebadged simply as GTIs and remained an option on the Clipper. There you have it: Volkswagen's complete understanding of the buyers who wanted to mix and match and have exactly what they wanted. The convertible buyer was not some old bloke in a flat cap, or even some young bloke smoking a pipe, they had changed.

Audi's luxury mini hatchback, years ahead of its time.

Although the '70s and '80s were all about the VW Golf, it is worth mentioning a teeny tiny hatchback that is now largely forgotten. The Audi 50 was part of the company's programme to build a wide range of models to appeal to all sorts of customers, especially those who wanted something economical. The 50 bhp engine gave the car its name and it was suitably compact too, yet it had safety crumple zones, a decent amount of room inside and the all important hatched back. Launched in 1974 and built in Wolfsburg on the Volkswagen lines it drew a lot of attention. Actually when the Audi badges were replaced by VW ones in 1975 and the specification stripped back to the bare bones, sales of the Polo went through the roof. Clearly sharing components was going to be the way forward for Volkswagen.

However, there really wasn't much point in the relatively more luxurious and certainly much more expensive Audi continuing, but it did until 1975. The Audi 50 was though a hint of things to come, because the homily, 'mini cars make mini profits' was certainly true of the original Mini. It may have been at the top end of the sales charts as motorists switched towards more economical alternatives, but didn't make much money because it wasn't expensive enough. Audi assumed that customers would pay for a bit more quality and class, but they were thirty years too early. BMW and their bouncing baby MINI, effectively a 0.5 Series BMW in all but size have led the way with premium pricing.

So back in March 1975 the Polo was nothing more than a low specification Audi 50, which finally came to the UK in October '76. Not the most exciting VW which struggled for attention over the years, but all it needed to do was behave like a faithful little mutt, do as it was told and not cause too much trouble and the owners would be more than happy. From February 1977 the booted

Derby version was introduced, which wasn't much to get worked up about. From 1981 the Polo got a revised body so that it looked at best like a miniaturised estate car, but to everyone else it really was a bread van, but with windows. There was though a slightly funky three door coupé, although really it was just another less long hatch. Launched in January '83 it might have had some red paint on grille like a GTI plus front and rear spoilers, a centre console and plastic trims on wheel arches and sills, but underneath the bonnet was a 1093cc 50 bhp, 4-speed slug. VW tried to sex it up a bit with a 1272cc, 55 bhp engine in September '83, but even calling it Coupe S, sticking four lights on grille, a rev counter, sports seats and steering wheel, could not hide the fact that this was another slow if prettier slug. The specification improvements still kept coming though as a steel sliding roof was standardised in September '86 along with the economy rather than performance minded 4+E gearbox. August '87 was exciting because of the alloys and twin jet washer nozzles.

No, its not a small van with windows it's a Volkswagen Polo.

VW nicked the steel sunroof back in Sep '88 and the Polo looked dark and dingy again. Despite a naff 'Parade' special edition it was a good job that the GT came along in November '90. Multi-point fuel injection was connected to the 1272cc engine and it pumped out a mighty 72 bhp. 60 mph came up in 14.5 seconds and top speed was 95 mph. Fitted with a catalyser and rectangular headlamps, wraparound indicators, red inserts in the bumpers and a three spoke steering wheel, things were starting to look serious for the old Polo. In fact the really serious Polo was the intercooled and supercharged G40, which produced 113 bhp. The performance was a highly respectable 122 mph top speed and 0–60 mph in 8.1 seconds. The suspension was firmed up and lowered by an inch, the alloys were 5.5 x 13" BBS, there was GTI like wheel arch extensions and side rubbing strips too. Inside there was some cloth with a sporty check design on it, plus a four speaker HO5 Panasonic pull out radio/cassette. In its short life all that changed in November of '91 was the fitting of white front indicators and partially smoked rear light clusters. Along with the rest of the range it was replaced in August '94 by an all-new Polo.

As much as BMW blossomed in the '80s this was also Volkswagen's decade providing good honest working man's transportation with a stylish twist when it came to the GTI or the convertible/cabriolet. The Rupperts were more than generally agreed that Golfs were a good thing after a Mark 1 1.6 automatic joined my Dad's fleet in 1981. When he asked me about a 318i that I could have collected some commission on, I told him to get a better value, cheaper to run GTI. He bought two and when I left the showroom and bought a GTI I then drove nothing else right into the late '90s.

I may offend Golf purists here, but the Mark 2 was the best Golf of all. Even when the Golf Mark 23 comes out in a century's time, which hovers and flies to Mars and back, it still won't be the second best Golf ever. That would be the Mark 1. The Mark 2 is tougher and chunkier. It isn't just the best Golf ever, it is the most representative German car of the 1980s which was more affordable than any other and affected more motoring lives for the better. As much as Henrietta and Jake would have one each that perfectly fitted into their West End lifestyle, it also suited the older Gentleman who'd had enough of exploding Triumph Dolomites like my Dad. Even when the Golf was getting on a bit and a whole heap cheaper, students and first time drivers and first time families all appreciated its reliability, toughness and practicality. And there was of course no other car quite like the GTI. Even though plenty of other cars may have been christened GT and I, nothing else came close and that includes the wonderfully urgent but rather flimsy Peugeot 205 GTi.

However, at this early stage of the Victory story there is still one little formality to negotiate, yes I still have to pass the audition.

Golf vs The Rest, well the Golf was up against just about everything in almost every sector of the car market in the '70s and '80s so here's a brief guide to some of those major non German opponents.

Volkswagen Golf vs The Rest

Austin Allegro – Badly built with a boot. Estate was a mini hearse and didn't come close.

Austin Maestro – Not bad, eventually had to use the Golf gearbox which says it all really.

Chrysler/Talbot Horizon – Good to drive but averagely built.

Citroen GSA – Proper bonkers Citroen, different but bigger and more troublesome.

Citroen BX – Clever hydraulic suspension, very rectangular, plenty to go wrong.

Datsun Cherry – VW levels of dependability but zero points for style.

Fiat 128 – Even more of a box on wheels and beat the Golf to having a hatched back, but oh the rust . . .

Fiat Strada – Built by robots which didn't stop the rot. Original model interesting to look at.

Fiat Uno – One of Giugiaro's so spacious and a big, big hatchbacked hit.

Ford Escort – The people's hatchback for those who couldn't quite afford a Golf.

Honda Civic – Massive range of efficient, sophisticated but truly ugly cars.

Lancia Delta – Italian Golf and another Giugiaro. However it was no Golf.

Nissan Cherry/Sunny – Generic reliable cars with awful names and styling.

Peugeot 104/305 – Dated 104, whilst 305 quite elegant and practical.

Peugeot 309 – A grown up 205 but not nearly as pretty or charming.

Renault 16 – Original misunderstood five-door hatch. Underrated but dated.

Renault 11 – Disappointing on every level. So dull.

Rover 214/216 – Thanks to the Japanese a decent Rover. Later hatches best.

Talbot Alpine/Minx/Rapier – Lots of space and glass and rust.

Toyota Corolla – Reliability on the button, but a total style bypass.

Triumph Dolomite – Very old, Italian style but British build quality.

Triumph Acclaim – Japanese to the rescue again. Mechanicals good, styling v.bad.

Vauxhall Chevette – Good basic car that was nice to drive, but so dated.

Vauxhall Astra – Opel's answer to the Golf and very good it was too.

Volvo 340/360 – Mature image means had none of the Golf's cross-generational appeal.

Scirocco vs The Rest

Alfa Romeo Alfetta GT/GTV – More Giugiaro with added Alfa appeal.

Alfa Romeo Alfasud Sprint – It's a mini Alfetta.

Fiat X1/9 – Versatile roof, great handling, but lousy at resisting rust.

Ford Capri – Lovable, unsophisticated, easy to live with.

Honda Prelude – Sophisticated and reliable, yet another victim of rampant corrosion.

Honda Civic CRX – Cute, good engines and great handling, lovely pocket sized projectile.

Lancia Beta HPE – Coupé masquerading as a High Performance Estate. Confused.

Nissan 280Z/Silvia ZX – 280 dated and hardly nimble. ZX largely invisible and not special.

MGB GT – Pensionable, thumped with American Regulation Federal Bumper ugly stick.

Mazda RX7 – Very pretty and clever. Too clever maybe and too expensive.

Opel Manta – A Capri with 'O' levels and really quite good.

Renault 15/17 – Dull, well it was based on the forgettable Renault 12.

Renault Fuego – Oddy bulbous. Turbo scarily quick.

Toyota Corolla GT – What was the point?

Toyota Celica – Later the better for style and transformation of Carina mechanicals.

Volvo 480 – Has pop up headlamps and there's a turbo, but it looks like a mini estate.

Volkswagen GTI vs The Rest

Alfa Romeo Alfasud – Closest in spirit and execution but build quality way off.

Alfa Romeo 33 – Sud updated but not very well.

Fiat 128 Coupe' – Looked like a hatch despite two door layout.

Fiat Strada 130TC – Abarth badge helped to fire up sporty image. Crude but fun.

Fiat Super Miafiori – Rust was a factor, made a lot of noise, but not much flair.

Ford Escort RS1800/Mexico/RS2000 – Old school rear wheel drive entertainment.

Ford Escort XR3/RS1600i/RS Turbo – Rivalled Golf for sales if not style or finesse.

Lancia Delta HF Turbo/Integrale – Looked the part and Integrale truly hardcore.

MG Maestro/EFi/Turbo – Amusing and surprisingly quick, comedy body kit though.

Peugeot 205 GTi – Thump in the back fast, and very nimble, but feels lightweight.

Peugeot 309 GTi – Very underrated, if it had only been prettier.

Renault 5 Gordini Turbo/GT Turbo – Point and squirt.

Renault 11 Turbo – Best thing about it was the Turbo, otherwise forgettable.

Sunbeam 1600Ti – Proper little rally car.

Sunbeam-Lotus – Actually homologated for rallying, oddly difficult to sell.

Volkswagen Convertible/Cabriolet vs The Rest

Fiat 124 Spider – Pretty and pretty old too. Troublesome.

Fiat Strada Cabriolet – Rusty basket surprisingly quickly.

Ford Escort Cabriolet – Uncomplicated, affordable and undemanding. Perfect.

Lancia Beta Spider – Expensive and rusty. Pretty and nice to drive though.

MG Midget – Ancient history that should have been buried a long time ago,

MGB Roadster – As Midget really.

Peugeot 205 Cabriolet – Despite roll bar still feels a tad flimsy.

Volkswagen Polo vs The Rest

Austin Metro – Good handling and ride, a more practical Mini.

Citroen AX – Frugal, five door door versions, diesel engines, but hardly solid.

DAF/Volvo 66 – Dutch oddity with estate option and stress free Variomatic gearbox.

Fiat 126 – Marginal motoring which finally got a hatch in 1987. Pointless.

Fiat Panda – Grown up 126, but not by very much, almost as pointless.

Ford Fiesta – Has five door flexibility and marginal Ford running costs.

Nissan Micra – Drab little box beloved of driving schools.

Peugeot 205 – Pretty and fun to drive, diesels great, budget motoring with style.

Renault 5 – Always nicely styled and fine to drive, but rust and durability are issues.

Toyota Starlet – Another Japanese box that was a doddle to drive and indestructible.

Vauxhall Nova – Hatches and saloons with old engines and dull looks but high sales.

In the Cassette Deck ...

 Grace Jones – Living My Life Arguably the first and pretty much the most important female rapper whose style could be described as fairly aggressive/seductive talking. Very well produced this is effectively low volume electro funk. Park up and play 'The Apple Stretching' with the electric sunroof open on a 5 Series and watch all the passers-by get into the groove. That really happened.

3 The Luxury Gap, plugged by Grosser Germans

Those great big S Club Sevens. Size does matter as does the kitchen sink specification sheets and of course Dreikugelwirbelwannenbrennraum.

March • New Car Profit: £6,110 • Used Car Profit: £2,146 • Total £8,256

The venue for my audition was The Dorchester Hotel. On Park Lane, Apparently finding the room where the interview was to be conducted was all part of the selection process.

Certainly dropping by at reception then finding may way to the fifth floor and room 518 was easy enough and must have proved that at the very least I had a sense of direction which would come in handy when it came to test drives. I certainly had a sense that meeting two strange men in a West End hotel room seemed a bit iffy. At best it could be interpreted as a clandestine business meeting, at worst an international drugs deal, or something more unsavoury involving one young man and two much older men. Certainly the fact that the curtains were drawn was not reassuring as the lights were set to mood rather than proper illumination. Refreshments were on offer and it was all delicate china cups, one lump or two and a pert little teapot.

I was preoccupied with the sheer oddness of the situation as I perched on the Queen Anne style chair, whilst my interrogators spread out on a chaise longue and asked questions. All the interviews I'd had so far in my life involved a sterile office and a great big barrier of a desk and usually just the one middle manager shuffling some papers on his desk. So although I didn't realise it at the time, this was a very clever way of working out whether I would be fazed by new situations and surroundings. They knew that selling cars would put me into some odd circumstances and I'd just have to cope.

Obviously I could drink a cuppa without spilling it and without raising my pinkie in the air like an affected twit. I must have looked half presentable too. One thing I never got out of the habit of doing was wearing a suit. Dad made sure I had a made to measure for my first job, fresh from the tailors in Commercial Street E1. After that I always wore suits and jackets right through my student years, just to irritate those who took being a student just a bit too seriously. Army surplus parkas and Arafat scarves was not me. By the early to mid '80s fashions had shifted and we were in a double-breasted, thin tie and pointed collars, which suited me fine, I'll come to my hair later.

Personally I think they could have introduced an even more testing element by requiring me to abseil out the window rather than leaving by the door. But before I left the man who would eventually be my sales manager, and the bloke who would ultimately tell me with some relish that I would be walking home, asked me what the secret of selling success was. Persistence. You didn't take no for answer. You kept on calling, you got in their way, you ground them down, you effectively gave the customer no option but to say yes, even if it was to get rid of you. However, this persistence thing only worked properly if you did it in a nice way. A charming way. A flirty, but firm way. I knew all that because my Dad had told me. Thanks Dad.

I deliberately walked away from the Dorchester towards Hyde Park Corner. To go the opposite way back up Park Lane to Marble Arch would mean walking past 56 Park Lane and the showroom. I couldn't face seeing all those lovely cars behind the plate glass if I was going to be denied the chance of trying to sell them.

A week later I got a fairly thin envelope containing some creamy Basildon Bond stationery with a BMW roundel on it that read, 'thanks but no thanks'. Then a few days later I got another envelope with creamy Basildon Bond paper and a BMW logo on it inviting me back for a second interview. Either this was an administrative cock up, or someone they regarded as a much better prospect had bailed out after the unsettling hotel interview. I wasn't about to question the confusing messages I was getting from my potential new employers. It could have been a test of course. Maybe they sent all successful round one winners these double bluff letters. If you pointed out their error perhaps you were a bit too pedantic and straight laced for the cut and thrust of selling. Whereas those who ignored it and just got on with the business of selling BMWs were the sort of creative characters pushing truthfulness and believability to the outside limits that they actually needed. I really didn't know and I certainly didn't care. I was never going to mention the letter to them just in case it reminded them about that candidate with the remarkably similar name (Rames Juppert) who they had meant to invite back.

The second interview was worth it because I actually got to visit the showroom this time and meet a whole new bunch of people asking me questions These included a bloke with a beard who would become my assistant sales manager, a person who wouldn't and a lady who was old enough to be my sister. They were ground floor management responsible for prodding and pushing their staff around and occasionally offering an arm around the shoulder or a pat on the back. I thought maybe I could distract them for a bit.

In the application I had made much of the fact that the company was called Cooper Park Lane, and I owned a Mini Cooper. The connection was John Cooper, the man who had not just won the world Formula One Championship a few times with a car of his own design which had pioneered engines at the back, he'd also invented the go faster Mini. Indeed his works factory where they made the racing cars was now the site of their Cooper Thames Ditton branch. When they bought John Cooper Garages out, they kept the iconic name.

I think that they were slightly impressed by that sort of knowledge. Knowing stuff about cars had not been a requirement at all. In fact, they made it plain it was rare for them to employ dedicated car sales people anyway. They wanted fresh meat, people they could mould to sell their way.

I may also have mentioned persistence a few times. Plus I said that my Dad trusted me to drive his Daimler Sovereign and so far I hadn't crashed it. Well I couldn't because it had been severely broken due to British Leyland's incompetence and was now semi-retired and largely ignored.

A week later I had a thick envelope full of terms of employment and a really nice letter telling me to roll up some time in November 1983 at Park Lane. Little did I know that the interview process was not quite over yet.

The first day though was seeing how the whole operation worked. Finding out just where the service department was, which turned out to be Brentford, several miles away rather than around the corner in Mayfair. Then there was the exciting subterranean world of the sales office. It was located directly below the showroom floor with no natural light but awash with body odours, adrenalin and cigarette smoke. It was also a time to find out who the important people were like the delivery drivers and the girl who actually ordered all the cars. Probably the most crucial thing on that first day though was making sure that we could all drive.

Yes we were three. Cooper Park Lane had taken on three new salesmen. Except that they hadn't. One would stay at the flagship new car dealership to fight it out with nine other salesmen, whilst the other two would be working at

Cooper St James, a brand new showroom that would be opening in January 1984, a few hundred yards away just off Piccadilly and staffed by three salesmen.

I didn't know where I was going to end up. But I didn't care too much. The new showroom at St James' looked like the better berth, being a fresh start and up against other greenhorns rather than the old pros at Park Lane, which seemed a lot more challenging. All I cared about was being handed the keys to a BMW 7 series and told to drive up and down the West Way for a bit. The West Way is a sort of mini motorway in the sky, the elevated part of the A40, which runs over North Kensington. If I crashed or drove like a lunatic then the dream was over.

A 735iASE was not a challenging car to drive, pull the stick into D and off it went. In a way it felt just like Dad's old Sovereign, except it was a whole lot firmer and far more likely to complete a journey without coming to an unscheduled stop. From the steering to the fixtures and fittings it felt mightily solid. There was a big shove in the back when I pressed the accelerator, as the BMW six cylinder's turbine like smoothness powered me past the dawdlers, buses and taxis. It was intoxicating. It was also an SE. Now Dad's 1978 Daimler may have been a top of the line Sovereign but the kit list beyond the power steering, leather, automatic, radio/cassette, electric windows, central locking and fluted grille and accompanying Daimler badges wasn't too much to get excited about. However an SE level 7 series lived up to its billing.

The A meant automatic gearbox and the SE stood for Special Equipment so it had absolutely everything fitted to it that could possibly be crammed into a car in 1983, plus as much as could be ticked on the options list. After all, this was a senior management vehicle and would be used for demonstration purposes, so it needed as many toys as possible. There was electric everything, including the front and rear seats. Most exciting of all was something called ABS brakes, which I got a live demonstration of days later in Richmond Park. The Sales Manager destined to run the new showroom took us out in another 7 and she gave it some proper stick in the Royal Park. To this day I can still feel the jolting sensation in my bottom.

Finished in metallic black it looked like pure evil and we were told that the reason why everyone would look at the car was the 1 BMW number plate. I suspect they mostly thought at best we were terrible show offs for driving up and down the West Way all morning, or rookie chauffeurs, or at the very worst, just a bunch of complete toss pots. Whatever they thought my first full dose of a great big BMW was an impressive one.

In theory big, luxury cars aren't supposed to be fun, or that good looking though the Jaguars were always handsome and fun to drive with a low slung sporty driving position. The extra exciting element was of course lots of steam, a muffled explosion and then waiting for the AA man. By contrast the 7 was more efficient, sharper and just a lot more German.

Originally a luxury car's job was simply to waft and roll, but clearly a BMW is different. After all it was advertised as the ultimate driving machine. So when BMW decided to start building a range of serious saloons in the late '60s they had to be up to the marque. The New Klasse and 02 (see Chapter 4) had set the standard and now they needed a bigger more comfortable car. This vehicle was codenamed the E3 by BMW (these E numbers will crop up with alarming regularity over the following chapters) but was identified by its engine size as a 2500, 2800 and later 3.0 and 3.3. It turned out to be big, beautiful and great to drive. The front-end arrangement of quad lamps and kidney grille established the look of BMW, which then lasted for decades. Best of all under the bonnet was a silky, smooth and powerful straight six. Now underrated, overlooked and hardly appreciated at all it deserves to be remembered and should indeed be celebrated for putting some style and the substance into the luxury car market. So why was this all-new saloon so good?

The cops loved the big old Baroque Angels. Nice blue light. Nice leather jacket too.

The three pointed star. How that badge must have dominated BMW directors' every waking hour. The New Klasse was all very well, but they wanted something bigger, better, grosser, more profitable and more Mercedes like. The last big Beemer was the hopelessly dated and hand built 501/502 series. It wasn't nicknamed the 'Baroque Angel' for nothing, because it certainly was beautiful but in a very old fashioned way with big swoopy wings and large soppy headlamps. It also moved in a very ethereal and angelic way, which is one way of saying that it was very, very slow. However, taxi drivers absolutely loved them for their roominess and so did the police, and here's why. Towards the end of the car's life BMW decided to tempt the Angel over to the dark side by installing a large V8 that instantly transformed it from one of the slowest to one of the fastest German production cars. BMW had managed to finally inject a bit of sportiness into the big old Baroque Angel, but in reality these models were 1930s throwbacks, which incredibly remained in production until 1964 and were well overdue for replacement.

Meanwhile as the 1.8 and 2.0 litre New Klasse chipped away at the lower reaches of the Mercedes range it was decided to make a full on assault at the Stuttgart based company's mid sized heartland. That decision was actually taken in early 1965 when BMW hired Bernhard Osswald away from Ford and put him in charge of this vital project. Already responsible for the 1800 TI/SA and the 02 series, Osswald was on message when it came to understanding what BMW was all about. Extensive market research had already established that the buying public were ready for an alternative to the establishment saloons from Mercedes.

Much was made by the German press on the launch of the E3 that it bore a dimensional resemblance to the latest W114/W115 Series (more codenames) Mercedes and that it also had identical straight six engine sizes of 2500 and 2800. There were other suggestions that if the kidney grille and lights were blanked off, the rest of the vehicle looked alarmingly like the latest generation Mercedes. Obviously BMW were rattling cages and had also made a rattlingly good car. The 1968 launch statement was a clear dig at Merc, "Our model was neither a muscle-bound body builder, nor a stolid citizen. We were thinking more of a field athlete – temperamental, sinewy, fit, nimble footed, agile, energetic and entirely youthful." Oooo, get them.

At this point it is worth taking a look at just what Mercedes had been up to so far. They really needed something to plug the yawning gap between the saloon W123s and the utterly over the top limousine 600. Ah yes, the W100 according to the model code effectively took on the world. The world amounted to the super league of road going luxury vehicles bought by the super rich and heads of state who wanted to make the grandest of entrances. With the 600 it was Mercedes vs the old world charm of Rolls Royce and the new world overstatement of Cadillac. Mercedes knew that technically they were up to the challenge. Indeed it was all about rekindling their heady pre-war position when any obscenely rich person or dictator wouldn't be seen dead in anything less than a Mercedes 770 model.

Launched in 1930 it was an 8-cylinder 7.7 litre monster that could develop 200 bhp with an optional supercharger. It was the vehicle that was nicknamed 'Grosser' (that's larger in German rather than a reference to someone who sells fruit and veg) but also a subtle dig that it really was a bit over the top and therefore fairly gross in a bad way. In fact, in 1938 it became even grosser when the engine output was increased to a maximum 230 bhp with a supercharger, enabling it to travel at speeds in excess of 100 mph.

Mercedes were determined to do it all over again, but a whole lot better. When motor manufacturers built so-called 'flagship' cars they seldom went to the lengths that Mercedes would do with the 600. Here was a car that would showcase their talent for technology and also make the lowliest taxi driver in a rattly 200D puff out his chest in pride and tell himself that he drove one of those too.

This is the family friendly 'small' 600.

Announced in 1963 the 600 was available in two versions: a 'dinky' four door saloon for every day use with a 126 inch wheelbase which seated five to six and an 'decadent' Pullman long wheelbase (153 inch) model that could seat seven to eight, but mostly it was just the head of state/cruel dictator and his Mrs. Not only that, there was a Landaulet version so that if there wasn't much chance of an opposition coup Mr and Mrs Dictator could throw half the roof section back and wave alfresco at their oppressed subjects. As if that wasn't enough 600s to consider, there was also a six-door Pullman that meant that the bodyguards could all come along for the ride and presumably be deployed in a defensive pattern very easily too. Oh and not forgetting that the 600 could easily be a place of sanctuary if fully bullet proofed, just one of many options.

The 600 was not an easy build like a Roller or Caddy. These had a big old fashioned chassis on which could be plonked whatever coach built body took their fancy. Mercedes believed in modern unitary construction so there was a subframe for the front suspension and crumple zones built into the huge body. That body was imperious, impressive and looked like a small continent, but with chrome. Lots of chrome, on the bumpers, around the wheel arches and window frames. Inside, it was well appointed but nowhere near as convincing or special as what a Rolls Royce could come up with, but then in car comfort and technology was what Mercedes were all about. Rolls Royce may have done class with ease, but Mercedes did clever with complete confidence.

It was the little things that set the 600 apart from ordinary cars, like the chrome door mirrors on both front doors which at the time was highly unusual (usually mounted on the wings), especially as they could be adjusted from the inside. The steering wheel adjusted for rake and reach too, so at least the chauffeur was going to be comfy. Indeed if he needed to hoof the spare wheel out of the car he wouldn't have to try too hard, because there was a neat little spring that popped it up from the right hand side of the boot.

There was a whole hydraulic system built into the 600, which utilised a pump that was connected to the engine. In turn it operated the windows, could open the boot lid and lock all the doors centrally. Not only that, it opened the fuel flap and air vents. If the rich owner ordered the sliding sunroof and a glass divider to keep the chauffeur out of the loop, these were all hydraulically operated. There was also division when it came to the heating and ventilation system, which was entirely separate for front and rear.

The whole magnificent edifice was tugged along by a huge 6.3 litre fuel injected V8 engine that produced a substantial 300 bhp. It was the company's first production engine of this configuration, which had a full time job powering all the separate compressors for the air conditioning, brake circuit, air suspension and that hydraulic power circuit. Incredible then that the 600 could get above 120 mph and return a frankly amazing 10mpg. Disc brakes all round helped bring it all to a halt and that air suspension could be adjusted to give pretty sporty handling. There was an air bag over each wheel backed up with rubber springs and the chauffeur could from the dashboard make it all softer, harsher, higher or lower. The future of motoring had arrived early, for those who could afford it.

The 600 was a phenomenal luxury car and arguably the best ever which was built to order and customised according to whatever the buyer wanted, the only limit was their imagination. Indeed John Lennon, Elvis Presley, Elizabeth Taylor and any number of ruthless dictators, including Saddam Hussein, had one or more. Only 2,677 were built and it remained on the price lists until 1981, but its impact went way beyond that small number. It was a charismatic, prog rock star of a super luxury saloon.

I wasn't the least bit famous or dictatorial, but I had a 600. It was one of my very favourite Dinky model cars. Long and red, it dominated my extensive collection of toy cars. Some achievement that a Mercedes could do this in miniature. A scaled down 600 though could of course have an even bigger impact. Say hello to the S-Class.

S-Class, this is a 300SE. Big isn't it?

1965 is when Mercedes made a clean break from their 'New Generation' medium saloons and came up with a large, imposing and elegantly styled vehicle for the rather better off. W108/109 was the model designation and the design penned by Paul Bracq was very similar to 'New Generation', but bigger. Indeed, there was a now a clear resemblance throughout the entire Mercedes range from the sporty SLs through to the gargantuan 600. Buyers found this reassuring and it always gave them something more expensive to aim for as they targeted the next model up. This was a lesson not lost on BMW and their own corporate design style. The 600 may have been out of most buyers' leagues, but the S-Class represented something slightly more attainable.

What the S-Class had in abundance was sheer presence and space. Convex side glass, and just more glass area overall, plus a lower rear floor meant that it seemed huge on the inside. There was also a 300SEL model, which had air suspension, which was four inches longer, giving back seat passengers extra legroom. Interestingly, the L did not stand for 'Long' as you would expect, but 'Luftfederung', which was German for air suspension. It was also given its own unique designation W109. Otherwise there was the usual combination of numbers and letters to distinguish each model according to engine size and specification. So in addition to the 300SEL, there was a choice of six-cylinder 250S, 250SE and 300SE. Three years later in 1968 though there was a big change as the 2.8 litre engine was standardised across the range to make the 280S, 280SE, 280SEL and 300SEL, confirming that you couldn't always trust the number to relate to the engine size. Indeed, the L in the 280SEL did not have air suspension at all, so presumably the L now meant long.

This is of course nitpicking when what buyers got was a high quality luxury express. By contrast it made the Rover P5 3.5 that Mrs Thatcher insisted on using as her Prime Ministerial motor well into the '80s look rather dated, cramped and shoddily built, even if it did cost less. Mind you, the old Rover's top speed with the wind behind it and that rather wonderful 3.5 V8 engine, would be 110 mph according to *Autocar* and it got to 60 mph in a tad over 10 seconds. Imagine then what a saloon that could charge on to 137 mph and get to 60 mph in 6.5 seconds would be like? Well that rocket ship was the 300SEL 6.3. But then again in 1968 the 6.3 cost a whopping £7743 whereas a Rover was just £2009. So was the 6.3 almost four times better? Probably. Here's why.

Mercedes 6.3 doesn't look mad, but it is. Standard driving living lights, very sensible.

At its most basic all Mercedes did was install its biggest engine, into its biggest production bodyshell. It was inspired lunacy to take the 6.3 V8 from the weighty 600 and put it into something more appropriate and almost svelte by comparison. By doing so they created what was clearly the first luxury super saloon. It wasn't just fast, it was extremely well behaved and refined due to the instantly responsive engine, standard automatic gearbox and the adjustable air suspension. On the outside though it looked like any other S-Class, unless you bothered to take a close look at the 6.3 badge on the boot, or took the time to notice that there were twin halogen headlamps and the additional driving lights at the front. Otherwise here was what car enthusiasts might refer to as a Q-car (very quick, with no outward signs of obvious quickness), but really it was a Grizzly Bear in Teddy Bear clothing.

Most famously a 6.3 was used to film Claude Lelouch's film *C'etait un Rendezvous* in 1976. In a nutshell, it's all about a mad dash across Paris at daybreak that took just under 10 minutes. It is much more exciting than it sounds which explains why it became a cult film. In the pre-video age you had either seen it at some private screening or on some dodgy bit of ciné film at some mate's house. Many believed that because of the low positioning of the camera and engine sounds it must have been a Ferrari V12 of some sort. But no, it was Lelouch, a 6.3 and some timely dubbing his Ferrari 275GTB going through the gears. Rumour has it, he was arrested when the film was first shown, but it was worth it to create the best real time, mad driving, lucky no one was pole axed by the great big Mercedes radiator grille, film, ever filmed.

Back to the rather more ordinary world of the S-Class, there was a radical reorganisation of engines and the introduction of a raft of V8s. Having introduced the engines for the W111 coupes and cabriolets it seemed logical to put them into the equally exclusive and prestigious saloon. First of all in 1969 the 300SEL had 3.5 appended to it with the installation of the new power plant. In 1970 the 3.5

was also put into the 280SE and 280SEL models that kept their original numbers, but got the 3.5 appendage. Just to confuse matters even further you could still buy the six-cylinder models. Then in 1971 there was a batch of 4.5 V8s all designed to comply with the increasingly strict American emission regulations. At which point you could get lost in the utter blizzard of numbers, letters and V8 capacities. Best then to look at what the S-Class actually meant then.

Well whether you call them the original S-Class, or W108/W109, this was the car that established Mercedes, or Daimler-Benz even, as the world's leading maker of prestige cars. No one else could make such a large number of upmarket saloons to such exacting quality standards. Maybe it had something to do with the fact that any minor bodywork blemishes could result in a full respray before leaving the factory. It was that attention to detail offset by sky-high prices and justified by a perennial waiting list that made all Mercedes great.

The S-Class became the world's favourite luxury car with more than 383,300 built up until 1972 as it became the acceptable face of Western capitalism. It was said that the old Imperialist undertones that came with a Roller or Caddy put off buyers in Africa. That was odd considering that there was a region called German East Africa, which later became Burundi, Rwanda and Tanganyika. Also in more recent history, what may have been branded National Socialism could not have been more imperialistic as Hitler made an attempt to enslave a continent or two.

That didn't seem to bother the African potentates presumably because they were not buying the top level Mercedes with their own money, as it would more often than not be misplaced overseas aid or some big fat bribe. With the country's rulers roaming around in Mercedes the inevitable trickle down effect was that the nation's entrepreneurs and taxi drivers all wanted one too. The colonisation of Africa via Mercedes saloons resulted in the cult of Wabenzi. Wabenzi was Swahili for wealthy people, often corrupt, who could afford expensive foreign cars.

BMW get serious with a proper executive express which has got the corporate kidney grilled four eyed face, a toolkit in the boot lid and classy interior. The future started here.

For BMW attaining this sort of status seemed a very long way off, but it wouldn't stop them trying very hard and brings us right back to the launch of their new big, luxury car. So as the debate raged about BMW's brave entry into Mercedes' previously exclusive territory, *Stern* magazine wondered, "A much more interesting question would be whether the big BMW is really a big car, or whether it is just a small BMW which has grown up a bit."

That was fair comment really because the whole design was pretty much a beefed up New Class, and that crazy German sense of humour did lead to the nick-name 'Grosse Klasse'. However, the bodyshell was all-new, the chassis had been tweaked and the new 6-cylinder engines had little in common with the smaller fours. Indeed, what the E3 did share with the New Class was similar packaging. So the all-independent coil suspension had MacPherson struts at the front and semi trailing arms at the rear. Under the bonnet was a slanted inline engine with a single chain driven overhead camshaft with a cast iron block and alloy head.

There was even more to it than that of course. Those front MacPherson struts were actually angled rearwards which meant less suspension travel and smoother ride. It also resulted in a car that was less likely to dive under heavy braking. The set-up also meant lighter steering although the worm and roller system from the four cylinder models, plus power steering was a valuable option. At the back, the coil springs were also repositioned which offered the enticing prospect of wider wheels and tyres. The 2800 model also had a limited slip differential, an anti-rollbar and Boge Nivomat self-levelling struts at the rear end. Bringing the saloons to a halt were 4-wheel ATE disc brakes which was one set of disc brakes more than the overtly sporting CS coupés which had to make do with drum brakes at the rear.

Wilhem Hofmeister did his usual top job when it came to styling. There was some New Class cues in there, but essentially this was large car that looked sharp and sexy. That big glass area, flat boot and bonnet plus the front end grouping of kidney grille and headlamps are still with us today. Inside, the main instrumentation was driver focused. This is then the BMW that ushered in another new era and weighing in at 2900 pounds meant that this was hardly 'grosse' at all.

The E3 must have been good, Formula One champ Emerson Fittipaldi had one.

So the E3 had the looks and the chassis, but most all it had the powerplant. There was no point entering this prestige end of the market if the engine was going to be coarse or gutless. Engineering genius Alex Von Falken came up with the M-52 engine with displacements of 2494cc and 2788cc delivering 150 and 170 bhp respectively. Like the 4-cylinder engines, the 6-cylinder had a cast iron block and an aluminium cylinder head with an overhead camshaft. But it had another feature as well, a trispherical turbulence-inducing combustion chamber. A bit of a mouthful, but it allowed the more complete burning of the air/fuel mixture with a minimum of residual hydrocarbons. That was big news in the American market and meant that all sorts of strange contraptions like air pumps and exhaust gas recirculators were not needed to clean up the emissions and strangle performance. Dreikugelwirbelwannenbrennraum! screamed the US advertising, which sort of stood for trispherical, turbulence bowl combustion chamber.

Zenith twin carburettors provided the fuel and they were available with either a four-speed manual, or a poor three-speed ZF automatic. The 2500 was nifty enough to get to 60 mph in ten seconds, but the intention always was to make M52s with even larger displacement units. The 180 bhp 3.0 litre in April 1971 was offered in twin carburettor and Bosch D-Jetronic fuel injected form and badged as the 3.0S and 3.0Si. Even more power was delivered with the 190 bhp 3295cc engine in March 1974, which was later revised in late 1976 with the installation of Bosch L-Jetronic fuel injection which produced 197 bhp. Indeed, this "Big Six" engine effectively carried on until 1993 in the 735i and 535i, which proves what a brilliant and advanced unit it was.

Everything you would think was going swimmingly at BMW. In 1968 their daily production figure reached 500 units per day. In that year more than 100,000 cars were produced and the company was starting to look very strong indeed especially when in 1970 they celebrated building their millionth post-war car. However, the customers who expected BMW to make sporting cars became confused by the more softly sprung 'big' car. Suddenly there were 5,000 E3s unsold and piling up at the dealers. Officially BMW blamed an overestimate of the market anticipating a 30% growth when there was only 12% increase and also poor export performance. In fact customer questionnaires revealed that the mature ex-Mercedes buyers were not impressed. They singled out the interior finish and BMW had to respond quickly. The E3 was never a cheap car and that was a problem in the United States.

Across the pond the clever solution was to combine the two models into one, call it the Bavaria and slash prices. The car appeared in 1971 and was actually the 2800 minus the leather upholstery and Nivomat rear suspension. A few items that had been standard on the 2800, such as the heated rear window and the neat tool kit mounted on the underside of the boot lid, were optional. Obviously, the Bavaria's most important feature was a lower price tag. At less than $5000 it was regarded as a bargain and bizarrely buyers then proceeded to load up the Bavarias from the options list. I wonder if that in any way influenced the company's highly successful approach to marketing their cars in the UK? In the meantime the E3 could only get bigger with the introduction of the L, which stood for lang/long.

The 3.3L appeared in March 1974 and was BMW's first entry into the limousine market since they had a go with the aborted 505 back in the '50s, but then they only made two of those. With the 3.3L the wheelbase was extended by four inches to 110 inches and the extra length could be seen behind the centre pillar and in the rear door. It had a fully loaded specification and an impressive turn of speed, getting to 60 mph in less than 9 seconds. In 1975 2.8 and 3.0 litre versions were also made available. The 3.3 Li was priced directly to compete with the Mercedes 450SE and more than 3000 of them were built.

Production ended in 1977 after 208,305 were built but not before the E3 had helped establish BMW in the upper reaches of the car market. Suddenly Mercedes had a credible rival. In the process BMW had developed a range of brilliant 6-cylinder engines that sealed their reputation. With the E3 the front-end design established the BMW family look whilst the interior pioneered the ergonomically correct drivercentric layout. BMW also put the tools in a neat little tray that screwed into the lid of the boot. So we have a lot to thank the E3 for.

Time though had not stood still for Mercedes, because as one S-Class left the factory for good in 1972 there was another one right behind it. The W116 may not have been prettier than the old model but undoubtedly it was better technically and became the flagship that led the company through the energy crisis and would power it into the 1980s as one of the strongest, most profitable and most prestigious in the world.

S-Class gets even bigger and a new number, W116.

Time was something that Mercedes were prepared to take to get the S-Class right and incredibly work had begun on the W116 way back in 1966. There is the suggestion that the arrival of the Jaguar XJ6 in 1968 had something to do with the long gestation period. The XJ6 was of course utterly brilliant in several key areas, namely styling, performance, handling and ride. No wonder it frightened Mercedes a bit, however the marginal build quality would have obviously made them laugh and the fact that the export version with the small 2.8 engine would regularly overheat and expire by the roadside. Building something more reliable than a Jaguar was not going to be a problem, or a big saloon with more room in the back for that matter. So all they had to nail was the ride and handling, or at least come close. Even if no Mercedes could ever create the whole interior wood and leather ambience, often on account of the wood not always being real and the leather looking and feeling like plastic. So the Jaguar was nothing to be frightened of, but the American engine emissions and safety regulations certainly were.

With that in mind the W116 grew up and was heavier and wider and longer by two inches in either direction. However, better side impact protection and improved crumple zones actually meant there was no more room inside for passengers and fractionally (one cubic metre) less luggage space compared to the old S.

As Audi would soon discover there was much to be learned by putting their prototypes into wind tunnels and the S was no exception. Everything on the outside from the wing mirrors to the smaller grille and rain deflectors on the screen pillars was designed to make the S more streamlined. The new S was much safer and little touches like relocating the spare wheel from the boot to underneath the floor to add more protection in the event of an impact and positioning the fuel tank above the rear axle with a filler neck that crushed rather than snapped in a crash, made all the difference. Lots of detail work went into the suspension and steering making this the safest car you could travel in well into the 1980s.

Inside it was the usual slightly austere but efficient story with plenty of padding and a large four spoke 'safety' steering wheel. Nothing like a Jag then, especially if the standard MB-Tex vinyl was not replaced by leather or velour, which in all truth wasn't very much better. But the seats were big and comfy and the whole package reassuringly solid, even if the rear legroom wasn't much better than an XJ6.

The first models were 280S, 280SE and 350SE followed a year later by the 450SE and SEL. The best of the S-Class bunch was the SEL with four extra inches (10cm) and all of that was given to the rear seat passengers. Everyone now agreed that Mercedes had a proper luxury car with a suitably powerful V8 engine. Unusually for such an indulgent and expensive car it was voted Car of the Year for 1973. Better that the S be rewarded rather than some basic family cart, which would be more able to deal with the looming fuel crisis.

However as SEL versions of the 280 and 350 models broadened the appeal, Mercedes did not do the obvious and make a green sprout powered S, or indeed cancel the whole model range out of sheer embarrassment at having so many profligate luxury cars in their model line up. No, they finally replaced the 300SEL with the 450SEL 6.9.

Launched in 1975 clearly this car had been held over for a year or so until the energy crisis had toned down to not being such a crisis, just more of a worry really, allowing big car buyers to start thinking naughty again. Certainly there was nothing naughtier than the 6.9, with or without the decimal point. The intention was to better the old 6.3 and that meant an even bigger engine was needed to cope with the larger body and all those annoying emissions regulations. Incredibly the engineers managed to simplify the engine and use a mechanical fuel injection system so that only the most basic filters, oil and plugs servicing was necessary up to 50,000 miles. The engine produced a substantial 286 bhp, which meant a true top speed of 150 mph, although only 140 mph was officially quoted. It was however slower to 60 mph, compared with the old 6.3, taking just over 7 seconds.

Being Mercedes of course this was no simple engine transplant, the whole suspension system had been rethought as a hydro-pneumatic system using pressurised cylinders filled with nitrogen along with oil filled dampers and gas struts. This was not dissimilar to Citroen's own advanced system and meant that it automatically self-levelled. Compared to the Citroen though it combined a supple ride with excellent handling with superior engineering, resulting in superior reliability. So if fitted with heavy armour plate the 6.9 could more than cope as regards acceleration and staying on the road under fire, although mpg was marginal at 13.6 mpg, a small price to pay for staying alive though. The only way to boost that figure was buying into an American specification 300SD diesel which was introduced in 1977 and would return a much more reasonable 25 mpg.

When production finished in 1979 the W116 had built on the success of the previous model and proved to have been an incredible sales success in what was one of the most difficult periods for the motor industry. With 473,000 plus in eight years no other luxury car came even close and this was what BMW were up against. They must have felt like giving up.

"Tomorrow's car today." That's what BMW's press office people promised when the all-new 7 series was unveiled in May 1977 and actually that is pretty much what we got. With the arrival of the E23 series the luxury car would never, ever be the same again. It wasn't enough that big cars would have big seats, big price tags and big engines. Now they had to have big ideas too and the 7 was clearly the thinking buyer's big saloon. As with so many great BMWs it was the climate of rivalry and even envy that created the 7. These Grosser wagens have been something of a Germanic obsession, a sort of mine's bigger than yours Fritz which has seen the competition escalate to the extent that arguably the grossest wagens in the world, Rolls Royce and Bentley, are now both in German hands.

Never mind Royalty and working class kids done good, who loved their Rollers, back in the '60s and '70s as we have seen the wheels of choice of potentates, plutocrats and the seriously sodding rich everywhere was an S Class. That must have hurt those proud Bavarians a lot, although their big saloon the E3 2500, 2800 and 3.0 was hardly a failure. Indeed the E3 had basically bankrolled BMW's expansion and sales were still strong as sales totalled 252,559 in all. However the mastermind of BMW's thrust even further upmarket was Chief Engineer Bernhard Osswald who also had to keep on top of 3, 5 and 6 series development. BMW design stalwart Wilhelm Hofmesier made the preliminary styling sketches and the first mock-up of BMW's big saloon was shown and approved by the board of BMW as far back as 1970. However production prototypes were not built until 1972 and anyway Paul Bracq who gave all '70s BMWs their sharkish features was due to give the big saloon a once over. That meant the shape wasn't finalised until the middle of 1974 and the final pre-production prototypes were not built until the end of 1975. By this time BMW were referring to their flagship as the 7 Series.

The brand new big BMW that they called the 7.

So what was so special about the 7? Just imagine if you could combine Brown's Lane (that's where Jaguar used to make cars) sportiness with Stuttgart (that's where Mercedes live) build quality and then top it off with some leading edge NASA type technology? Well, the result would be something not unlike the 7 Series. The brave new BMW world that was the late '70s model range now had the final piece in the series jigsaw with the flagship 7 to go along with the 3, 5 and 6 series. So what were the details?

Well the front suspension was clever and without going into boring detail (MacPherson struts with knobs on) it was more compact, therefore had bigger brakes, wouldn't dive in an emergency situation, was more stable and had sharper steering. Indeed drive an E23 today (oh yes BMW were up to 23 on the E numbers by now) and you will be amazed by the smoothness and sportiness. This is a complete contrast to the wallowy rubbish that passed for luxury motoring back in the '70s. And then there were the engines. Halfway through the 7's gestation period the fuel crisis happened. As war waged in the Middle East and oil supplies were suspended a rethink was required in the power plant department. BMWs had to be smooth and quick, so the six-cylinder layout was guaranteed, but economy was the watchword. Revised combustion chambers and manifolds, plus innovations to cut down on fuel wasting internal friction initially produced three M30 units. The 2.8 and 3.0 litre had Solex four-barrel carburettors delivering 170 and 184 bhp whilst L-Jetronic injection fed the 3.2 litre 197 bhp. That's how we got the 728, 730 and 733i and just in case you are wondering the mpg was only just into the low 20s for the carburettor cars whilst the fuel injected 733i struggled to 19.4.

Petrol injection across the range was inevitable and by 1979 the 728 now had an i on the boot, whilst the 730 was dropped and the 733i was given the moniker it should have had in the first place, namely 732i. The range was topped by the 218 bhp 735i.

A fundamental part of the 7 Series credo was high technology. DME, Digital Motor Electronics, made their debut on the 7 Series in 1979 as the Bosch system carefully controlled every aspect of the engine's performance; yes it was the beginning of the black box era. ABS brakes that we all take for granted now were standardised on the 735i in 1982 and optional on the rest of the range, bringing them to a juddering, but carefully controlled halt. That service interval indicator which meant that the car told you when it needed the attentions of a BMW service bay also became a dashboard fixture, along with the mpg econometer and the check control panel by your right knee that let you know that all the vital automotive organs were operational.

Of course the 7 did everything else you expected a luxury car to do. Firstly you couldn't ignore it. That sharp profile and kidney grilled front end had real presence. There was also a decent amount, but never quite enough rear legroom inside. Best of all, it handled and motored like a BMW should. 135 mph from the 735i and tidy handling that meant you thought you were flinging a 3 Series around.

The 7 Series was tweaked over the years and indeed just in time for me to start selling them. That five-speed manual must have been a relief in 1981 after rowing around with a four-speed. In 1983 fuel consumption was reduced by between 15 and 20 per cent, mainly through a weight loss, and a mildly reworked smoother front end that took about 13 per cent off the drag coefficient, from 0.44 to 0.383 if you are bothered. Also contributing was the introduction of the ZF 4HP 22 four-speed automatic gearbox, with lockup on the top gear. Now the 7 really was a luxury performance saloon to be reckoned with.

Buffalo leather absolutely everywhere in an Executive model. Next to it an old 7.

It really is a struggle to come up with many four door '70s rivals for the 7 without going really exotic or way upmarket. In fact there were really only two serious contenders. The Jaguar XJ6 had essentially shown the 7 the way proving that big saloons don't have to be staid and could be a thing of real beauty. Unfortunately by the mid '70s the Jag was dated, underdeveloped and badly built. Even so BMW must have been jealous about that 5.3 V12 which was something they couldn't compete with. Even Mercedes didn't have a twelve cylinder in the S class, but they did have a gutsy V8. The S remained the prestige saloon to aim for. Even so BMW had some very creative ideas of their own to tempt buyers away.

BMW had big-engined ambitions that stretched back to the middle '60s and joining two four cylinder units together to make a V8 seemed the obvious answer, but it was too big and heavy. Later the idea of joining two M60 small blocks together to make a V12 seemed feasible. It worked brilliantly inside 7 Series prototypes and delivered 0-60 mph in 7 seconds, but was a victim of that damned oil crisis. Instead a turbocharged version of the 733i, called 745i, was developed. The model name is due to the fact that a turboed engine is calculated to be worth a 40% power gain over a normally aspirated engine so, $3.2 \times 1.4 = 4.48$.

I once took a left-hand drive 745i in part exchange against a new 7. It was bright blue and driving the huge manual car through London was interesting. I can't remember what happened to it, but some car trader must have bought it and then probably sold it to a criminal on the Costa del Crime as the family runabout.

Later the 745i was sold with 3430cc displacement and logically according to that algebraic formula should have been 748i. Meanwhile the South African version of the 745i actually had the 24 valve 277 bhp engine last seen in the M1 super car, the M5 and latterly M635. Wow.

Less of a wow though was the 725i with 150 bhp, which was introduced in '83 and only survived in high tax markets like Belgium and Italy. In 1984 in the

UK though we got the full monty with the longest BMW model designation in history: the 735iA Special Equipment Executive. The American equivalent was the L7 (also the name of a grungy all girl group from the '80s and it is also '50s America slang for square). Apart from electric rear seats and full house spec list, there was Buffalo leather everywhere and walnut wood trim where you least expected it.

Despite building all those super saloons and even those not so super detuned 725is for the killjoys, the 7 Series didn't seriously threaten the S's luxurywagen supremacy. At least the E23 paved the way for the next generation 7, E32 that really did put the frighteners on those stuck up Swabians (Mercedes). The E23 may now be old edge, shark nosed, arrogant, and aggressive and some of those high tech electrics may be on the blink, but unlike many Jaguars they aren't rust buckets. Sadly they are not as pretty or lovable as Jags so few survive. Buying tomorrow's car today has never been more difficult.

The Audi 200. Remember that? Thought not, hence tiny picture.

At this point it is worth mentioning a German luxury car that attempted to crash the BMW/Mercedes duopoly in 1979 and that most people have completely forgotten about. The Audi 200 arrived in the spring of 1980 available as a 5E with a 136 bhp 5-cylinder engine, or more excitingly a turbo version that produced a substantial 170 bhp. It had a more aggressive four headlamped front end and some spoked alloy wheels. Otherwise it offered no more room than a 100, so as a luxury barge it was never going to offer much to buyers in the market for that sort of vehicle. Especially as it was front wheel drive, which still had strong family hatchback associations. However, when the turbo engine was paired up with Audi's four-wheel drive system, it started to make some sort of sense. Then in 1985 full galvanising meant that the bigger Audis became cars for the long term. Certainly a four door Quattro was a glimpse into the future for the company, but it still had some way to go to get near a 7 or an S.

The new S-Class was stuck in a wind tunnel with impressive results.

Mercedes' response to the E23 in 1979 was even more awesomely competent and in tune with a new era. It was now identified as the W126, and with it Mercedes were now able to face up to the full impact of the 1973 oil crisis. They were going to have to balance all that was expected of an S and that began with an s, speed, safety, spaciousness, along with a relative degree of frugality. That meant that Mercedes engineers went back into the wind tunnel to improve aerodynamics even further. The drag coefficient dropped significantly compared to the old model and the Cd figure fell to 0.36 which would be the slipperiest figure for a saloon car until the new Audi 200 came along three years later. Whereas the Audi screamed, "look at me I'm so slippery" styling, the S had none. It just looked a bit smoother than the old S and was more obviously wedgy. It was though 2 inches (5cm) narrower than the older car, which certainly helped it cut through the air more cleanly. It was also a good idea to go on a diet, as with less weight to haul around the engine would operate more efficiently. Thanks to the latest computer aided design technology and the use of advanced materials like High Strength, Low Alloy steel for most of the floor pan, depending on the model they were between 100lbs to 600lbs (45.5–272.73kgs) lighter.

Also the engines needed a bit of work too so that they would operate more efficiently. The V8 engines, 3.8 and 5.0 litre used 10% less fuel overall due to improved fuel injection systems. Buyers could if they wanted even specify an Econometer to appear on the dashboard so that they could monitor the fuel consumption. This was also something that began to appear on contemporary BMWs.

Safety was a continuing priority with even stronger passenger cells with clever touches like the door edges being overlapped in their frames so that they would not jam solid in a crash. Mercedes were also designed to resist rust, so as not to compromise structural integrity and therefore safety. Consequently zinc-coated steel was used in all the likely corrosion areas such as the sills. In 1981 Mercedes were the first manufacturer to offer a driver's airbag and a passenger side seat belt tensioner. Meanwhile ABS brakes were an option but fitted as standard to the top of the range 500 models. Available in the standard SE and longer SEL wheelbase lengths right from the beginning along with 6-cylinder and V8s this S-Class was a fully formed model range. However, after six years came a mid life makeover and a bunch of new engines.

The 5 litre V8 was carried over and two new 6-cylinder models, the 260SE and 300SE, were introduced along with some fresh V8s as the 420SE and 560SEL. So all the hard work involved in saving fuel seems to have been undone by the introduction of the 560SEL. Here was a return to the 6.3/6.9 super luxury saloon market. As well as the big engine it had masses of standard equipment, some of which you would expect to find on a luxury car, such as air conditioning, electric sunroof, heated door mirrors and self levelling rear suspension, plus a heap of new technology that some luxury car makers could not yet comprehend.

Out of the wind tunnel, this wind cheater with its concealed wipers, flush headlamps and reprofiled door mirrors, but with flash alloys rather than low drag plastic wheel trims.

The 560 had ABS brakes and ASR traction control which would soon become widely available on the E-Class saloons, but it was the speed sensitive suspension that set it apart from any competitors. When the 560 hit 85 mph a sensor in the automatic transmission would automatically lower the suspension ride height to reduce wind resistance, which would dramatically improve stability.

At Park Lane we did from time to time get the odd S-Class part exchange although there were not very many. The one that really stands out though belonged to The Who's management company. So presumably Roger, Pete, Keith and John may have at some point been passengers. I loved The Who and Quadrophenia *had been an important part of my life for a while and I remember sitting in the back and playing with the electric curtain which swooped across the windows and thinking that perhaps they had done the same in an idle, bored rock star way. It was an impressive lump of 500SEL but it wasn't a car I really wanted to drive. That big squashy steering wheel I found quite off putting, along with the fairly characterless interior. Mind you, over-stimulated rock stars could be pretty dangerous so maybe they were better off inside something they wouldn't be inclined to smash up.*

There were plans to introduce the next generation W140 S-Class in 1987; however, Mercedes got wind of what BMW were up to so its launch was put on hold, for four years. Clearly the new 7-Series was a force to be reckoned with, but were they right to be worried?

Luxury in the '80s could have been a striking miner's family with a square meal on the table, or the exotic locations involved in a Duran Duran video, but automotively it really meant a three-pointed star on the bonnet. That's because the case for the flying lady (Rolls Royce) was fading fast, whilst the leaping cat (Jaguar) could sometimes go a bit lame and could often be found at the vets. Buyers who wanted reliability, comfort and some technological toys to play with, all wrapped up in a classy package would automatically invest in an S-Class and BMW knew this.

As impressive as the E23 was, it didn't quite look the sophisticated mid '80s part anymore. Also simply having a six-cylinder engine range wasn't good enough either. No, the whole luxury car world order changed on the day that the E32 was announced.

Everyone in the motoring press knew that an all-new 7 Series was coming and that it would be a technological tour de force. The rumour mill churned out stories about four-wheel drive systems and photo chromatic windows that darkened as the sun got brighter. Most intriguing of all was a 750i Sport with low suspension, bucket seats and spoilers. What a shame that never made it to production. Never mind because what did arrive never disappointed anyone.

First of all it looked great. Critics of the E30 (3 Series) and E28 (5 Series) reckoned that they dated within a few years of launch and it seemed that BMW were determined to style something that would look good enough to buy a decade later. And so it proved. The E23 looked ancient by the early '80s and sales started to suffer quite seriously.

In 1984 I was part of a UK sales force taken ostensibly in September to sample the Oktoberfest. In between beers and on a visit to the factory we were taken to an interrogation room in the four-cylinder building and told in no uncertain terms that the E23 would be around for another few years yet. Being Germans they were absolutely right. Of course it was never in your interest as a salesman to suggest to a customer that the model they might be considering would be obsolete in the coming months. Even so, some of the customers were on the more mature side.

Dickie Henderson was one. Now long forgotten (you may have to ask your grandparents what he meant to them), he was an all-round entertainer in the UK during the '50s and '60s which meant that he could do a bit of everything. Tell a joke, do a dance and sing a song. Just ask some of these so-called stand up comedians to do anything more than tell a gag and be cynical, or insult the first two rows of the audience and they would be stumped.

Dickie knew his audience and respected them and one winter's afternoon his audience was me. He turned up in a blue Vauxhall Royale Coupé, a magnificently huge car that had velour seats, which would swallow you up and a rear tailgate that lifted up majestically to allow room for several sets of golf clubs. He also turned up with his agent. As Dickie looked through the brochures and colour charts the agent went through the financial implications of it all, the part exchange price for the Vauxhall and a contract hire rate on the new car. Yes, Dickie wanted a 7 Series and settled on a 728i. He had hardly said a word, but beamed happily throughout, firmly shook my hand and thanked me profusely as if he had been presented with a Variety Club of Great Britain Award. A really lovely man.

Another nice old gent I met in the showroom was a bit more spiky. Ever heard of the Carry On films? Course you have. Well right at the beginning of every one of them is statement of fact, 'Produced by Peter Rogers'. In the West End for a meeting he popped into the showroom for a chat. He owned a BMW already and seemed to be suggesting that his local dealer in Buckinghamshire was not exactly doing him any favours. Carry On films were famously made on tight budgets that included shooting summer scenes in the bleak mid winter with grass painted green. So he wasn't about to waste more money than he had to on a new 7 Series. I went away and found a few 732is in stock, always our worst seller. Not good value like a 728i and not a top of the range 735i, it fell in the middle. Overlooked and under appreciated they were routinely registered as management demonstrators. Consequently if someone really wanted one it was possible to get quite a lot off. Mr Rogers liked the on the road price I quoted and signed on the dotted line.

We chatted amiably about films and writing scripts. I thought I could do innuendo and double entendres to quite a high standard and he said by all means send him a script. A week later when he was back in London I delivered the 732i to the Dorchester and left the key with the doorman. Half an hour later I got a phone call.

"James, you didn't tell me it was sh*t coloured."

Bronzit wasn't a particularly popular colour and most people regarded it as a slightly dull metallic gold. He didn't find it funny, but then neither was Carry on Emmanuelle.

So the staid E23, which only appealed to mature semi-retired gentlemen in the entertainment industry, was eventually replaced by the wonderfully handsome

E32. BMW made full use of their wind tunnel to cut the sensationally bad Cd figure of the old car from 0.42 to 0.32 for the new model. Bonded front and rear screens, virtually flush side windows and a curvy profile to the wings all played their part. Indeed there was even a streamlined under tray positioned between the front spoiler and axle and not only that the fuel tank was reprofiled. The sharknose styling may have gone, but the kidney grille and twin headlamps were still there. Indeed the headlamps were smaller than before but actually produced 30% more light with an ellipsoidal reflector. It had a low waistline, which added to its sporty demeanour, and although this was an in-house styling job, there may just have been some input from the Italian styling houses who also pitched for the job. So no wonder that the 7 still looks good today and that means whatever day, year or decade you are reading this.

The really rather handsome E32 BMW 7 Series.

BMW were determined to keep that body beautiful, as the bumpers didn't just bump they were part of a complex impact absorption system designed to cope with the 80% of accidents that occur below 10 mph. The new 7 was much tauter than before with dynamic rigidity up by 50% which made the car feel much more stable. Even so there were 30% fewer body welds and 20% fewer panels. Inside it was still ergonomically impressive, but those who thought that it was still a bit tight in the back would now have the option of a longer wheelbase with 11cm more room. So the new 7 looked the part, but how did it go?

Much was made at the launch of the 7 in 1986 about the advanced windscreen wiper technology that kept those slithers of rubber clinging leech-like to the screen, cleaning more glass than ever before. BMW also immodestly proclaimed the all-new air con system to be the best in the world. Those details are important in a luxury car. But something that had often been overlooked was the way a luxury car actually handled.

Driving an old generation BMW, be it E21 or E23, was never boring.

Although the ride of the big car was great and the handling borderline sporty, push it too far and that big tail could certainly wag and either give you a shock or leave you in a ditch. To improve traction and keep the car level under acceleration and braking the rear axle was loaded to 50.9% so at least the weight distribution was even. The rear trailing arms were made stiffer as were most of the bushes. This was the E23 reworked for a more demanding generation, but there was also the old six-cylinder engine line-up to consider. Out went the 732i, but the old 2.8 was bored out to 2986cc with the output climbing by 13% to 197 bhp creating the 730i. The 735i unit was revised and delivered 220 bhp. A complex gas flow programme on the cylinder head and the latest generation Bosch Motronic engine management made all the difference. Top speed of 145 mph and impressive mid range punch got the 735i from 50 mph to 75 mph in 9.4 seconds. That was fine, but if BMW were truly to take on and beat the world's best the new 7 needed more, much more in the way of cylinders. The world braced itself for the arrival of the awesome V12 750i.

A 750i complete with the most plastic looking alloy wheels ever designed. At least there was a full fat aluminium V12 under the bonnet.

Greed was certainly good in the '80s and you could never have enough of anything and the 750iL was reassuringly expensive. At £53,000, it was £250 more than the biggest V8 that Stuttgart could muster in the shape of the 560SEL. The Daimler Double-Six HE cost a trifling £30,200, but it was old shape and very old tech by comparison. If you want to get technical BMW's V12's all-alloy unit had the main block cast in high silicon aluminium which meant that the cylinder bores could be etched to expose the silicon crystals and protect the metal. The V12 configuration was chosen over a V8 because it would be more refined and with a target output of 300 bhp the size would have been 5.6 litres and that would have caused installation and weight problems. Indeed, BMW did not go for the easy or cheap option, with a closed deck casting that was pricey but made the block stiffer. Chain driven camshafts at one per block and reshaped pistons, plus hydraulic tappets were all part of the spec. Managed by a mark 4 version of the Bosch Motronic system the engine produced 300 bhp at an impressively low 5200 rpm with the top speed limited to 155 mph although 62 mph was reached in just over 7 seconds. Yet the whole unit was impressively light at 240kgs and the two halves of the engine had their own life support (engine management and catalyst) systems. Not surprisingly the V12's cleverest party trick was the ability to shut down one bank of cylinders for 'limp home' mode, while still managing to crack 120 mph, if there was a problem.

With the 750i BMW achieved what they had always wanted and that was to embarrass Mercedes. By early 1987 it outsold the S-Class and by the end of '88 sales had topped 20,000. In sheer performance terms the Mercedes unit was still there or thereabouts. When it came to refinement the V12 engine in the Daimler may have been twenty years old, but it still set the standard for unfussed and silky smooth progress. Yes, you could hear the V12 working hard under the bonnet, but what put the 750 at the top of the luxury car pile was the overall package. It was one that BMW sought to steadily improve with all the toys that the rich buyers expected. ASC (anti slip control), BMW Hi Fi, Park Distance Control, driver's airbag, double-glazing and soft close bootlid all enhanced the ownership experience over the years. However, there was something of a gap in the range. It seemed a giant leap between the 735i and 750i that other manufacturers, especially the emergent Lexus, were all too happy to fill. The answer to a 750i with little low down torque was a V8 with torque to spare.

However, if we are going to look at the V8s that takes us into the 1990s which is not where this book was supposed to go. So as the 7 aged gracefully into the '90s it was not being left behind. The new generation S-Class never did sweep the competition away. Too big, too complex and too dull, the 7 Series still looked lithe and handled like a 5 Series, which was good. However, rivals were improving and the Lexus in particular was setting the standards for refinement that left Crewe's finest (Rolls Royce) wanting. Above all the 7 remained the ultimate driving machine. The E32 shook up the previously staid world of luxury motoring and injected some overdue attitude. What was most impressive was the fact that the E32 came almost from nowhere to set the luxury car agenda for six-cylinder, V8 and V12 models.

The new face of luxury, the Audi V8

However, the luxury car market was getting even busier as BMW and Mercedes also got a proper homegrown rival at the end of the '80s in the shape of the Audi V8. Here was the company's proper entry into the premium marketplace in October 1988. The new V8 engine was 3.6 litres and was made from light alloy, had four valves per cylinder and produced 250 bhp. A big engine and high tech were not new, but a permanent four-wheel drive system certainly was. The styling was the conservative side of dull, not so much understated, as underwhelming. It was a just a bigger Audi 100 and for the moment that would not be good enough, but it was a surefooted four-wheel drive move in the right direction.

However Audi's ascent to the top table of premium saloons was a nod to the far future because for the moment it is still 1983, an Audi 200 was a fairly meaningless model to me and anyway it was going home time. After a long day taking it all in we were in an underground car park in Mayfair. As my fellow sales apprentices made do with a 318i automatic and a 520i automatic, what was left for me? I half suspected that they would uncover a part exchanged bubble car from around the back, or perhaps one of those Taxi specification Baroque Angels. Or maybe I would have to make my way homewards by public transport deeply regretting my decision not to buy a return ticket that morning. However in the office they found a key and it belonged to a 735iA SE. I'd hit the jackpot. I doubt that after one day they thought I deserved it. Never mind, I was driving home in a car that at the time cost as much as a small flat in an unfashionable part of London.

It didn't have the 1 BMW number plate thank goodness, but otherwise it was exactly the same. Even better it was dark and the dashboard lit up just like fruit machine, but a very classy one, like the sort you'd find in the foyer of a Monaco Casino. The highlight wasn't any of BMW's myriad controls, it was the Blaupunkt New York sound system which beguiled me the most. The extra speakers helped too. Having previously made do with a Radiomobile and just the one speaker wedged into the parcel shelf of my old Mini, this was surround sound before anyone had thought to call it that, with speakers in every door plus the rear parcel shelf and on top of the dashboard. For a music head like me, six speakers were pretty much in car nirvana. I turned it up and flicked around the stations, prodding at the tiny illuminated buttons. All I got was unsatisfactory chatter and inappropriately poppy music. What I really needed was a cassette of my own choosing and resolved to put a handful into my otherwise empty Samonsite brief case.

This was turning out to be a very good job.

BMW E3 & Mercedes S vs The Rest (The '60s)

Austin 3-litre – Ugly runt of a car even though it had the big Healey/MGC engine under the bonnet. That didn't help this unaerodynamic heap to reach much of a velocity though. Looks like an overgrown Austin 1300, but with rear wheel drive. The only good news was loads of usable room inside.

Citroen DS Pallas – Complicated but heavenly to look at and drive. See round the corner headlamps and trick suspension made this cutting edge tech, despite a design dating from the '50s.

Daimler Majestic Major – England's Baroque Angel with attitude. Old fashioned swoopy styling offset by serious 220 bhp V8 delivering 120 mph. Odd.

Humber Hawk/Super Snipe – Big old saloon which wouldn't hold a candle to an S Class. Well actually it would hold a candle, but nothing more sophisticated than that. Very 1950s overuse of chrome.

Jaguar XJ6 – Beautiful, cheap and every bit as advanced as the E3. Export aimed 2.8 model worst of the lot and would boil its top all too easily. 4.2 much better and still loads cheaper than an E3 and S Class. Build quality got ever iffier into the '70s.

Rolls Royce Silver Shadow – Facing up to the S-Class and almost as square, but technically decades apart. Olde worlde image with the Roller whereas the Merc was all brave new, high tech world.

Rover P5B – Iron Maggie's favourite barge. A big old bruiser of a motor just like the ex-PM with a gutsy Buick V8 under the bonnet that made the old girl seem very nifty. Coupé the one to go for. Now very cool to own, back then looking its age.

Vanden Plas Princess 4-Litre – Yet another dated Brit and the presence of Rolls Royce engine from a military armoured car was not much help, though it had a huge appeal to motoring snobs who couldn't afford the real thing.

Volvo 164 – Even in the '60s Volvo were trying to charge upmarket, but buyers would rather break down in a Jag 2.8, than be saddled with this old tank of a saloon. It will last for ever, but that is something to be depressed about rather than celebrated.

BMW E23 7 Series & Mercedes vs The Rest (The '70s)

Aston Martin Lagonda – Very Lady Penelope. Even more complicated than a 7 with a Starship Enterprise flight deck. Looks like a large wedge of Chedder. Overripe and smelly.

Jaguar XJ6 4.2 – The nearest in spirit, rather than build quality to the 7s. Fun to drive, sporty, cheap, comfortable but shoddily put together and not that roomy inside. And low tech too.

Maserati Quattroporte – Completely mad Maserati with rear seats. Italians can build scooters, supercars and buzzy Fiats, but not luxury barges. A rare and oddly proportioned sight, which was not unlike a Jag.

Rolls Royce Shadow II – Best car in the world? Hardly. Firmed up Shadow II still a blamange. Wideboy/scrap dealer image unfortunate. Flying Lady still opened doors though.

BMW 7 Series & Mercedes S-Class & Audi 200/V8 vs The Rest (The '80s)

Bentley Turbo R – Bentley got vital high performance cred in '80s/'90s, Edwardian styling combined with rocketship turbo performance was always highly amusing. Epically expensive though and it made a 750i look like a bargain.

Daimler XJ6 4.0 – Upmarket Jaguar with more chrome trimmings. Awful boxy XJ40 shape, Series 3 with V12 power much more of a match for the 7, especially the 750i. Digital dashboard not very nice, build quality better, but not in the same league as the 7.

Honda Legend – Japanese version of the Rover 800. Enough said? Lots of standard kit though, and it will be reliable.

Jaguar XJ – As Daimler. Better than old XJ but not as handsome.

Opel Commodore/Vauxhall Senator A Carlton with a cheese grater grille. You either love or loathe the look, but you can't ignore the decent performance. Built in Germany but that did not give it much executive cred, although it could out pose a Granada. It was also a copper's favourite.

Peugeot 604 – Big, dull, well equipped. Er, that's it.

Volvo 700 – Lots of straight lines and most would buy the gargantuan estate rather than the pointless saloon.

In the Cassette Deck...

 The Smiths – Meat is Murder With Morrisey's whining voice and Marr creating sonic sound scapes with his guitar it was never less than interesting and mostly was wonderful. Some may have found it depressing and it is not ethically the right tape to play when piloting a 735i Executive with all that Buffalo leather. Overall the Smiths sounded as northern as Spandau were southern.

4 Klasse Act – 2002
a Sportsausführung Oddity

How BMW finally got its act together and came up with the super cool 2002.

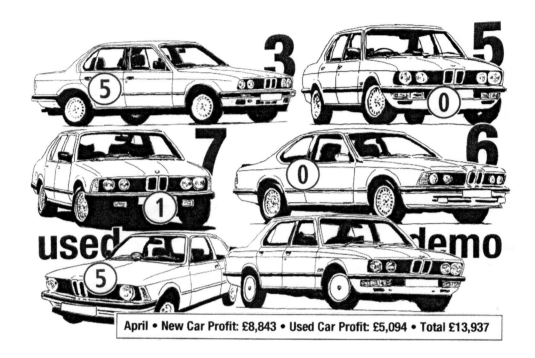

April • New Car Profit: £8,843 • Used Car Profit: £5,094 • Total £13,937

Selling BMWs still seemed to be a long way off. Although I never got the 7 Series at going home time again, any sundry 3 or 5 Series that happened to be hanging around the garage was perfectly adequate to get me home. Being able to drive and not crash was important, but I still had an awful lot to learn. A series of away days followed. First off it was the service and parts department in Brentford.

Here was a location that was as far as you could get from the 'streets are paved with gold' high life in Mayfair. Although it wasn't far from the posh inner suburbs of Ealing, Chiswick and Richmond, this particular section of the Great West Road was a sprawl of industrial estates and factories. All exhaust fumes, deafening dual carriageway traffic and a thick layer of grime that covered both the buildings and the people. It was a world and social strata away from where most of our customers lived and worked. Brentford would always be an issue when it came to closing a deal. Few wanted to drive into purgatory just for an oil and filter change. There may have been a courtesy Transit Minibus to Osterley Park Station, but it wasn't the Park Lane experience they were hoping for.

It was important to find out first hand what happened at the service department and how they also prepared the new cars. This was also a chance to meet a couple of salesmen who were working there on a basic wage. That was because they had been very naughty. Drink driving is of course now quite rightly regarded as just about the worst thing you could do short of murdering someone. To some back in the '80s it was viewed as just a bit of bad luck to get caught though year driving bans were the norm. It had been carefully explained to me that drink/drive was instant dismissal, but it was reassuring to know that if management thought you were good enough they'd hold your job open. In return you had to work in Brentford for the period of the driving ban on basic pay. When I visited there were two salesmen joyfully helping out with servicing department bookings. One who was effectively a super salesman and consistently top of the heap was due to return to the showroom after just six months, he was that good. The other wasn't and would serve the full twelve months. So that's what I learnt in Brentford.

Further west in Bracknell I spent a week at BMW's headquarters learning the difference between a 525i and a 525e. Product knowledge was the key to success, without it you were just a blithering clueless idiot. In fact, learning all the colours and associating them with the swatches in the brochures actually led to a minor miracle. By knowing my Burgandrot from my Henna Rot, I was temporarily cured of colour blindness. That's probably because my new career depended on it.

Much more fun though was driving around London and shopping other dealers. Part of the less formal and more guerrilla approach to training saw us mucking other BMW dealers about. Asking for swingeing discounts, making ridiculous part-exchange proposals and going on meandering test-drives, before giving a false name and address and a telephone number belonging to a Chinese take away.

We even had the benefit of the group's used car buyer who left his office for once to spend some quality time with us and reveal the dark mysteries of just how to look at a customer's car for part exchange purposes. It had begun to dawn on me that this was often the most crucial part of the deal. Selling a car was easy enough, but actually giving the customer anything near the money they thought their pride and joy deserved could be the deal breaker. There was also the issue that if you missed something then the car was worth less. Or possibly even worthless. It was pointed out to me that any shortfall over the initial valuation meant we would have to make the difference up out of our pocket, but in many cases we would probably pay for that fundamental mistake by getting the sack.

So this small quite hairy man (a year later I found out just how hirsute he was, when stripped naked and booted off a bus in the middle of Munich), could be found in his office scratching his beard and squinting through tinted glasses, with a permanent Rothmans filter tip cigarette on the go. Often there was a telephone cradled to his ear, so presumably he was doing something. That is when he wasn't having his rapidly growing hair trimmed by the secretary that he shared with the managing director.

Yes it was a curious little set up yet we were eager to hear what he had to teach. He took us outside into the cold West End and walked us down lines of parked cars suggesting which ones may have seen the inside of a paint shop recently. When we reached the end of the road he said, "I could murder a pint." He nodded at the adjacent public house and that was the end of that master class. With the image of being banished to the Brentford Gulag fresh in our minds we sipped orange juice as he downed something much stronger. He then talked about horse racing and started to read the form at the back of a newspaper. Clearly we were on our own. Well not quite, we were given a book each.

The sales manager went into a cupboard and took out three books. Two straight histories, which my colleagues picked up straight away. They were detailed but dull. I got the one I wanted which had an airborne CSL Batmobile on the front and it was called 'The Ultimate' by Jeremy Walton. It detailed the racing history of the marque and for me that was crucial. It was partly why people wanted to buy BMWs, they looked fast, they were handsome, with smooth and powerful engines. All this still mattered even if they were buying a lowly 316. Few knew the history, or may have cared, but for me it was important to know exactly where BMW had come from in order to understand where they were now. The more I read the more I understood that if it wasn't for the New Klasse, BMW would have been very old news and I might have been working for Mercedes.

It's true. One model saved the company and built a dynasty. The 'New Class' BMWs kickstarted the blue and white roundel revival. The truth is that BMW as we now know and understand it didn't really exist before 1962. The New Class when it arrived was the sharp, sporty and technically cutting edge machine we now expect BMW to produce every few years as a matter of course. Back then it was a complete and utter revelation. Without the New Class we wouldn't have BMW or the Series saloons and coupés that we have come to appreciate as the ultimate driving machines.

BMW's 700 was the link between the Isetta and New Klasse (half motorcycle, half proper car) which kept sales alive and had enough room for four adults and their dog.

Before the New Class, there was what we might as well call the Old Class. BMW had done well to survive in the tough post-war climate but by the late '50s they had a bizarre and barely profitable model line-up. The 503 and beautiful 507 V8 sports cars were low volume vanity projects. Those so-called 'Baroque Angel' 500 saloons were luxury statements that maintained BMW's reputation for prestige products but also tarnished it, as the model got older and increasingly outdated. Meanwhile it was the licensed bubble car Isetta 250/300 and bigger 600 that actually kept the company afloat whilst the tiny 700 that looked much more like a conventional small car rather than a motorbike with a roof was the only model with limited potential. Meanwhile bike sales were in the doldrums and money was very tight. BMW badly needed a hit.

The company began thinking about a 1500cc-sized car back in 1955. They wanted a new family car and cutting the existing 3.2 litre V8 from those Angels in half to make a 4-cylinder 1600 seemed the sensible thing to do. Disguised as an Alfa Romeo the road tests suggested that the car BMW had in mind was just too big, complicated and slow. So by 1958 BMW had decided that they wanted a comfy 4 to 5 seater with a sporty character and a big boot. Trouble was in 1959 BMW made a loss of 15 million Deutschmarks. At this point BMW could have become British.

Sir William Rootes who previously had turned down the opportunity to acquire Volkswagen, admittedly when it was mostly rubble, now eyed the BMW operation for his own purposes as a distribution point for the various interrelated Hillmans, Humbers, Singers and Sunbeams that made up the Rootes model range. Closer to home Mercedes was also interested in buying out BMW, but the proud Bavarians wanted to remain independent so went in search of finance. Enter the Quandt family who are still the financial force behind BMW today (2011). Their investment enabled the company to throw away all the work they had done so far and start afresh with a new approach to the family car. This was 1960. Smaller, lighter, with an all-new 4-cylinder engine the project was not given the usual code number, but was called Neue Klasse, or New Class.

BMW building their most important car ever.

At the heart of the new car was to be a four-cylinder power plant. Engineer Alex von Falkenhausen did not need to start with a clean sheet. In 1958 he had designed a 1.0 litre overhead camshaft four-cylinder unit that was destined for the back end of the little 700, but never used. This was the company's first four-cylinder since they had built the old side valve Austin 7 under licence back in the 1920s. The engine had to be small which allowed the transmission to sit ahead of the passenger compartment for maximum space. Lying at a 30-degree angle this meant the bonnet could be lower, the centre of gravity was almost perfect and servicing accessibility was good too. This engine had an overhead camshaft, aluminium cylinder head and a single Solex carburettor which helped produce a strong 80 bhp that translated into a 92 mph top speed and 62 mph arrived in 15 seconds, which was good at the time. The four-speed gearbox was light and precise whilst the low gearing was suited to autobahn cruising in the homeland.

The 700 also donated its rear suspension set-up. Having pioneered semi-trailing arms it suited the 1500's layout perfectly. The arms acted on upright coil springs and telescopic shock absorbers. Even more important was the pioneering use by the 1500 of MacPherson strut front suspension. At the bottom end of the struts the coil springs were linked to the outer ends of the lower control arms, which consisted of transverse beams. Without getting too techie here, the handling was excellent with just a little understeer, with great road holding, excellent weight distribution and that all helped it maintain decent high speeds. The ZF worm and roller steering was light and tight at 3.3 turns lock to lock. It could stop too, courtesy of solid Dunlop brake discs. In the early '60s this all amounted to truly fabulous performance.

The New Class not only went and handled brilliantly it looked great too. Boxy certainly, but also very fresh, functional, well proportioned and airy. Wilhelm Hofmeister established the look of all future BMWs for several generations by incorporating a flat bonnet and boot, greenhouse cabin, rounded corners and that famous 'dogleg kink' to the thin rear pillars. All BMW had to do now was sell it.

Those paying attention so far may have noticed that the New Class project began in 1960, there was a Frankfurt Motor Show debut in September 1961 and it was launched in 1962. A two-year development cycle in the '60s when 5 years plus was the norm? Quite. The 1500 was not ready. According to the rules of the German car industry association a vehicle presented at a motor show must enter production within 6 months, otherwise there would be a fine. An inspection by a member of the association at the factory prompted frantic activity. A production line of 700s was cleared and some twenty hand built 1500s placed on the track. Workers fussed around them fitting sundry bits of trim. The inspector saw what BMW were up to, but let them get away with it. The truth was that by the time 1500s were being 'properly' built, the quality which BMW were known for and they expected customers to pay for, was sadly lacking. Indeed, in every market the 1500 was a pricey proposition and on the closely fought home turf it cost the same as the Mercedes 190.

A fully built New Class busy saving BMW.

Some of the major problems included shot steering, seized final drives and snapped con rods that punched holes in the side of the crankcase. Yes they were that bad. A crack engineering team found 124 defects and to the company's credit they sorted it all out. Quality control now rejected cars and they never left the factory until they were right. How else could BMW have expected customers to pay what the industry thought was a mad price anyway for a substandard car? Like it or not BMW's premium pricing policy was born with the New Class. So the 1500 certainly did its job of re-establishing the marque and was discontinued in December 1964 after some 24,000 had been sold, its place taken by the 1600.

The first addition to the New Class was the 1800 in September 1963. A strip of chrome here, some bright fancy hubcaps there and luxurious trim only slightly set it apart from the 1500. More important was the engine under the bonnet that had been bored and stroked. The capacity was now 1773cc and a twin barrelled Solex carburettor delivered 90 bhp. The gear ratios on first and second were revised, plus a ZF automatic transmission was offered. To make it an even better driving experience ZF power steering and ATE vacuum assisted brakes were standardised. Much more exciting though was the 1800TI (Turismo International-nationale). The compression ratio was raised and the output went up to a more useful 110 bhp.

BMW 2000Tii – the high performance model.

This was soon followed by the 1800TI/SA (Sportsausführung, that's Sports version). With twin Weber carburettors and a reworked engine, which unofficially produced 158 bhp and was hooked up to a 5-speed gearbox. Just 200 of these were built and although it was street legal, the intention was competition and all the customers were recognised racing drivers and teams, although World Champions Jack Brabham and Phil Hill actually used them as road cars. BMW's first real post-war performance car was finished in metallic grey and was soon nicknamed by those pithy Germans as the 'silver-grey understatement'. Indeed it was good enough to win the 1965 Spa 24 hours race.

Even better 2.0 litre power was transferred from the CS coupé in January 1966 to create the 2000 available in standard 100 bhp tune, or as a TI with 120 bhp. Indeed the TI won the 1966 Spa 24 hours with homologated parts from the SA. Meanwhile, those who didn't go racing and only wanted plusher trim could go for the TI-Lux.

The last significant changes occurred in 1968 when the 1800 was transformed by using the 1600 crankshaft and 2000 block to produce a rev hungry short stroke unit, which was smooth, quiet and incredibly popular. Sales jumped by 30%. Then the 2000tii arrived with Kugelfischer injection, which produced 130 bhp, but only 1952 were ever built. When the New Class celebrated its tenth birthday it was time for a change and the new 5 Series effectively became the new New Class, but that's another story for Chapter 6.

The New Class faded away very quickly and the staid four door is now overlooked and that's a great shame. That roomy cabin and fabulously sharp styling almost suggests that this was BMW's first front wheel drive car, but no, it was clever packaging and a distinctive design. Overall the New Class legacy is a long one. Not only did its profitable sales save the company, the model set design standards and helped define the company's brave new image. Most important of all the TI/SA model got BMW back into serious competition. Indeed that inspired factory tweaking led directly to BMW setting up the Motorsport arm. Even more incredible is that the four-cylinder engine in highly modified Turbo powered form even went on to win the Formula One world championship in 1983.

Audi 80, the original one from 1966.

Whichever way you look at the boxy BMW saloon, it was and still is a class act and it really did not have many direct rivals. Initially though the revived Audi brand in 1965 was equally, though far less prettily, square and there were no proper model designations. Later on the little saloon was called the 72, reflecting the 72 bhp power output and in 1967 came the 80, on account of it having 80 bhp and then three months later in came the well-equipped Super 90. However, as an indication of just how unreliable German model designations can be the 60 with a 55 bhp engined joined the line-up. Meanwhile the 72 and 80 were replaced by the 75. There was at least a range of far less sporty Audis to rival the new BMWs and that included a Variant estate car, although they would eventually launch a response to that model in the shape of the Touring.

So far though, Audi had relied on a DKW designed body and Mercedes engine to relaunch the marque that was always regarded by chief engineer Ludwig Kraus as a 'bastard'. He wanted something much better and had been under instructions from Volkswagen to simply oversee those make do models and not worry about further or new developments. However, he was determined to make real Audis and after the success of the stylish 100 (see Chapter 6), it was a short step to replicating that in a slightly smaller package, hence the 80.

Here's an Audi 80 in a field.

Here was the second all-new Audi, launched in 1972. It featured a four-cylinder engine that was to form the heart of all the future Volkswagens. Indeed, this car was the basis for VW to cut their development costs and a few years later the 80 would be adapted to become the original less than pretty Volkswagen Passat. Despite that the 80 was the car of the year for 1973 beating such innovative cars as the Renault 5 and Alfa Romeo Alfetta. That may have seemed unfair at the time, especially as one was the most significant European hatchback and the other the sweetest handling small sporty saloon possibly ever.

By comparison, the 80 was a dull but worthy winner of a prize, although as an acknowledgement of Audi's undoubted durability and long term sustainability it was well deserved and very prescient. At first the 80 was just a simple two door saloon, then it was joined by a four door two years later and it was most notable for being rot proof. Yes the 80 was corrosion resistant thanks to a zinc powder coat in vulnerable areas along with some PVC underseal. Over the following six years more than a million were sold, 1,103,766 if you actually wanted to keep count. Audi had found their niche. Now it was up to BMW to find theirs.

The truth is that the compact sports saloon didn't actually exist until BMW properly invented it. Jaguar, Alfa Romeo, possibly Rover and Triumph might

argue otherwise, but nothing was as purposeful and agile as when BMW went all
'02 on us.

2002, the side profile of a legend.

Four doors were very good on the New Class, but sometimes two doors are
so much better. Just take one look at the perfectly proportioned 2002 for conclusive proof. This wasn't just a good-looking car, or just a cool one, it is the
defining BMW of the 1960s. This is the one that established the compact sports
saloon/cabriolet/hatchback blueprint that would lead to the fabulously successful
3 Series and pretty much world domination for a small privately owned
engineering company based in Bavaria.

So to recap, in the beginning there was the 'New Class'. BMW's year zero
was 1961 when a smart, purposeful and spartan four door banished all memories
of the Isetta bubbles and OAP Angels. The new range of saloons badged as 1600,
1800 and 2000 managed to capitalise on the economic miracle and capture
profitable sales from the affluent middle class. That meant BMW got saved from
bankruptcy and there was cash to spend developing more BMW products. The
head of sales, Paul Hahnemann, already had a clever theory that would later be
pretentiously identified as 'niche' marketing. Effectively he wanted to create
BMW models that could be positioned in the market without any direct competition.

So the first product to plug that yawning gap arrived in March 1966 when
a new model range was announced. The 1600-2 signified the arrival of a two
door, entry-level saloon. It was always the intention for this model to be the basis
of a large range of cars. So never mind pioneering niche marketing, BMW were
also busy developing the platform concept that Volkswagen would later stretch to
breaking point with cross pollinated Audis, SEATs, Audis and Skodas. Back in
the '60s the ambitions were simpler. The monocoque shell was smaller (10 inches
shorter) and lighter (2073lbs) than the New Class with a two-inch shorter

wheelbase. The main chassis components came from the 1800 four door with MacPherson strut suspension up front and semi trailing arm independent rear suspension with front disc brakes and rear drums. However the 02 had a narrower rear track at 52.4 inches which also matched the front. Power was provided by a 1573cc, 85 bhp, overhead cam engine. Over the following 11 years there would be four different body styles, three engine sizes, a turbo and eight contrasting power outputs.

2002tii in three door Touring format. Yes that would make it a hot hatch.

As soon as the 1600 engine was dropped into the 02 everyone noticed just how much faster and more agile the smaller car was. So it was only a matter of time before things started to get hotter. In September 1967 the 1600TI was launched (the TI stood for 'Touring International'), with twin Solex carburettors and a higher 9.5:1 compression, which boosted output to 105 bhp and delivered a top speed of 109 mph. That model was not around for long before the introduction of the benchmark 2002. This was the best seller that established the brand in Britain and the USA. Power was down to 100 bhp and just a single carb. But that was only the cooking model because in 1968 the 2002 ti delivered 120 bhp with twin carburettors. That model in turn made way for the 2002 tii, the extra i stood for injection. The Kugelfischer system helped pump out 130 bhp and magazine roadsters at *Autocar* were even able to obtain a creditable 0–100 mph time of just 28.2 seconds.

So in Europe there were a lot of decidedly hot 1600TI, 2002ti models and also the lukewarm 1802. As for cold 02s, well there were a few of those. The 1600-02 was the entry-level model from 1966, which had prehistoric 6-volt electrics and was rebadged as the 1602 from 1971. As if to apologise for the profligate 2002 Turbo the 1502 was BMW's response to the oil crisis. Using the 1602's engine, the compression was lowered to produce an underwhelming 75 bhp. Not many were sold in the UK as it lingered on the price lists between '75 and '77 when the new E21 3 Series established itself.

Variations on the 2002 theme, Touring and the Cabriolet.

Rather than trying to single-handedly fight the oil crisis BMW were rather more successful at lopping the roof off their smallest model. There are few prettier saloon based '60s cabriolets than the Baur 02 (Baur – the company who carried out the decapitation). That central pillar does not look intrusive, or out of place. Indeed it offers all sorts of targa topped possibilities with the roof panels in or out and the rear hood up or down. How exciting. You felt safe, the bodyshell was almost free of the scuttle shake and it looked the business. However, the cabriolet wasn't the first 02 to see the sky. Back in 1967 a fully open 1600 and 2002 were offered by coachbuilder Baur, but only to our lucky European cousins. It looks a bit too open and was obviously a bit more shaky, but it proves that roof on, roof off, or roof half off the 2002 was always a stunner.

Just as you can fall out with someone over just how pretty a cabriolet is, you can argue all day long about just who invented the hot hatchback, but BMW have a more convincing case than most. They hired stylist Giovanni Micholetti to add a rear door to the 2002 and the result was the Touring. Introduced in 1971 it only enjoyed a brief three years on the price lists until '74. The shape isn't to everyone's taste and the concept isn't as practical as some would like with that high loading sill, sloping tailgate line and intrusive suspension turrets. But never mind it was a first glimpse into a hatchback dominated future and the 2000 Touring even came in some very exciting flavours. A tii version delivered 60 mph in just over 8 seconds and if that isn't a hot hatch then what is? The tragedy is that in the UK we only got the standard 100 bhp single carb model. There were also low output 1600 and 1800 models in Europe.

Although strictly the Touring isn't a 02, it is a crucial part of that period of history and can't be separated. It didn't sell in huge numbers, around 30,206 were built, so maybe the world wasn't ready for the Touring. By 1988 though buyers were all too keen to be seen in a bread van shaped E30 3 Series, but this time with four doors and a tailgate. Again, it was hardly a Volvo estate, but then that wasn't the point, BMW had reinvented the sports estate that just about everyone has since copied. Slightly more on that in a later chapter. For the moment though let's concentrate on the really, really, really fast 2002s.

The ultimate performance 02 was undoubtedly the Turbo. It was the first turbo-powered car that you could actually go into a showroom and buy. However, potential customers needed a lot of cash because at £4221 it wasn't far off the cost of a Jaguar E-Type. 51 buyers in the UK were impressed enough to place orders and put up with the fact that they would be sitting on the left. What they got was a 2002 which was still comfortable, refined and quiet. However, once the throttle was opened in anger, not much happened. Then suddenly the world went all blurry. The 1990cc tii engine with Kugelfischer injection had its blue touch paper lit when the BLD truck turbocharger (as supplied by KKK), kicked in. It managed 130 mph flat out and ultra rapid acceleration that saw 60 mph arrive in something over 7 seconds. There are some scary road tests written in the '70s, but actually the 2002 Turbo was a stable, tight little package which stopped well on its ventilated front discs and allowed enthusiastic drivers to dial in oversteer at will (wag the tail around like a hooligan). Brilliant. A wet round-about though was another matter.

Use a mirror to find out just what model this is.

Not only did the 2002 Turbo make the pulse race, it looked the part in a quintessentially '70s way. Whereas the standard 2002 was understated, the Turbo was a total show off. Finished in white there were Motorsport tricolour side stripes and cheeky ambulance style reverse print Turbo lettering on the spoiler so that drivers glancing in their rear view mirror would be in no doubt about what was about to hurtle past them. Mind you the Turbo needed that deep windbreak on the front and rubbery lip on the boot to keep it planted on the floor. Also, those fabulously fat arches were filled with alloys, wider tyres and also hid the lowered suspension. It was a beast of a car, but unfortunately it was also an endangered species.

Launched in the late summer of 1973 the 2002 Turbo met the fuel crisis full on when war broke out between Israel and Egypt that October. After ten months production it was discontinued and just 1672 had been built.

I honestly thought that at Park Lane I would be swamped by old 2002s and perhaps be in a position to buy a nice one for a few quid and keep it. Even in the early 1980s the 2002 still seemed to be very practical, delivering more than adequate performance and despite the number of years that had passed, a quality product. Some saloons from the '60s might look half-decent, but it all falls apart on the road and in your hands as bits of trim drop off. The BMW 02 isn't like that. There is a decent sized boot, an enthusiastic but smooth four-cylinder engine and a light yet precise four-speed gear change. You sit upright and the masses of window glass means that the all round view is brilliant. Best of all an 02 chassis lets you know what the whole car is up to. It is utterly controllable yet there is room for oversteering antics on demand. Add to that the solid feel of the doors and squeak free interior and you understand why the 02s were so expensive. Whereas the 2002 was and still is a class act, a ropey old MGB remained tat.

Yes the number of 2002s, 1502s and Tourings I saw was minimal. It was eight years since the very last 02 was built and no one seemed to care much for the 1502s. Hardly any turned up at part exchanges at Park Lane and none with me. However, there was a very interesting phenomenon at the time when owners who lived 'oop North', drove them 'darn Sarf'. This was so that they could get around £150 more as there was still a strong residual West and South London demand for old Bimmers. So maybe £150 in the Miner's strike racked regions north of Watford, but £300 trade in the Smoke (London) and then in the classifieds for anything north of £499.

So I'd missed the boom when everyone was part exchanging their old 02s for the all-new 3 Series. Indeed the set who had climbed aboard BMW's new small sporty, understated, fast and cool 2002 had moved on to the E21 3 Series and were now moving into the latest E30. Life would be very good for me and selling small BMWs was never that difficult. So bring on the next chapter.

New Class vs The Rest
Alfa Romeo Giullia Ti/Super – Last seen failing to catch three Mini Coopers in *The Italian Job*. They did catch rust though and most are red powdery wrecks now. Discs brakes and five-speed box are civilised and help lively performance.

Lancia Flavia Berlina – As boxy as the Beemer and even more expensive, so hardly any around in the UK. Another Latin victim of the UK rust inducing climate. Complicated flat flour engine is very sweet.

Rover 2000TC – As cutting edge as the BMW with great handling, safety and bolt on body panels. Broke away from the Auntie image and did for Rover what the New Class did for BMW. So how come BMW eventually ended up designing Rovers?

Triumph 2.5 PI – The BMW connection is Micholetti's work for Bertone and BMW and also styling the elegant '60s Triumphs. Fuel injection systems utterly unreliable. Smart middle class buyers loved these, but guess what? BMW still own the Triumph badge at the time of writing.

BMW 2002 vs The Rest

Ford Escort RS1600 – An Escort Cosworth in all but name with the legendary BDA engine. In blistered arch Sport Pack trim it would look as mad as a Turbo. Great opposite lock fun. But is it the real thing?

Alfa Romeo GTV – A coupé really, but it had a body to die for, rust usually killed it though. All the usual superb ingredients from Bertone body to that resonant overhead cam engine.

Reliant Scimitar GTE – As endorsed by HRH Princess Anne, this is the closest in spirit to a tii Touring. It won't rot as the body is plastic, but there were some iffy electrical connections. Association with three-wheeled Robin knocks image.

Vauxhall Viva GT – Don't laugh I could have included the Morris Marina GT. In the right hands of legendary racing driver Gerry Marshall, a Viva was something to be feared. Otherwise this was all show and not a lot of go.

MGB GT – This is what the 02 made obsolete. Tweed cap not required because of the tin top, but never the most inspiring drive when they weren't breaking down or falling apart.

In the Cassette Deck...

 Tom Waits – Swordfishtrombones A truly weird and wonderful recording. It doesn't sound like anything else from the '80s, or any other period in history, although it could described as proto-punk American vaudeville. Here was a tape that either traumatised or invigorated passengers. 'Frank's Wild Years' could well have been about me, if my name was Frank. Best enjoyed in a rusty part exchanged 2002.

5 Chariot to Inspire

Everyone wanted a 3 Series. Nigel bought one and even Mrs T popped into the showroom for a closer look. There's Audi 80s and Merc 190s too.

May • **New Car Profit: £11,001** • **Used Car Profit: £1,617** • **Total £12,618**

He didn't really want to come fully into the showroom. He seemed unwilling to climb the steps up past the reception desk and onto my territory. But there I was face to face with Hollywood actor, Nigel Havers. Actually, apart from Chariots of Fire, *I was rather more familiar with his father Sir Michael Havers. My legal training had left me with an abiding interest in all things judiciary and that included the Attorney General. To me, Nigel Havers was a potential customer while the receptionist was in that dreamlike state fondly imaging a scenario that presumably involved walking down the aisle.*

He told me who he was, although I already knew, and that he definitely wanted a BMW but was not quite sure which one. I jotted down his contact details and trotted off to the cupboard next to the stairs for a bunch of brochures. It was a very strange encounter and I really didn't think that he would buy a car at all.

Several telephone conversations later we had a budget and a BMW he liked, the 6 Series. However, his budget, which was substantial enough, would still not buy a brand new one. Indeed, I was still so convinced that Mr Havers wouldn't buy a car that I told him to go down to our Brentford service centre to look at a 635 that had been in a smash. That is a dangerous thing to do. I had been trained to never ever let customers go anywhere on their own to look at a car and especially a smashed up one. It can put all sorts of ideas in their heads, especially to go elsewhere and buy something else, which is in one piece. In this instance it had the opposite effect. He rightly decided that rather than tolerate a patched up 6 Series, a brand new BMW made much more sense.

Ladies and gentlemen, Mr. Nigel Havers, not pictured with a BMW (it's an MG) and as he appeared in the hugely popular 1980s ITV drama series, *The Charmer*.
© London Weekend Television © Yorkshire Television.

Back in the showroom we pored over the specification sheet and put together a rather wonderfully equipped black 323i two door. He did ask whether he could have a few quid off and obviously the answer was no. This was Park Lane after all and we never, ever gave discounts, especially on 3 Series to anyone, even if they were film stars. However, I had a chat with the sales manager and we could certainly chuck in a nice Blaupunkt radio. Everyone was happy. However, to me this was just another profitable sale. Even when the car was built and delivered I didn't even hand it over and get my picture taken shaking hands across the bonnet. I had a test drive to do somewhere else at the time so my Assistant Sales Manager did it. On reflection though that sale to Mr Havers summed up an era and defined 3 Series customers at that point in time and at that particular location.

If anyone was going to be the poster gentleman for the new upwardly mobile generation it was Nigel Havers. Suitably posh, very polite and seemingly well off, he was the template for thousands of blokes like me in double-breasted suits and carefully teased hair. Whereas to all the Princess Di lifestylealikes, which included our receptionist, he was the one that they all wanted to marry.

What interested me at the time was exactly what their South Kensington resident's parking permit was attached to. Of course Lady Di herself famously had a patriotic little Mini Metro, but what should she have been driving? Well, before she was the Queen of Hearts she was of course at the very least the Princess of the Sloane Rangers. Do I need to explain that term? Well Sloane Square is an expensive address in the West End where posh people lived during the week. Then at the weekend they would chase off to their country houses, often in Range Rovers, hence the adoption of the Range part of the name. The owners of the Range Rovers were more often the parents of the younger Sloanies who also lived there. For a while in the late '70s and '80s there were numerous articles about this sect and Peter York, previously the Style Editor of Harpers & Queen *magazine was the co-author of the incredibly successful Harpers & Queen's* The Official Sloane Ranger Handbook.

So if mummy and daddy drove a Rangie, what would they have? As a starter car it could be a Mini, a Metro, maybe a Fiat Panda or something else that was easy to park and also dent. When they grew up a bit and had jobs in the City, or perhaps more indulgent parents who were funding Jocasta or Jonathan's college course, the car would get bigger and better. Because they cared what other people thought then a Volkswagen Polo was a good place to start, more often though it was Golfs and ideally a GTI. Modern, classless and reliable, any Golf would do as it wasn't a car to show off in. It did however have a lot of respect and the little red GTI badges were priceless. However, those who wanted to grab a bit more attention would always go for a BMW. The 3 Series was small enough to get in the residents' parking bay and tough enough to cope with the cut and thrust of West End motoring.

Every SW postal district was teeming with Golfs or 3 Series and now Nigel had one too. It wasn't just the quintessential '80s car, it was the very best car that you could buy in any era full stop.

It may seem a bit late to mention what my first demonstrator car, or demo was, but it's highly relevant to this chapter. Although salesmen may convince themselves that it was their own car, really the motor they drove was just a short-term fling. It amounted to a brand new model every three months, which then got sold and replaced by another. Of course there there was a bit more to it than that because if they were out of favour and slipping down the sales league then the model and the specification may not live up to their expectations. Initially I had no expectations at all, but I thought that Brentford might hold a clue to what I would drive.

The Park Lane Service Department had a brace of old 3 Series, which were loan cars. I say old, they had been registered in early 1983 as the very last of the old shape models. Their official model designation was E21 and compared to the new E30 that I was going to sell it did look a bit dated. These 316iA loan cars were regarded as idiot proof. They had small 1.6 litre engines with A for automatic gearboxes. Perfect for the old dears and duffers having their BMWs rebuilt after bouncing off a bollard in a multi storey car park.

What I found hard to deal with was the colour, beige. The old hearing aid hue seemed very odd, but perhaps this was a job lot of final production examples that they couldn't really refuse, especially with a big discount. That little automatic was perfect for tooling around the West End, but wasn't destined to be my demo. As a contrast to a Special Equipment 7 Series it was all you really needed. At the time, with a heated rear window, radio/cassette, front head restraints and velour trim, it had as much as any other European manufacturer could offer. Even so, with the new E30 model on sale, the still very excellent E21 3 Series now looked like a very old car. But it wasn't always this way.

In 1975 the new 3 Series proved that there was an insatiable demand for a small two-door saloon with superb build quality, understated styling and a range of great engines. The decision to put a short, silky six-cylinder engine under the bonnet was certainly an inspired one. Here was the vital link between the sporty, but fairly spartan 02 series and the subsequent sophisticated compact executive that was the next generation E30. It was also the vital key in BMW's aspirational model line-up that saw customers progress from the entry level 3 through to the 5, 6 and then 7 series. The E21 became BMW's cash cow and the blueprint for a new model that every other manufacturer has since copied, but as yet, has never bettered.

BMW realised that their core market customers in Germany, the US and UK were getting richer in the 1970s. Consequently they were demanding much more from their cars when it came to performance, safety, comfort and equipment. 02s were basic, sporty cars that almost by accident became iconic compact saloons. BMW had aimed the 02s to appeal to a different kind of buyer. Certainly the design and engineering aims for the new car had fresh priorities. The product chief Bernhard Osswald wanted more interior space, improved ride, better fuel economy and greater levels of passive safety.

Front and rear end of the 316 and 318 with single headlamps.

Five years in development and 35 million Deutchmarks later the 3 Series emerged in July 1975. Yet for all that time and expenditure there really didn't seem to be a lot to get very excited about. With the familiar four-cylinder engine, strut suspension, rear wheel drive and trailing arm suspension was it really very much more than a made over 02? The only technical upgrade to get excited about was the rack and pinion steering. Keen enthusiasts may have noticed that the double caliper brakes were switched for singles, although the rear drums were larger. Certainly the E21 was bigger and heavier than the 02. The wheelbase was 63mm (2.5 inches) longer and the 320 model was 90kg (198lbs) heavier than the 2002. The suspension set-up was also on the soft side, but it was a more stable set-up with stiffer rear springs to reduce pitching. The European line up comprised a 316, 318, 320 and 320i. Essentially these were 02 units with Solex carburettors and automatic chokes and the 320i had an electronic Bosch K-Jetronic injection system. All models were available with a four, or an optional five-speed gearbox. A ZF three-speed automatic was optional from the 318 upwards.

From the styling point of view you could start to see the family resemblance now. Stylist Paul Bracq had come up with another shark nosed masterpiece that looked like a scaled down 5. The interior was also pretty much 5 Series and therefore ergonomically perfect with clear dials and a centre binnacle angled towards the driver.

Some BMW customers felt that the four-cylinder E21 was a bit of a slug in performance terms and they went off to buy specialist tuning parts. However, there was a sizeable majority who wanted their performance delivered more smoothly. The old 02 series was always intended to have low powered 1.3 and 1.6 power, but instead circumstances brought about the wonderful 2002 and turbo. BMW did not want to get caught on the hop again so right from the very beginning it was always intended that the 3 would be able to accommodate larger engines. There was some internal debate about whether this new generation of power plants should have a big four cylinder, V6 or straight six configuration. It was decided that the straight 6 delivered more power throughout the rev range compared with a V6 and would be smoother than a 4. The M-60 engines were different from the big block sixes. They still had aluminium cylinder heads, cast iron blocks and deep crankcases. However the cylinders had thin walls, the crankshaft was cast iron rather than forged steel, while a single overhead camshaft was driven by a cogged belt. This was a lightweight unit at 170kgs (374lbs) and made up for the E21's general podginess. Available from September 1977 it was fitted to the 320/6 and the 323i. The 320 delivered 122 bhp courtesy of a single Solex carb and the 323i 143 bhp with Bosch K-Jetronic injection.

Interestingly, BMW boss Von Kuenheim was so impressed by six-cylinder sales which rapidly accounted for 50% of 3 Series production that he considered dropping four-cylinder production altogether. However, Dr. Radermacher in the marketing department helpfully pointed out that the lack of a true entry-level model would be unwise. I witnessed first hand how buyers were drawn in by the cheapest and least powerful version and how they would often weigh up whether they should simply go for the 320i in basic trim, 316i with a sunroof, central locking and a radio, or possibly sell a kidney and go for a 323i.

323i. 6 cylinders and four headlights.

Indeed, the 323i was BMWs attempt to emulate the appeal and performance of the 2002tii with an impressive 0–60 mph time of just over 8 seconds. Rear end grip though was minimal. I found that to my cost on a very gentle negotiation of a roundabout in East London when for no apparent reason I found myself facing the oncoming traffic. It was a lovely red 323i that I had been borrowing and clearly accelerating in any situation other than on bone dry tarmac was unwise. Yes a 323i was either fun, or frightening depending on your mood or ability. At least the 323i had four disc brakes to bring it to a halt. The 320 was less charismatic, no less thirsty and relatively expensive to maintain.

Not a huge amount happened to the 3 Series over the years apart from some detail changes that are mostly too insignificant to mention. British spec 3 Series though were always better equipped than the European versions and by 1980 an electric driver's door mirror, tinted glass and locks on the fuel cap and glovebox were standard. In September 1980 the 1766cc European 318 engine was fitted to the 316, which retained its badging. Briefly the UK got a batch of 316is, which had the 1766cc unit producing 105 bhp with K-Jetronic injection. It remained on the price lists even when the E30 arrived and was obviously a way of using up left over bodyshells. Five speed gearboxes as standard on the 6-cylinder cars from 1982 was probably the most important technical change and really that was a test bed for the forthcoming new 3 Series.

Although the bodywork stuck rigidly to the two-door saloon format there was none of the variety that distinguished the 02 Touring. However, from 1977 to 1983 the coachbuilders Baur built their targa versions of the 3 Series, which were officially referred to as hard top cabriolets. Not the most elegant open top solution, however that roll bar provided a lot of rigidity and meant that the handling was far better than many open top cars of the day. Meanwhile Karmann who built the 6 Series coupé bodies produced a full convertible prototype which never made it to production. In all, around 4600 Baur models were built and it was still pretty much the classiest and best small open car anyone could buy in the late '70s and early '80s.

Towards the end of its life there were some special edition models, which had the six-cylinder engine and Recaro sports seats, plus some distinctive two-tone paint that still looked acceptable in the early '80s. In historical terms the first 3 Series was the cradle of the M60 engine, spawned the Formula 1 engine, was the catalyst for Alpina series production and it also defined what the 3 Series was all about and established a dynasty, which was pretty impressive.

The new 80 from 1979, which was rather rectangular.

Meanwhile Audi were revising their small family car as the longer and wider second generation 80 was launched in autumn 1979, and then quickly established itself as the company's best selling model. Looking even more like a scaled down 100 they were building 800 a day. Customers could also order a whole range of engines from a 1.3 to 1.6 and most significantly the 80 would get the fuel injected Golf GTI engine, but have the less sexy moniker, GLE. However, the closest in spirit to BMW's sporty two doors was the big engined 80 five-cylinder 2.0. Also there was the short-lived 2.1 litre five-cylinder 136 bhp unit. Both of these models were eventually renamed 90 in 1984. Audi wanted a new sporty image even if the 80 and 90 looked identical, but then the four wheel drive Quattro with the four rings down the flanks really gave BMW something to think about. Whereas the standard front wheel drive version was rather ordinary, the Quattro version was sensational when it came to handling and performance.

Of course, diesels were also on the menu for European buyers, something that never sullied the sporty 3 Series price list. Audi was a more practical proposition and a standard 1.6 and the turbocharged diesel represented the frugal side of 80 motoring. But I would never get to see one of them, just as the number of E21s I would have to deal with would be relatively small. It was all about the new E30 3 Series. After all that was the model people were buying in the biggest quantity and hopefully they would buy them from me.

This was the model that really took BMW from being a small, technically clever carmaker who made desirable sporty cars, to a company with a vehicle, which seemed to translate successfully into every worldwide market. The E30 was compact, exclusive, and yet affordable. It didn't matter than an entry level 316 looked almost identical to a top of the range 323i. What mattered was the badge and the quality and the engineering. Whether buyers wanted a saloon, estate, super saloon or convertible there was a model just for them. The E30 was and still is one of the most important cars ever to be built in Germany. Here's why.

The new 3 Series took six years to develop, yet at first glance when it was launched in the UK in March 1983 not a lot seemed to have changed from the old E21 days. Claus Luthe was responsible for the styling, which was neat and functional, but no quantum leap from the previous generation. It was also just 35mm (just over 1 inch) wider than before, a touch shorter at 4325mm, compared with E21's 4355mm. Despite many hours in the wind tunnel aerodynamically the Cd figures were less than impressive at 0.38 for the fours and 0.39 for the six-cylinder models. However, it was the specification, build quality, refinement and ambition that were the key ingredients that made the E30 so special.

Technically it seemed to be more of the same with a familiar range of four- and six-cylinder engines with confusing nomenclatures. European entry level was a 1766cc carb-fed 316 that produced 90 bhp. The 318i benefited from Bosch L-Jetronic injection to pump out 105 bhp. The 320i now delivered 125 bhp also courtesy of L-Jetronic, whilst the top of the range 323i revelled in a Bosch Motronic set-up with breakerless electronic ignition and 143 bhp. Actual engine changes included a lighter ribbed crankcase with a flange between the engine and gearbox that reduced vibrations to the cabin area. There were also lower tension valve springs and narrower camshaft bearings, which reduced internal friction. In particular the fours got lighter pistons. The 316 and 318 also had the benefit of a new four speed Getrag gearbox and a new ZF unit with five speeds.

3 Series 2-door, cleverly parked so we can see the back and front.

Chassis wise much was done to cure the rear end waywardness that had blighted the E21. So up went the wheel size by an inch from 13 to 14 inches and widths meant either 5 or 5.5ins rims. The front suspension was now similar to the 5 Series set up featuring MacPherson struts. At the rear the coil springs were modified so that they mounted directly onto the trailing arms. Indeed, the arm angle was reduced so that there were less toe in changes under roll and there was longer spring travel. So what that all amounted to was that the new 3 was no longer tail happy. It stopped better too with bigger front discs whilst the 323i received the added reassurance of rear discs. ABS anti-lock brakes also became an option on the 320i and 323i.

That was all very fascinating, but from a sales point of view the most important thing about this new range of 3s was the inclusion of two extra doors.

An American spec 4-door, we know this because it has those really silly bumpers.

Customers had to wait until August 1983, but the extra £350 and the 8 inches (20cm) that the B pillar had to be shoved forward, seemed worth it in order to get four doors. The E30 expansion programme had begun as the family of related models began to grow and capture more and more customers. As well as attracting the local Sloanie the appeal of the 3 Series went way beyond that very specific postal district. The acronym YUPPIE described the young upwardly mobile, professional (not a very good acronym then). Well actually Young Urban Professional might fit better, but it was the upwardly mobile bit that was crucial.

BMW was certainly the car to be seen in, because at that time in the early '80s it was still an exclusive marque, but more importantly it had a sporty and high tech image that left Mercedes and Jaguars looking fussy, old fashioned and out of touch. Mercedes in particular were driven by the establishment. As well as the YUPPIES the good company car driver was starting to pay attention because suddenly a BMW could be squeezed onto the user/chooser list. Rather than make do with a top of the range Ford Sierra it was now possible to score vital company car park points bragging rights by turning up for work in a 3 Series. Often that did mean avoiding some of the tick boxes on the order form and learning to love the standard steel wheels.

Actually company car fleet managers who authorised the cheques soon realised that a BMW 3 Series needed at the very least a sunroof to retain its value. Selling a BMW without a sunroof rarely happened. Although I do remember trying to convince one gentleman that the 320i he was buying for his daughter would be a much better proposition with a sunroof.

"Mr Ruppert, if she had the roof open, boys could dive inside." He was deadly serious. She was pretty, but not that pretty. He got what he ordered – a 318i with an intact roof and presumably as a result he also had an intact daughter. But that was a long time ago.

Keeping company car drivers happy was only part of BMW's aim, what they really wanted was complete market domination. So it was no surprise when the E30 started to mutate. By 1989 there were no less than 17 derivatives.

A 3 Series Convertible by BMW.

Baur of Stuttgart created 3 Series convertibles first seen in 1977. Distinguished by the roll bar, framed side glass and two separate opening sections, the soft rear hood was complemented, possibly complicated, by a single glass fibre lift-out panel. Despite the arrival of BMW's own full convertible in 1986 sales of the Baur conversion continued.

Touring. Not that practical, but certainly pretty.

The Touring name was revived in 1987 when an out of hours project reached production reality. It was a bit more practical than a saloon, but couldn't quite be called an estate, so that's why they called it a Touring. Here is then the lifestyle estate car, which is so familiar now, but was a novelty back in the late '80s. Practical, but not so practical that the BMW could possibly lose its sporting edge. No one else could get away with it (especially those rear light clusters, which turned the loading lip into something of a letter box opening. UK deliveries began in March 1988 as a 320i, 325i and latterly 318i and 316i. Model wise though this is simply scratching the surface. There were more 3 Series where that came from.

If you thought that there were more than enough E30 derivatives on sale in the UK, those who lived in Europe were even more fortunate. How about a Touring with running gear from the four wheel drive 325iX? We only got the 325i version in left-hand drive layout and figures from BMW show that just 43 of them were registered in 1989 before it was dropped in 1990. There was also a very unusual high economy, low revving eta version of the 3 Series fitted with the six-cylinder 2.7 litre (from the 525e) engine. This 325e model was added to the range in mid 1984 and was available in both two and four door variants. Italian market customers got a tax break 320i Sport rather than pay through the nose for a 325i version. Diesel wasn't a '90s thing for BMW they had oil burners for years and way back in 1987 a turbocharged version of the six-cylinder M60 unit resulted in the smooth and frugal 115 bhp 324td.

Arguably the oddest E30 of all was the production concept Z1 that was available in the UK in left-hand drive only. It was effectively a 325i in pretty composite drag, except that there wasn't much drag at all because of the smooth underside. Indeed the clever Z axle filtered through to the next generation E36, whilst the disappearing doors simply disappeared into the shell. More on that later.

Of course the whole point of BMWs is that they are ultimate driving machines and from day one there was always something to amuse and entertain.

At first buyers had to make do with the E30 version of the 143 bhp 323i. After a new camshaft, distributor and inlet manifold were fitted in October 1984 the output went up to 150 bhp and the 0–60 mph time fell to just over 8 seconds, which wasn't any improvement on the E21 version. The 171 bhp 325i in 1985 put that deficit right by getting to 60 mph a second quicker. The UK market Sport model in 1986 had an M-Technic body kit and suspension that included gas filled dampers, stiffer springs and thicker anti-rollbars. The wider BBS alloys 6.5J were uprated to 7J x 15s. A limited slip differential also helped out, but it was never going to be the ultimate driving machine. Oh no, that accolade could belong to the only one E30.

M3.

Ah the M3. There really isn't enough room to write about the M3 here, however we do touch on its phenomenal racing success in the appropriate chapter. If any BMW deserves the credit for raising the profile of the Motorsport badge it has to be the M3. In many ways this was the people's M car as the M635i, M5 and the M1 before it had been expensive and rarefied products. Instead of limited production wondercars, what BMW really needed was a high-speed sports car by the thousand (5000 to be precise) in order to qualify for Group A racing.

Work had started on the M3 as far back as 1981 with BMW's four-cylinder engine that was already over 20 years old and was still a staple power plant in Formula 2. This was connected to a shortened (by two cylinders) twin-cam four valves per cylinder head from the M1 and M635. The block was lightened and its size was a generous 2302cc producing 200 bhp. BMW also designed the engine with siasmesed pistons working together, duplex chain driven overhead camshafts, Motronic fuel injection, a lightweight alloy sump and separate oil cooler. The gearbox was different without an overdrive and a higher final drive to compensate. However, the most notable difference was the dogleg first gear, which meant that first is where second usually is. Helping the changes was an uprated clutch with a bonded lining.

As for the suspension it was revamped with a new layout and thicker anti-roll bars front and rear. Gas pressurised dampers, uprated rear springs and 15 degree rear trailing arms all made a difference. Also new stub-axles with larger wheel bearings were transplanted from the 5 Series. A power steering system with a quicker rack made the M3 more responsive.

Revamping the engine and suspension was only part of the Motorsport makeover and every panel apart from the bonnet was modified or replaced, indeed the whole bodyshell needed to be changed so that it could accommodate a roll cage. The blistered arches were made of steel and now contained BBS 7 inch wide alloys for the road and ultimately even wider ones for racing. You had to be eagle eyed to spot the larger rear window, which had a sharper profile whilst both the front and rear screens were bonded in place to stiffen up the bodywork. Mods that were easier to spot included the front spoiler, rear wing, side skirts and also a raised boot line. That all meant that the not particularly aerodynamic E30 body dropped to a more reasonable drag coefficient of 0.33.

Bringing the M3 to a halt was an adapted 5 Series braking system featuring larger ventilated discs at the front and solid ones at the rear with reinforced single-piston calipers and uprated Bosch ABS brakes.

M3 Evolution.

Inside, the M3 was only slightly different to a standard car with sports seats and a three spoke Motorsport steering wheel. As for the instruments a tiny M badge in the middle of the binnacle signified that there were some major differences. The speedometer was calibrated to read 160 mph, while the rev counter went all the way to 8000 rpm. Tinted glass and electric door mirrors were standard and all the usual fripperies, apart from an automatic gearbox, could be ordered. What was different from a standard UK car was the fact that this was available as a left-hand drive model only. However, that didn't put off buyers.

It is incredible to think now that the BMW board were concerned that the M3 looked too aggressive. Apparently the announcement of the even more evil looking Mercedes 190E 2.3–16 persuaded them that it would look like a pussycat by comparison. Well a pussycat that had an official top speed of 146 mph and would get to 62 mph in 6.7 seconds. Announced at the Frankfurt Motor Show in September 1985, the M3 was finally available to buy a year later.

BMW had to constantly uprate the M3 to keep it competitive hence the arrival of 500 Evo or evolved road cars that had the required modifications they needed for the track. The very first M3 Evolution was announced in early 1987 and was a very subtle update, with a more prominent front spoiler and an extra blade on the rear wing with a lightweight boot lid. That was it. No, really it was.

March 1988 saw the arrival of the rather more radical Evolution II as the output of the engine was boosted by 20 bhp to 220 bhp. This was achieved with a revised Motronic system, new camshafts, pistons, lightened flywheel, a raised compression ratio and new air intake. Along with a higher final drive and wider 7.5 inch alloy wheels the top speed rose to 152 mph. Also more high tech light-weight materials were being used in its construction on the boot lid, rear side windows and rear screen, cutting the weight by 10kg (22lbs).

And finally in December 1989 the Evo III really was the ultimate driving machine. The engine size was upped to 2467cc, it had bigger inlet valves, sodium cooled exhaust valves and a revised cam which on the road meant a rise of 18 bhp to 238. As well as the mechanicals the front and rear spoilers were now adjustable by virtue of additional flaps helping to keep the Evo III on the ground. That's important when the top speed went up to 154 mph and officially the 0–62 mph time dropped to 6.5 seconds. Incredibly, even the vents on the kidney grille were reprofiled and rubber inserts were located in the headlamp and grille mountings and bonnet surround to aid airflow.

Weight was kept down to 1200kgs (2645lb) by using a smaller 62-litre fuel tank from a 325i, lighter bumpers and thinner side and rear glass. Inside passengers had to do without grab handles or map lights. However they did sit on new front sports seats with fixed headrests. However, no weight gaining, power-sapping extras, from air conditioning to electric windows were offered.

There were special edition M3s too which capitalised on its competition success, such as the Europa Meister. It all amounted to signed driver plaques and leather special seat trim and colours. One of the rarest was the UK only Ravaglia finished in Mosano Red with half leather seats. At least it was named after an M3 driver and you could see the point of it, whereas the convertible seemed a lot more like a marketing and money making exercise. Even so, it was completely hand built by Motorsport. Available from mid 1988 the convertible was something of a compromise, but a very beautiful and accomplished one that had to do without the rear wing and made do with just the standard 3 Series boot lid and spoiler. With an electrically operated roof it can be seen as a direct response to those Porsche 911s that did not have a roof. Obviously though it was much rarer.

The M3 could not have been a better performance brand builder for BMW. Unusually for what is a limited production, homologation special, the M3 sold by the transporter load and 17,184 went to very happy customers.

The future shape of BMWs? Say hello to the Z1.

There was yet another variation on the 3 Series theme that was also left-hand drive only. In 1985 BMW founded a new division called BMW Technik GmbH. It was the company's think-tank staffed by engineers, technicians and designers from BMW who had freedom to innovate. The first project for the so-called 'ZT' team was inventing ground breaking car parts rather than a complete vehicle. Their ideas were then implemented into the Z1 concept. The 'Z' comes not from Zappa or Zeberdee, but from 'Zukunft', the German word for future.

The Z1 was nothing more than development 'mule' for the future technology that would find its way onto more conventional production BMWs. However, at some point it was decided to release the vehicle into the general population. It was no ordinary car and uniquely constructed with a steel backbone chassis providing all the structure and strength, making the bodywork merely cosmetic. 13 bolt-on plastic panels made up a distinctive and very purposeful wedge shape. The floor comprised a foam cored composite sandwich and above the thick sills what grabbed all the attention was the disappearing doors that dropped down at the push of a button. Oddly the drop down doors never did make it into any future BMWs, but the Z axle suspension did.

So what is a Z axle? Well it is a multi-link suspension set-up, which is infinitely tuneable, and the set up claimed to give much better road holding. It is essentially like double wishbone suspension but each arm of the wishbone is a separate item. These are joined at the top and bottom of the wheel spindle thus forming the wishbone shape. Except that the Z axle isn't strictly wishbone shaped, it is Z shaped hence the name. In BMW's own inimitable words it was actually called the central point guided, spherical, double suspension arm and even at one point the central pull rod axle. According to BMW it gave almost perfect control of the camber and toe in changes. It generates a small degree of toe in at high cornering speeds. So as the rear offside wheel loads up, it results in added stability. This is effectively rear wheel, or passive steering, technology in action.

Essentially it made the Z1 very sweet to drive and the 325i engine pulled it all along very smartly. Launched in 1989, there did seem to be a willing market for a high tech roadster and that probably explained the optimistic £36,925 price tag. I was invited to buy some Z1s with the expectation that there would be a waiting list and that they could be sold at a comfortable profit. Well there wasn't and I didn't. For once I did the sensible thing and didn't join the showroom speculators, as all they got was their money back, just. The world was changing and even a futuristic BMW roadster, which cost more than twice the price of the equally new Lotus Elan at £17,850, was going to struggle. A world financial crisis was looming and there wasn't money to waste on clever open topped sports cars.

If there is one market no one expected BMW to tackle it was the hot hatch one. No they didn't produce a hatch, but they did build the 318iS. Taking advantage of the new M42 16-valve block that produced a healthy 136 bhp, which equates to almost 76 bhp per litre, runner up only to the M3 in power terms. Firmer sports suspension was an asset and it would get to 60 mph in just over 9 seconds and run up to 125 mph top speed just like all those Astra GTEs and Golf GTIs. Except that it was so much classier and the price premium was around £2000–£3000, so worth every penny.

It wasn't all over when the fatter E36 arrived in 1991. The E30 still had important work to do by keeping convertible and Touring buyers happy until 1994. At that point the E30 could gracefully retire satisfied with a job well done. Over the years, BMW made no radical changes. The 1987 facelift was so subtle it was easy to miss and amounted effectively to just getting rid of the chrome. Little changed because it just wasn't necessary. Regular evolutionary changes were the order of the day to keep the 3 Series fresh and desirable. Catalytic converter prepared engines and the revised M40 four-cylinder units were the major changes otherwise gradually more comprehensive specifications and tempting SE packages kept the UK buying public interested.

2.4 million buyers could not be wrong. The E30 3 Series proved that pre Rover, BMW had their finger on the car buyer's pulse. Their appetite for aspirational, well-built, compact and sporty was almost insatiable and BMW could charge almost what they liked. Even today an E30 looks classy, purposeful and confident. That success did not go unnoticed.

At some time early in 1984 an announcement was made at the daily sales meeting that a Mercedes 190 was on the premises. We were advised that it would be a really good idea to take it for a spin. That's because when a customer said they were test driving a 190 tomorrow we could tell them all the reasons why that would be a very bad idea.

It was a part exchanged left-hand drive 190 in white. To be honest none of us had the time to fool about in a Mercedes. We all had 3 Series to sell and we really didn't rate what would become its greatest rival. So four of us crammed inside and went for a brief tour of the West End. Certainly it wasn't that spacious in the back. The interior was as dour as any other Merc and with four up it didn't seem that quick. To us it was Mercedes like all the others, but smaller. But then again we were car salesman, so what did we really know? We were also biased towards the Bavarian marque and quite right too. The 3 was a much more sporty and versatile proposition. The 190's handbrake amused us because after years of sticking a silly umbrella stalk under the dashboard or relying on the daft foot operated parking brake, they seemed to finally admit that sticking it between the seats made sense. We reasoned that a newly qualified accountant, or possibly a small shopkeeper would be delighted with a Merc that was a bit less bulky to park, but it really wouldn't turn the heads or empty the wallets of our predominantly young, ambitious customers. For Mercedes though it was a massive move in the right direction.

Mercedes wanted a share of those young thrusting professionals throughout Europe but they also felt the need to downsize as a response to the deeply scary Energy Crisis of 1973. Even so, trawling through press releases revealed that Mercedes were keen to stress that they had been considering something smaller before the price at the pumps went nuclear. Even so they must have spent a lot of time just thinking about how they were going to make the Mercedes magic work on a smaller scale as nothing seems to have happened until at least 1976.

Designated the W201 it was a concoction of new technology projects from multi link rear suspension to some rather radical rethinks, which even involved a front wheel drive layout. It may have been the fact that the initial development vehicles were based on Volkswagen Golfs which had been stretched a bit to cover the running gear. However by 1979 it was decided to stick with the more traditional layout, as front wheel drive did not seem to offer any interior advantages as the W201 was still going to be much bigger than the newly fashionable small family hatchbacks. Plus parts sharing between front and rear wheel models is never going to work especially as the engine was going to be the very familiar 1997cc four cylinder first seen in the W123 from 1979.

So if the mechanicals were going to be trad, so was the styling. Started in 1977, the team lead by Bruno Sacco had full approval just a year later, but it was another two years before the prototypes finally hit the Autobahns. Badged as Ushidos, this was obviously some sort of German joke to suggest that the Japanese were entering the compact executive marketplace. In another decade that wouldn't seem so funny, but for now Lexus had not been invented as a word and Ushido could still confuse a dumb motoring journalist. Except it didn't. Registering the cars in Aachen rather than in their hometown Stuttgart did not fool anyone, and meant that published pictures of these Jappo-German saloons were still captioned 'New Mercedes' in the car magazines.

This New Mercedes was certainly a lot sleeker and more contemporary than what they had on sale at time and was a reflection of the fact that time spent in their wind tunnel had not been wasted. Instead of looking like a teardrop blob there were lots of clever details that would help the 190 slip through the air without very much fuss. A sloping theme at the front with the bonnet, grille and headlamps caused less disturbance to the airflow, whilst a spoiler did its job below. Indeed, there was a fairing underneath the engine and a remarkably flat floorpan which all helped keep the air running smoothly. The high rear boot and creases in the roof and rear wings also suggested that slide rules and little wooden models had optimised the airflow co-ordinates. And finally the dish like hubcaps that Mercedes were famous for became even dishier as polycarbonate plastic now covered the whole wheel.

This was clearly a Mercedes and although the designers could have gone all out aerodynamically, the windscreen was still quite upright and there was no escaping the unfashionably large grille, which was topped off with the three-pointed star. The drag coefficient was a pleasing 0.33 for the engineers, which was impressive, as they didn't try too hard. Whereas the Audi 100 did try really hard and scored 0.30, which means it was very slippery through the air.

A crucial part of making a smaller Mercedes meant it ought to be lighter, well lighter for a Mercedes anyway. There were more plastics than before in the bumpers, door handles and lots of other pieces of interior and exterior trim. However, it was only marginally lighter and Mercedes were unwilling to compromise on safety, so at the centre of the W201 was a massively strong passenger cell with crumple zones at either end and a large crossmember below the dashboard. Although Mercedes were not giving any thought to future resale value and its used car prospects, there was an unusual amount of body protection. Mercedes knew that rust would weaken the structure and compromise safety so there was a lot of galvanized steel, wax injection and plastic

A very sensible Mercedes 190.

shrouds on the door bottoms and under the wheel arches. Build quality then was never going to be an issue and there was even a bit of engineering innovation to get excited about.

At last Mercedes were paying attention as to what BMW had been doing and how their saloons handled. The suspension was new with MacPherson struts being fitted to the front with a wishbone arrangement and the coil springs mounted separately which all helped to save weight. The rear suspension was a complicated set up with five suspension links in all on each side. This meant a much more flexible system which combined with more familiar coils and dampers. The intention was to make a very sophisticated car, which matched the top of the range S-Class.

So far, the opinion of four car salesmen in a white 190 (that it was nothing special and nothing to worry about) making the tyres screech around the W1 postal district, seemed about right. In its first year or so the 190 was perceived as expensive, cramped and poor value, so the E30 BMW continued to dominate the small executive car sector that the 3 Series had invented anyway. So although it had taken a full year for the 190 to get to the lucrative British market in 1983, its impact was marginal. Before its arrival though Mercedes were already making changes and introducing new models to broaden its appeal.

The centre or B Pillar was slimmed down so that seeing out was easier, which also gave them the opportunity to modify the door seal so that the occupants no longer got damp. New manual gearbox ratios and switchable Sport/Economy automatics were welcome upgrades, whilst a Diesel 190 meant that it could finally take its place in the taxi rank. Actually the engine was Mercedes' most advanced oil burner ever, being highly efficient, fast and refined. One day all diesels would be like the 190, but at the time few cared except those who charged by the kilometre, sat on a beaded cover and didn't care that the steering was unassisted and the gearbox held only four gears.

Mercedes did though go after the seriously quick 3 Series having considered entering the wacky world of Group B rallying. Here's where the Brits come in, because the contract for developing the engine was given to Cosworth Engineering. The plan had been to coax 320 bhp out of the engine, but clearly someone at Mercedes came to their senses and cancelled the programme. They still had the engine though and it was decided to make it civilian friendly and produce the 190E 2.3–16 in 185 bhp form. That was quick enough as it managed 145 mph and got to 60 mph in a hot hatch time frame of 8 seconds. It also looked different as Mercedes had gone back to the wind tunnel and shaved a bit more off the drag coefficient which now stood at 0.32 thanks to a new front spoiler, side skirts and a low level boot mounted wing. The wheel arches were also flared so as to squeeze in wider tyres and the suspension was lowered.

Mercedes 190E 2.3–16 Evolution, basically a black hole with alloys.

To prove how special these 190s were Mercedes took them to the Nardo test track in Italy and indulged in a bit of record breaking setting 12 world records for speed and endurance. This was followed up in May 1984 with a promotional race featuring Formula One drivers from several eras who competed against each other at a reopened Nurburgring. Of course Aryton Senna won. In fact, despite a long delay between the initial announcement of the Cosworth and its launch because of engine production difficulties, it actually turned into something of a hit.

Mercedes had planned just 5,000 of them so that they could be homologated for racing, but actually more than double that number ended up being built. The interior had a dogtooth check pattern to brighten things up a bit, but more important were the huggy sports seats front and rear. So it was the Cosworth engine which helped the smallest Mercedes become respectable. Indeed the 190 started to get better with revised 2.5 litre engines in both diesel and petrol forms and by 1987 the diesel had a turbocharger.

Constantly uprating the 190 in response to 3 Series tweaks from 1988 there were lower body side panels and 16 valve engines. Going racing in the increasingly popular German Touring Car Championship led directly to the 190E 2.5-16. Despite being a 150 mph supercar, the 190 still looked less special and did not have the appeal of the 3 Series which remained the model they had to chase.

Luckily they did this in a fairly spectacular fashion when in 1989 Mercedes unveiled the Evolution version of the 2.5-16. They built limited numbers to qualify for Touring Cars and it came with wider wheels, fatter arches and a more pronounced rear wing. Evolution II was an even more decent sequel, which featured a fairly spectacular rear wing, which in the annals of legendary downforce devices ranks up there with the Porsche 911 Tea Tray. This architectural wonder had a fixed upper and adjustable lower wing for maximum effect. There was even a wind deflector on the upper section of the rear window. Not only that, the front spoiler was deeper and instead of being a dumb piece of immovable plastic it could be adjusted slightly too. The alloys were six spoke monsters and the lowered suspension made it look much meaner than the original Evo.

However, although the Evolution looked businesslike and was finished in metallic blue/black and was powered by a 235 bhp engine it was not hooligan quick. The limited top speed was 155 mph and it would get to 60 mph in just over 7.0 seconds, which is still quick, but not astounding. Uncouth speeds were really not the point when it came to the 190. Here was a car that was all about reliability and understated style. The 190E 1.8 did its job as an entry level teaser and four irritating, know it all salesman in a left handed import really did see the 190 for what it was, a superbly built Mercedes for beginners. Longer term though it turned out to be a lot more durable than the four cylinder 3 Series that rusted and were opposite locked into various hedgerows and suburban dwarf walls.

Just as Mercedes were finally getting to grips with the 3 Series, so were Audi with the third generation 80, also known as the B3 to anyone who actually cared. It was a far more rounded soap bar shape, with a surprisingly tiny boot, that really established a visual link through the range from 80 to 100 and 200. Like the 100 it had class leading aerodynamics so it cut through the air with a wind cheating Cd factor of just 29. Like its big brothers the 80 had a fully galvanised body (guaranteed for ten years) which meant that they would be around a lot longer than most E30s and easily as long as a 190. Also designed to make their passengers last longer was the Procon-Ten safety system which was designed to reduce the severity of collision injuries caused by the driver's head hitting the steering wheel.

The soap bar shaped Audi 80.

Procon Ten was neatly illustrated in an Audi TV ad whereby a paperclip was bent into the shape of a steering wheel and then inserted into the top of a matchbox. The sliding inner drawer of the matchbox protruded slightly and that is what was pushed into a wall to simulate an accident as the pretend 'stationary based' steering wheel was pulled back by the drawer. Geddit? It won an award in Cannes you know. In real engineering life where no paperclips were harmed steel cables were used to pull the steering wheel away from the driver's body and towards the dashboard.

The smaller engine was increased to become a 1.6 and was then replaced by a 1.8. A 2.0 engine in 1989 would make the 80 a bit more sophisticated and just a bit quicker and there was a turbo diesel too. However a 16-valve engine badged as the Sport was the quick one, but really the performance glory was left to the 90. These models exclusively had the five cylinder engines in 2.0 (11 5 bhp) and 2.2 (136 hp) capacities the bigger one getting the option of Quattro four-wheel drive. In fact the engine size was upped to 2.3 in 1989 to cope with the power drain of the catalytic converter. There were also Sport versions of the 90 had 20 valve engines, which produced 170 bhp. It had lowered suspension and wider tyres. However, the 90 was living on borrowed time and the designation was dropped in 1991.

Audi 90 Quattro which added alloys and spoilers and four wheel drive and a bigger engine to the 80 format.

Audi though were eyeing the 3 Series market ever more closely by stretching the model range into profitable new niches, such as the coupé in 1988 which was much criticised for its handling and ride. Whilst the original square cut Quattro 20V power slid from 1989 into the early '90s, the S2 Quattro version was no Quattro, but that's another story possibly for another chapter.

However, the 80 went on to evolve into the '90s with the cabriolet and Avant estate in '91 and '92 respectively. For the purposes of the book we shouldn't be interested in the next decade, but actually both these developments were fascinating as Audi now had an almost complete set of models to match the 3 Series.

Open top Audis had not been around for more than 50 years. A concept version of the topless coupé was shown at the Frankfurt Motor Show in 1989 and by 1991 it was a full production model. Unlike the coupé it looked absolutely gorgeous. Compared to the standard saloon it piled on the kilos, weighing 135 kilos more, all in the name of structural reinforcement. However, once powered by a 2.8 six-cylinder engine the 3 Series now had a very credible rival. Yet this wasn't just a 3 Series clone, which came with all sorts of tiresome Yuppie baggage. No people actually liked the 80 cabriolet.

They liked it even more once it was adopted by the Queen of Cabriolets, HRH Princess Diana. Rumour had it that post divorce she had wanted to get herself a big bad Mercedes SL. However it was deemed rather too German, by the not at all descended from Prince Albert Francis Charles Augustus Emmanuel of Saxe-Coburg-Gotha, British Royal Family.

The 80 had the understated elegance that the 3 Series had long since lost and a roof that was dead easy to use. In a West End overrun with 3 Series the 80 was a breath of fresh air. It was good enough for the Princess of Wales, especially the newly independent Diana, making a break with tradition and away from the stuffy Royals. It was a serious move upmarket from the silver Ford Escort she had been given by Prince Charles in the early 80s.

Audi Cabriolet as it appeared in 1989 as a concept.

Audi took another cue from their Bavarian countrymen. Seeing how well the chic and not particularly spacious estate car had done as the 3 Series Touring, Audi clearly thought that there was room for another lifestyle load carrier. No one has ever properly defined lifestyle, but it seems to be the sort of scuba diving, surfing, rock climbing, outdoorsy type things, though quite how you would get all that stuff in the back of a Touring or Avant is open to question. Obviously giving these small estates names which held no promise of capaciousness was good protection under the Trade Descriptions act. The Audi Avant was available with a range of engines from little 4 cylinders through to 6 cylinders diesels and even a supercar RS version to take on BMW's M3.

BMW may have offered a Motorsport saloon and cabriolet, but they never thought to consider speeding up their mini estate car. Luckily Audi did and again although this is outside the remit of a book that should finish in 1990 it is worth taking a peek at just how Audi were rapidly moving out from under the shadow of Volkswagen.

Audi realised that all some enthusiasts have ever wanted is a 5 door Porsche. Not so much a supercar as a superwagen, the Audi Avant RS2 had a full Porsche engineering makeover that saw the 2226cc 5-cylinder engine produce 315 bhp. There were new camshafts, injectors, a bigger intercooler, free flow exhaust and a turbocharger that was 30% bigger than standard and mapped to provide 1.4 bar of boost. Incredibly the Audi engine was tough enough to take that comprehensive reworking. A six-speed gearbox marshalled that power whilst Porsche 968 Club Sport brakes made it all come to a halt. Porsche also supplied the five spoke 17-inch alloys, door mirrors and the indicator clusters housed in the big bumper/airdam.

The resulting performance was nothing short of astounding and getting to 60 mph in under 5 seconds in a lifestyle estate was positively brutal. Keeping it all on the road was Audi's brilliantly efficient Quattro transmission giving levels of grip that made so much of the 315 bhp useable. It was difficult not to be impressed by such an awesomely competent package concocted by two companies with legendary engineering abilities. However the RS2 was flawed, with noticeable turbo lag at lower revs, a lack of steering feel and a less than precise gear change. So it wasn't perfect but then the RS2 didn't have to be. Neither did my company car. It just had to be a BMW, and the fact that it was brand new was just a massive bonus.

My first demo car turned out to be a 316i finished in a bright Sapphire Blau, or Blue as we say in English. It was specified with a manual sunroof of course. Not only that it had alloy wheels, which looked really cool, compared to the standard steelies. The four speed gearbox did seem a bit silly even in the early '80s when this was supposed to be the Ultimate Driving Machine. Then again it was the very first rung on the BMW ladder, leading to the giddy heights of a 5, 6 or 7 Series. In London though I would rarely get to use third or even second most days. At least I could listen to the radio, which was more than some poor customer who just about managed to scrape together a deposit for a brand new 3. He or she could not have expected any entertainment at all. Indeed, if they ticked the 'radio preparation' option, all that would guarantee was a couple of speakers, some wires and a pull up aerial, all for fifty quid. So I was lucky to get a radio. No cassette, just an on-off switch and a tuner. The lowliest level Blaupunkt named after European City, or maybe seaside town like Skegness. Yes it was the Skegness I had. But at least I wasn't on a bus, as according to Mrs Thatcher, "A man who, beyond the age of 26, finds himself on a bus can count himself as a failure."

Actually it is debateable as to whether she said that because there seems to be no actual source for it. Although this is not a political book, the issue of driving and vehicle ownership has become highly politicised. To drive a BMW in the

1980s was a statement of independence, some significant wealth and a commitment to trading up to a better model, or next 'Series' as personal circumstances
improved.

A BMW was not just a capitalist's car, it was an entrepreneur's one, a risk
taking, ambitious, individual's way of saying that they were doing rather well. A
Saab meant you were a Socialist dentist. Volvos were for dabblers in antiques. A
Mercedes belonged to the company accountant. An Audi suggested that you
couldn't quite afford a Mercedes. A Rover was a cry for help.

Janet Brown as Mrs T.

*I once met Mrs T in the showroom, well actually I didn't, it was Janet Brown
who spent rather a lot of time during the 1980s pretending to be the Prime
Minister. A comedienne as they used to say and impressionist, she let me know
very quickly who she was and what she wanted. A four door 318i. Price was the
sticking point and this lady obviously was not for turning. I told her how much
I admired her late husband, Peter Butterworth, veteran of several 'Carry On'
films. And then she was gone.*

*My 3 Series was the most saleable car in the building. With metallic paint,
alloys and a sunroof, few cared that there was a gear missing as my car was the
model everyone could afford and it had all the right extras too. My colleagues
were allocated a 318i automatic and a 520i manual as our final destinations sort
of became clear.*

BMW 3 Series vs The Rest (1970s)

Fiat 131 Miafiori 2.0 Sport – At least the plastic trim around the wheelarches
and grille didn't rust, because everything else did. Fun in its own way this boxy
two door never had the street cred of an RS2000 or the sheer class of a 3 Series.
A bit of a joke then, except for the 16-valve homologation only Abarth Rallye.
But there were only ever 400 of those.

Alfasud Sprint – Whether you go for the two door Sud TI or the coupé Sprint, what you get are fizzy little engines, fabulous styling and rampant rot. A joy to drive and look at there is plenty of charisma, but almost no build quality. Four headlamps just like a six-cylinder E21, but five speeds from day one.

Ford Escort RS 2000 – Working class approach to the performance saloon market and very successful it was too. Upmarket Custom model much preferred to the steel-wheeled basic version. Fast enough, chuckable and with full Rallye Sport credentials it is at the opposite end of the styleometer to the BMW.

Saab 99 Turbo – Two doors and turbocharger were a recipe for fun. Many have been turbo lagged into the ground by several careless owners. In its day smooth and civilised with a good turn of speed, just like a six pot Beemer. Softer Saab image no match for the aggressive Bavarian.

Triumph Dolomite – There is the Micholetti connection of course (he styled BMWs too) and there is even a slight kink to the rear door pillar. The similarity ends there. Clever Sprint engine, but chassis not nearly as sorted as a 3 Series. Build quality often utterly appalling.

BMW 3 Series, Mercedes 190 and Audi 80 vs The Rest (1980s)

Alfa Romeo 75 – Great engine, shame about everything else really. Alfa were light-years away from the 156 inspired revival. This absolutely proved they could not do executive cars, or anything else for that matter. Orang-utan driving position and pasta build quality.

Lancia Delta – It was a Golf rival really, although there was a Prisma saloon which wasn't at all sexy or desirable, just square. Integrale version got as close to the M3 as anyone else, but fit and finish very low rent by comparison.

MG Maestro – Whether it was the 2.0EFi or Turbo the reasoning would have been that the addition of the MG was enough badgework to separate it from Austin associations. Nope. Despite being nice to drive and the Turbo terrifyingly quick it was no 3 Series.

Peugeot 505 V6 – A weird one and more of a rival for a 5, but this proves how little competition the original E30 six cylinders had. Rear wheel drive, but more about packing the family in comfort than on the limit joy. Comfy, decent handling and very, very French.

Saab 900 Turbo 16V – The Swedish entry never quite hit the mark, although it was tough and very speedy indeed. Styling not for everyone especially the dumpy saloons. Very underrated, but the nice Scandinavian image appealed to many who didn't like the arrogant Bavarian.

In the Cassette Deck ...

 The Cult – Love Those who worried (me) that traditional rock was on the wane were pleased that young gentlemen could dress like the progeny of Keith Richards with paisley prints and scarves and everything. Oh yes and there were lots of loud guitars and plenty of wailing. Led Zep reinvigorated for the '80s then. Cheered up the interior of a dour 190E no end.

6 Built to survive the Apocalypse. Vorsprung and all that . . .

A new breed of tough saloons for tough times, except for the NSU Ro80 of course. Mercedes W123 and the first BMW 5 Series.

June • New Car Profit: £17,619 • Used Car Profit: £2,926 • Total £20,545

Park Lane became my permanent home. The Sales Manager took me to one side and told me the news, but I could not decide whether it was good or not. What had swung it was a flippant answer to a direct question.

    "What are you doing?"

    "I'm having fun."

    Apparently that was the right thing to say accompanied by a cheery grin and a straightening of the tie. I'm sure I was being sarcastic at the time, but someone had staked their reputation on keeping me in the Park Lane showroom.

    Suddenly there was quite a lot to be frightened of, especially the nine other salesmen, or sales executives as our business cards read. It was a weird subterranean world with no natural light. In the '50s and '60s it had been a Ford showroom and all the cars were stored downstairs and a lift was used to get them to showroom level. The lift that had taken Ford Consuls from basement to ground level had long since been torn out and replaced by office dividers and cubicles in the middle.

I got my own cubicle, a beige push button telephone and most important of all, a wad of cards. These cards were A5 sized and coloured either yellow or white. The yellow ones were fairly new, up to five years old, but the white ones were like parchment. They were dirty, smudged and the edges were bent double and dated back to goodness knows when. They contained customer details. So people who had bought one, possibly two or more BMWs had all their personal and automotive details on the card. On the reverse were notes about all the contact that had taken place over the years. Some of the scribbles were a bit personal, like 'mad' so these cards were a bit like a doctor's notes. They belonged to my predecessors and according to the current salesman the very best cards had been redistributed by the outgoing salesmen or just pinched.

So I was left with a bunch of cards that were rubbish. I soon discovered just how rubbish when I started to 'follow up' on the information contained in them. These old customers were now mine, even if they were dead. Yes the cards contained all sorts of stories, both comic and tragic. My innocent enquiry as to how their 1968 BMW 1800 was keeping could trigger a tirade of abuse about an ex-husband or wife. Or worse, genuine sobs as they remembered a late loved one. If the telephone still connected with the right person the best I could hope for was an incredulous owner moaning about the fact that tyres actually wear out and exhausts will rust through after a decade.

I did briefly speak to 5 Series owner George Graham, ex Arsenal double winner now plying his trade in management at Millwall. At the time he probably needed a proper centre back, rather than a new car, so I didn't get very far and even offering my own 'sweeper' services didn't go down well. I was as sick as a parrot, but not really very surprised.

Following up the cards wasn't going to help me sell a car. With two teams of five salesmen I was on alternate afternoon and morning shifts. So half a day could be spent taking phone calls and showroom enquiries on rotation and in direct competition with my colleagues. The other half of the day was conducting test drives and following up enquiries.

The dream scenario was a 'Walk In'. That's when someone walked into the showroom and said, 'I want that red one there.' That very rarely happened. I just kept my head down and kept on bothering people who had only recently had the pleasure of meeting me. Yes I was being persistent and it did pay off.

It took a while to sell a car and it wasn't an especially memorable sale, being based largely on the bottom line. A discount, in other words. It was a 528i and it was blue and I still don't remember an awful lot more about it or the person I sold it too.

The 5 Series back then (E28) wasn't a particularly exciting model and in the early '80s despite a revamp it was never a strong seller in the UK. The buying public may have understood the 02 despite the amount it cost, but the relatively expensive New Klasse was never going to be an alternative to a Cortina, or more realistically a Rover or Triumph. That's because when buyers wanted a premium saloon they usually bought a Mercedes, Any ditherers needed a lot of convincing to change but the new medium sized BMW was the model to make them think again. In fact the E12 5 Series managed to set a quality, sportiness and style for an upmarket middle sized executive car that every other manufacturer has since copied. BMW also proved how far they could develop exciting performance variants, hence the first M series in the shape of the M535i. The E12 is probably BMW's least heralded car, yet it deserves a very special place in their history.

1972 was an important year for Munich and BMW. It was the year that the City got the Olympics. It was also the year that BMW's magnificent four-cylinder building was completed along with the adjacent eggcup shaped museum. 1972 also marked the introduction of the vitally important 5 Series. With it came a new model identification system and a four door 520 saloon to replace the 1800/2000. So 5 identified the body size and the 20 stood for the 2.0 litre engine last seen in the 2000tii but with redesigned trispherical cylinder heads like the sixes. It was available as an 115 bhp twin carb unit, or with mechanical fuel injection, which produced 130 bhp and was badged 520i.

An original 5 Series.

Paul Bracq's lines looked, crisp, fresh and less boxy than the old New Class. Slightly longer by 5 inches yet an inch narrower, the 520 was a heavy car at 2780 pounds and the 520i 2820 lb. That meant it was relatively slow getting to 60 mph, in just over 11 or 12 seconds depending on whether it was a 520 or 520i. Mpg averaged around 22, which was not that impressive. Like the old new class there were MacPherson struts, but now they are angled rearwards by 12 degrees and there was more wheel travel for a better ride.

The 5 Series became a much more serious contender in 1973 with the arrival of the 525. Always destined to accommodate a six-cylinder engine it came from the 2500 and produced 145 bhp. Then in February 1975 the 165 bhp 2.8 was installed. Both models had rear disc brakes, but neither was that economical, hence the arrival of the fuel crisis inspired 518 in 1974. This used the 1766cc engine from the old 1800 and actually returned worse fuel consumption than a 520.

Spot the difference revamp. Well the kidney is a bit more prominent.

For 1977 the 5 Series got a mild makeover as the kidney grille was raised, the bonnet was made more distinctive with a central ridge and there was a tad more chrome around the grille. At the back there were new tail lights, whilst the fuel flap was relocated on the nearside wing. More importantly BMW developed a model with America in mind. In the US market Audi had emerged as serious rivals to the 5 Series and obviously the smaller Mercedes too. The 5000 was a version of the European 100 and sold rather well. It frightened or rather intrigued BMW enough to consider a front wheel drive research programme. So the 2.0 litre M-60 unit was reengineered for transverse operation. They built several prototypes, but did not take the idea any further. It would have been interesting even if the front drive approach would have gone against the company's long held rear wheel drive is good, front wheel drive is less satisfactory, statements in press releases and advertisements. Still the US market did get a different model in the shape of the big engined 530I which was the first BMW created specifically for that market.

Featuring a detuned version of the 2985cc unit it produced 176 bhp, got to 60 mph in just over 10 seconds and returned 19 mpg. It was regarded as something of a class act and a real rival for the equivalent Mercedes W123. However, the 528i that replaced it was much faster, getting to 60 mph in just over 8 seconds and more frugal returning around 22 mpg. Even faster than that though was the M535i.

In the beginning there was the M1. Trouble was you had to be a Formula One driver in the Procar series, very rich or very patient if you wanted to buy one. Read more about BMW's first supercar in the later Wundercar chapter, but essentially it was difficult to pop down to your local showroom and acquire an M car. BMW probably thought that this situation should be rectified. So the series that BMW chose as the M car for the people was the E12.

This decision was not as bizarre at it at first seems. The Motorsport division had used the 5 Series as their basis for customer specials. As an employee at the former BMW concessionaires I can vouch for the appearance of a CSL engined E12 in the underground car park that belonged to the Chairman. Built in 1974 it had uprated suspension with roll bars and specially valved Bilstein shock absorbers. Certainly there are records of official Motorsport makeovers in 1978 for the E12s fitted with 197 bhp 633 CSi engines along with close ratio gearboxes and limited slip differentials.

M535i on the Autobahn.

In 1979 the 100% official M car was an E12 bearing M535i badge work. Interestingly under the bonnet was a version of the M49 engine last seen amidships in the M1 and providing the power for the 635CSi. The state of tune was more responsible, but then the 218 bhp and 224lb-ft of torque produced at 4,000 rpm by the 3.5 litre unit was not to be sniffed at. The close ratio gearbox with a dogleg first was similar to the unit available with the 528i but with a taller final drive. The suspension was standard except for some specially prepared Bilstein dampers. Bringing it all to a halt were ventilated front and solid rear discs plus the four piston calipers. In speed terms you could get to within a whisker of 140 mph and 0–60 mph in a fraction over 7 seconds.

Already quicker than the heavyweight 635i Coupé the most noticeable thing about the M535i was just how unnoticeable it actually was. The understated M class demeanour definitely started here. The wheels were BBS cross spoke alloys and at 6.5" wider than standard. There was an air dam at the front and a black lip on the boot lid, both were deletable when customers ordered their cars, but otherwise there was little to distinguish it from a specced up 528i. If you wanted to draw attention to yourself however, there was always the extrovert option of the red, purple and blue Motorsport stripes. Inside Recaros were standard along with a leather trimmed sports steering wheel that came from the M1 supercar. Not only that, electric windows, central locking, sunroof and electric wing mirrors were all part of the package.

A mere 1410 were made with 450 right hookers landing in the UK before production was discontinued in 1981. The principle had been established and the 5 Series had every right to be branded as a super saloon.

Just as the 5 Series package appealed to the Motorsport division, Alpina also thought that there was plenty of room for improvement and explosive performance, hence their B7 model. Previously offering two packages – the B6, a 200 bhp six-cylinder and the B2, a 230 bhp 3.0 litre – Alpina took the turbo route with the full production B7 in 1978. The 3.0 litre car produced 300 bhp, which translated into a 0–60 time of under six seconds whilst the top speed was 155 mph. If you thought that was impressive Alpina also created a limited edition B7S in 1981 and '82. Sixty of these cars finished in Sapphire Blue with those distinctive Alpina stripes finished in gold had a turbocharged 3.5-litre unit, which produced 330 bhp.

By 1981 the E12 looked tired, but it had done its job of establishing BMW as the maker of sporty and solid executive saloons which is more than could be said about the NSU Ro80. Here was a car that was meant to be the future and it still looked twenty-first century in 1977 when production finished, leaving in its wake lots of smoke, shards of metal and very big repair bills. Here was a very smart car with a very misunderstood engine.

The handsome and clever, but flawed NSU Ro80.

Without doubt, the NSU Ro80 was a technical tour de force when it was launched in 1967 and crowned 'Car of the Year' for 1968. Not only did it have a Rotary engine, it was helped along by a semi-automatic three-speed transmission. Press a button on top of the lever and it changed gears via a vacuum system without the hassle of pressing a clutch. Steering was easy because it was powered by the engine, plus it was pulled along by front wheel drive at a time when this was a rarity on larger cars. The long travel strut suspension meant a very smooth ride and the disc brakes all around kept drivers out of trouble. It really did look like it had been sent from the future but not in a negative Terminator sort of way, until that is buyers started using them. At which point the Ro80 terminated itself rather too easily.

A Rotary engine does need some sort of explanation. First of all you have to visualise the rotor, which is a sort of triangle with slightly bowed sides. This is housed inside an engine, which looks like a great big fat number 8. So each face of the rotor acts as a collector of the fuel/air mixture as it passes by the inlet, which then compresses it and is then driven around by the ignition of the spark plug, which then pushes out the spent gases through the outlet. The Ro80 engine had two rotors and it was the seal between the rotor tips and the housing, which turned out to be the weakest link.

The not so clever and troublesome Rotary engine.

Drivers knew they were in trouble when first the car would seem sluggish, then the fuel consumption would shoot up and there would be rather a lot of smoke. Finally, when the engine became reluctant to start the owner would take it to the garage where the service manager would have to draw a lot of air through his teeth, shake his head and start filling in warranty claim forms. Early cars used carbon seals, which wore out far too quickly, sometimes after just 15,000 miles. NSU then switched to a cast iron based material, which was technically known as IKA in 1969. The trouble was that this new material proved to be too brittle so that the seal edges would chip and break up. Then from 1970 Ferotic, an iron and titanium compound, was used and it was a huge improvement.

Not only did early cars get through a lot of engines, they also consumed a lot of oil. That's because the movement of the throttle triggered a squirt of oil into the carburettor, which in turn lubricated the rotor. That meant a Ro80 consumed a massive pint of oil every 300 miles so effectively it would never need to be changed, even though the constant topping up amounted to the same thing but in a rather more roundabout way.

When it wasn't breaking down the Ro80 was a very safe place to be. Like contemporary Mercedes there were front and rear crumple zones built around a central safety cell. This was combined with very deep sills, which was designed to protect passengers from side impacts. Not only that, there was also a dual-circuit braking system which meant that there was always 70% braking efficiency if the whole system should fail. On top of that, a heated rear screen, fog lights and reclining seats all came as standard.

The styling was pretty much twenty years ahead of itself with a sloping bonnet and a high boot line, which started to find favour in the later 1980s. Also the slim door pillars and large glass area which was trimmed with stainless steel and aluminium was well advanced of the car stylists' game which was moving towards a more brutal right angle architecture in the 1970s. The front wheel drive layout and flat floor meant that there was loads of room up front. Incredibly NSU only built 37,400 examples and around 10% of them came to the UK. NSU had a very generous warranty policy and would replace the engines without too much quibbling and some owners had as many as ten units replaced.

However, the huge cost of keeping buyers happy and supplying replacement engines meant that NSU were in deep financial trouble and looking for someone to help them out. Volkswagen came to the rescue, snuffled out all their models and merged them with Audi. Indeed squint a bit at the later Audi 100 and it is obvious that aerodynamics and styling was carried over from the Ro80, so some of its brilliance did survive for future generations. Sadly the Ro80 was a heroic failure until, that is, some bright spark decided to replace one compact engine with another. Unfortunately it was the V4 unit used to power in the Ford Corsair and Transit van. Not quite the upmarket image or refined performance that drivers of the exclusive NSU had hoped for.

NSU could trace their origins back to 1873, manufacturing knitting machines. Neckarsulmer Strickmaschinenfabrik, to give the company its rather full title, diversified into bicycles in 1886. Motorcycle production commenced at NSU in 1901, and five years later the first motorcar was built there. Car production stopped again in

1929, to allow the company to concentrate on building more profitable two-wheelers, before the war got in the way. It was almost thirty years later, in 1958, that production of cars recommenced in their hometown of Neckarsulm.

Which brings us to Audi, or more precisely Auto Union. A name plate that had not been used since before the war returned in 1957 with the launch of the Auto Union 1000. This was a further development of the F series DKW. Admired at the time for its graceful, curvaceous styling, the Auto Union 1000 also spawned a very attractive coupé, the 1000 SP that looked a bit like a scaled down Ford Thunderbird.

So without getting bogged down in the complex financial dealings that surrounded the company, Daimler-Benz got a controlling interest in 1958. Then a year later the 741cc 3-cylinder DKW Junior was launched, and proved very popular. The Junior's successor, the 1963 F12, had truly up to date styling and front disc brakes (rare on a small car at this time). When the Auto Union 1000's replacement, the all-new DKW F102, also arrived in 1963, the group at last had a range of modern passenger cars, but with crude two-stroke engines (you have to add oil to the petrol and these were effectively noisy, unrefined motorcycle type units). This did not sit comfortably with a company like Daimler-Benz who wanted to concentrate on luxury cars and commercial vehicles. So Auto Union had a for sale sign in the window.

In 1962 Heinrich Nordhoff, chief executive of Volkswagen, agreed to a takeover. The Wolfsburg based company realised that this would give them a much needed increase in production capacity, as well as ownership of one of their more serious competitors. By the end of 1966 Volkswagen had acquired enough shares to make Auto Union a wholly owned VW subsidiary. At least they knew how to sell cars that people actually wanted to buy, even though VW had issues of their own with an ageing product line (the Beetle). So work went ahead on completing the F103 – an existing F102 with a new high-compression four-stroke engine developed during the period of Daimler-Benz control. To help keep the production lines going in the short term however, Volkswagen introduced the 'Beetle' to Ingolstadt, where between 300 and 500 were assembled each day for over four years. It was an effective means of maintaining full employment when the outdated Auto Union models weren't selling.

Audi 72, the model that restarted the company.

In September 1965 the first four-stroke car to emerge from Ingolstadt was ready for public launch. That was celebration enough, but much more significantly it also bore the Audi badge. Audi was back, and the model range developed rapidly, initially based around the original four-stroke car, which became known as the Audi 72 (based on its engine output). Resurrecting the Audi name meant that there was a fresh start and some clear blue water between the smoking DKW two-strokes and the more sophisticated Audis. Later versions of the new range were the 80, Super 90 and 60, and at the end of 1968 the 72 and 80 were replaced by a new Audi 75. Meanwhile after lengthy and sometimes acrimonious discussion, Volkswagen completed the takeover of NSU AG at Neckarsulm, and the establishment of the new company, Audi NSU Auto Union GmbH.

The future was something that Audi could now look forward to. Ludwig Kraus, technical director of Audi, had a clear picture of how he felt the next generation Audi saloon should look. However, new model development was exclusively a matter for VW engineers. Therefore Kraus set about designing the new car in secret. The clay model was 'accidentally' discovered in the styling studio by Board Chairman Rudolf Leiding. No one was sacked because he was so impressed he asked Wolfsburg for special permission to undertake 'body modifications', and then suggested that the VW Group Board of Management might care to come and inspect the result. They approved and the prototype was designated as the Type 104, although it was given the internal model designation C1, which never seemed to have the same raw appeal amongst enthusiasts as BMWs E numbers and Mercedes Ws.

Audi 100. Not a sheep-like choice of executive car at all.

The new Audi 100 was launched in 1968 and the 100 referred to the engine's output and made some sort of sense before the company later on switched over to what were effectively paper sizes, when the 100 would become the A4.

Much of the clean styling could be credited to the influence of Mercedes-Benz when they owned the company. Long term, the objective was to get a slice of the profitable executive and luxury sector of the market. Audi's USP (unique selling proposition) was going to be advanced technology. In January 1971 the first double-page advertisement appeared containing the slogan which has since been so closely associated with the Four Rings: 'Vorsprung durch Technik' which literally means 'The Technological Edge'. In Britain the phrase became memorably associated with holidaying Germans getting to Spain in record time without breaking down and putting their towels on the sun loungers before the Brits could get their Rover SD1s off the cross channel ferry, which is fast fowarding a chapter and two model generations ahead.

In 1968 the 100 was part of Audi's brave new world, even though they shared showroom space with Beetles. Even so Audi were now moving up in the world into the upper midsize class. The engine was 1.8 litre derived from the 90 model and was available in three power outputs of 80, 90 or 100 bhp.

Second generation Audi 100. On the right is the Avant hatchback model.

Here is a car I know intimately. The 100 was the first car I drove and introduced me to the wonderfully well-built world of German cars. Just as British ones were becoming discernibly flaky, with lots of cheap plastic, rattles and doors that clunked rather than thudded, build quality was clearly a priority. The addition of an extremely pretty coupé version only enhanced the 100's reputation as a stylish and very individual way to travel.

By the time that production of the first generation 100 ended in 1976 more than 800,000 had been built, which was far more than Audi had ever predicted. Actually 1976 was a quiet year for Volkswagen and just the one new model was launched, a new 100. A two and four door model with 1.6 and 2.0 litre engines, it looked a lot more stocky than the previous model, otherwise it was more of the sensible same. Also to set it apart was a unique five-cylinder 2.2-litre engine, the first of its kind in the world and obviously it sounded great. The Avant model was not an estate as it later became, but a great big hatchback. Audis were getting serious but they still had some way to go, that is some way to go before they would be taken as seriously as a Mercedes.

Mercedes was in a class of its very own, pun intended. No one did saloons like Mercedes. Like the rest of the car industry they didn't have much in the way of complete factories in 1945. Those that weren't seriously bomb damaged were divided among the Allied Occupational Zones. Considering what tough and uncompromising cars they would go on to build Mercedes started with something simple, a light commercial vehicle. Based on the old 170 model, it was soon joined by similar pre war saloons.

What was remarkable is the speed at which the company re-established production and its sporting pedigree with a prestigious range of products. So as the 170 diesels did the donkeywork as taxis there was time to develop cabriolets and coupés based on the elegant six-cylinder 220 model. They even went big with a 300 limousine and a slightly smaller 200. Meanwhile the company went back into motorsport with the 300.

Mercedes Ponton 180D. Taxi!

As for bread and butter saloons it was the Ponton models from 1953 that paid the wages. It was a silly name, which translated into English as 'Pontoon' which was no less ridiculous, but referred to the way the car was built which is still difficult to understand, but essentially the chassis was incorporated into the bodywork. This was the first modern mass market Mercedes that helped establish not just the company's reputation for excellence in building cars, but was crucial in building a profitable dealer network in America. Although there were convertibles and advanced fuel injection models, what came next defined the marque.

Fintail.

'Fintail' is not a daft as Ponton, because it more accurately describes the clipped rear wings that distinguish it, however Mercedes anoraks may prefer to use the official model designation W111. Here was a whole range of mid sized saloons that arrived in 1959 and lasted for nine years. The design may have looked a bit dated when they were phased out in 1968, it was the fins that had gone the way of the '50s DA (duck's a**e) haircut, but in so many other areas they were incredibly advanced.

Whereas most manufacturers didn't think there was much they could do about accidents and crashes, Mercedes were much more proactive. Back in 1951 they had patented a design for a body structure that consisted of a central rigid passenger cell, sandwiched by front and rear crumple zones, effectively the bonnet and boot. The idea was that the energy of the accident would be absorbed in these areas. That was remarkable enough, but Mercedes when applying these principles to their new Fintails incorporated many other safety features. The door locks were anti-burst items so that they would not fly open in an accident. Inside there was extra padding on pieces of trim that the driver and passengers could come in contact with such as the steering wheel and dashboard. There was some plastic wood on some models, which was of questionable taste if you liked your Jaguars, but as Mercedes pointed out, in an accident it would never splinter. Not only that, trim edges were rounded off and softer material was used for the switches. Even the rear view mirror would break off if there were an impact whilst the large wraparound windscreen would pop out if need be.

Crash test dummies.

As well as the active safety features that no one else had at the time there were the more subtle passive elements that contributed hugely to driver and passenger safety. Before that windscreen had a chance to pop out it offered a wonderfully panoramic view. Even if it got dirty the new design of windscreen wiper technology meant that they overlapped in the middle and swept outwards leaving the forward facing parts of the screen squeaky clean. If for a moment the view out proved less than stimulating Mercedes ensured that the ventilation system was very effective and crucially gave the driver and passenger individual controls. Meanwhile the vertical strip speedometer was either loved or loathed, but it could be argued was another factor in helping the driver to concentrate.

These Fintails were impressive models and were available in a number of specifications, but you really had to know the Mercedes brochures intimately to tell the difference. Essentially the more chrome there was and the bigger the wheel trim, the more likely you were looking at an S or SE rather than a basic model. It is possible to get bogged down in the engine sizes and specs, especially as the range extended at both ends of the price range, so let's try and unravel it all.

At one end of the Fintails was the 190 which arrived in 1961 with four-cylinder petrol and diesel engines. These certainly looked a bit different, as the bumpers were simpler, just a single piece of chrome, and the bonnet was shorter to accommodate a smaller engine. Also, instead of the distinctive rectangular headlamps there were just two slightly apologetic cheap round lamps, perched on top of each wing.

In the middle were the 220s with six-cylinder petrol engines, some with fuel injection. The top of the Fintails was the 300SE. This had an alarming amount of chrome, around the wheel arches, sills, and a strip down each side tailed off with twin shiny exhaust pipes. Technically though there was a lot more to this Fintail than a bit more bling. It was a model apart in its own right and so earned the designation W112. The powerful 3.0 litre fuel injected engine gave almost sports car acceleration and the four-speed automatic gearbox ensured that progress was smooth, which was also helped by the self-levelling air suspension and power steering. Bringing it all to a halt was a set of servo-assisted Dunlop disc brakes operating on all four wheels and with a failsafe dual circuit system.

300SE as a coupé. Gorgeous.

Yes the 300SE was wonderfully impressive and even had some real wood on the dashboard proving that the rich have thicker skins to take any splinters. Oh yes and there was air conditioning as an option, an electric radio aerial and delayed courtesy lights which usefully illuminated the interior for a precious few seconds while you adjusted yourself for the sublime drive in front of you. The 300SE was an awesomely accomplished vehicle and made the contemporary Rolls-Royce and Bentley products look old fashioned and expensive. With this model Mercedes were clearly moving away from the mainstream saloon and growing into another marketplace altogether. The 300SE was stretched and there was also another class leading Class of Mercedes.

If the S-Class was going to be the First Class saloons then there was room for a Business Class model too. In 1968 the world got to see the W115 four-cylinder and W114 six-cylinder models. All the good things about the old Fintails were there, such as safety and the engines, but not the fintails. Indeed these saloons were more compact in every dimension, yet inside were just as roomy. The styling was decidedly square thanks to Paul Bracq, being free of any fussiness with a single side-rubbing strip as the sum of all the embellishment. It could be viewed either as bland, or superbly confident and restrained. This was something car buyers would have to get used to, as it would set the design trend for decades to come.

New Generation saloon, no fins and beloved by taxi drivers the world over.

Mechanically there was a major overhaul with revised suspension, gearboxes and engines. The interior was a lot more up to date with a proper round speedometer, loads of padding and switches grouped in the centre console to keep them out of harm's way. Mercedes called it the 'New Generation', which of course of it was. There were lots of models to choose from and some subtle trim differences that only salesmen and particularly enthusiastic customers would ever know. This wasn't the sort of car that would warrant a poster on a small boy's bedroom wall, unless that is they had advanced plans to become an accountant. So you could have a 200, 200D, 220, 220D, six-cylinder 230 and 250. Obviously it would never stop there as high spec 250S model and emissions requirements in the USA over the next few years meant all sorts of alternative engine sizes and outputs doubling the number of New Generations. It was nomenclature hell, as the combination of numbers and letters multiplied though always with a purpose in mind.

One very interesting avenue that Mercedes explored though was coupé variants of the saloons. Something that BMW never did with their mid-sized 5 Series although Audi did have the beautiful 100 Coupé. Mercedes being Mercedes they offered a swathe of models with bigger doors, which did without a door frame and had a lower roofline. Effectively the W114 was a budget version of the more expensive W111. Mass produced and just as elegant it was designed at a time when it seemed the American market was officially falling out of love with the convertible. Because when they weren't strangling engine outputs, the regulators, especially in California, were keen to protect the perfectly preserved heads of their citizens from any further damage, other than that inflicted by plastic surgery.

The New Generation got a facelift in 1974 when bonnets became flatter, grilles a bit shorter and fatter and guttering more extensive to keep the windows, side windows and rear screen clearer when it was raining. Yes it was the little details that would surprise and delight buyers such as the rear light clusters which, interestingly, were ribbed. Yes it really is fascinating as Mercedes engineers had discovered that this design made it harder for muck to cover the light. Clever. Also very clever was the realisation that diesel had a big future and not just for those who had beaded seat covers and lots of things dangling from their rear view mirror.

Yes taxi and diesel habitually went together on account of the increased mpg figures achieved by the compression engine, even if it rattled like a locomotive and belched smoke like one too. However, as the 1973 oil crisis took a grip on the world, running a diesel suddenly seemed like the sensible thing to do. Especially if it was going to be a class act like a Mercedes who had high ambitions for what many regarded as just a humble 'oil burner', a dismissive way of referring to a diesel engine. So Mercedes set about reinventing it with a radical five-cylinder design. Well, they did not actually invent the concept, because the British engine builder Gardner had developed one that was often used to power buses. The Mercedes 240D, 300D for the American market, was nothing like an old charabanc. Indeed, it could be ordered with an automatic gearbox, air conditioning, power steering and all the other luxury car fittings that would be taken for granted in 30 years time. Right there though Mercedes had invented the modern executive express. The thing is though, they were about to reinvent it all over again in 1975.

The W114/115 had been an astounding success in Europe and most importantly in America. Mercedes had managed to keep up with the safety and emissions legislation in the most demanding and profitable market in the world. More than 1.8 million had been made and the two most popular models had been diesels. Selling these models had never been a problem and often there was a waiting list. In fact, production of the old car kept running well into 1976 and they were still commercially available in 1977. At least Mercedes were not complacent and came up with the W123, arguably the ultimate easy to live with Mercedes.

We know this because it was constructed in a different way. Instead of the body being lowered onto the engine, it was actually dropped in from above. A special catch allowed the bonnet to open extra wide to swallow it up. This meant practically everything was accessible, so looking after a W123 was going to be easier and cheaper, whether you looked after it yourself or got a local garage to do it. Not only that, your W123 was also going to take a lot longer to crumble to dust as there was a five-stage process that started with a zinc phosphate coating and finishing with a petroleum based preservative sprayed onto the completely assembled underside of the Mercedes. Also, body panels were now designed to be easily accessible for simple replacement if they were damaged.

For these reasons alone, in any post apocalyptic world which seemed a real possibility in the cold war '80s, it would not be a Beetle, or a Toyota Corolla, that would keep on running through the rubble, more than likely it would be a W123, possibly in Taxi spec.

In the metal it looked like a shrunken S-Class, which was no bad thing, hardly radical and supremely practical. Here was a shape designed to last a decade, maybe several decades with the little touches that few other manufacturers even considered. Never mind the ribbed light clusters, which were resistant to muck, the doors overlapped the sills, which meant that your 1975 flares or maxi dress would remain pristine.

Quality was paramount and an increasingly mechanised production process was going to help that and of course there would be more safety features. So the body shell became even more rigid for improved roll over protection plus with better side impact protection and extra reinforcement to the bulkheads. This not only kept everyone in a much safer place, but also if it could be repaired afterwards then it was easier and cheaper to do.

Mercedes W123, another firm favourite with the world's taxi drivers.

Mercedes had realised early on that a straight head on crash was a rarity. Mostly drivers would take some sort of evasive action, which meant that the damage would be offset on the wing. Consequently the steering column would deflect sideways away from the driver whilst the parking brake linkage was not a straight, spear like rod, but a chain that would crumple. Not only that, the seat belt latches were attached to the seat so that they maintained a constant and the safest possible position. Everything else inside the cabin was well padded and these features combined with a trickle down in advanced suspension and steering technology from the S-Class and all round disc brakes.

The engines were a carry over from the W115s as four- and six-cylinder petrol and diesel with small changes to improve efficiency. The biggest changes came in 1979 when new lighter engine units were introduced along with redesigned gearboxes. With longevity and cost effectiveness in mind the servicing schedules were extended from 6,000 to 12,000 miles. Many of the modifications to the four-cylinder engines (200, 230 and 230E) involved making them more refined and quieter for improved driver and passenger comfort.

Mercedes had plenty of six-cylinder models of their own badged as 250, 280 and the fuel-injected 280E, which were adapted and modified for various markets. Even more impressive was their fully developed range of diesel engines – the 200D, 220D, 240D and 300D. Mercedes addressed the lack of performance of diesels, which hindered sales in North America, so set about installing a turbocharged 300D unit, which had been developed for the S-Class. The engine was fitted to the estate version, the Touristik, in 1983 and it quickly became a best seller. Europe never got the 300TD but it certainly got the estate.

Estate cars had once upon a time been quite posh, coach built specialist vehicles originally called shooting brakes, quite often half timbered in a mock Tudor way and designed specifically for the landed gentry to go into the country and shoot things. Later on they became all metal and commercial travellers found them easier to get all their samples in the back. The middle classes latched onto the Volvo estate as a safe, practical and upmarket way of having a much larger boot. Certainly for antique dealers it was better than being seen in a van. Now with the Mercedes estate a whole slew of society had another purchasing option.

Although it would seem to be the logical thing for manufacturers to do, adding an estate version to the line up was never a certainty. Often the results were not that pretty or practical. BMW certainly took their time waiting until the late '80s, but Mercedes were never frightened of appealing to another profitable niche market. The Touristik was shortened to T and was the company's first official estate car, although many coachbuilders had produced relatively expensive five doors.

W123T, *the* upmarket estate car.

Mercedes took the standard W123 saloon floorpan and then reinforced it at the rear so that it could take the tailgate door. It was good looking coherent design in contrast to some estates that looked like an extension added by dodgy builders. It was topped off with distinctive chrome roof runners that allowed the area to be converted into a rack for anything that would not fit inside. Not that the interior was that huge, especially compared to a Volvo. At least the rear seat could not only fold, but split too. Even more cleverly it could become a people carrier if the customer specified a rear facing bench seat that folded into the floor and was comfy enough for a couple of kids. It was certainly possible to load up the boot safely as there was a hydropneumatic self-levelling rear suspension system.

As well as the estate, Mercedes continued to offer variations on the W123 theme with fewer doors. The coupés arrived in 1977 and like before the doors were pillarless with a lower roofline and a shorter wheelbase so obviously it was less practical. But hey, that is the price you pay for a good looking if slightly staid coupé. These were coupés that accountants would approve of, especially the America only Turbodiesels. A broad range of engines and models 230 and 280 in C and CE specification, plus a top of the range 300CD completed the line up.

W123 Coupé, obviously.

Here was another glimpse into the future when there would be a massive demand not just for diesels, but also distinctive high quality cars, which didn't need to be very sporty at all. The W123 was the most remarkable and most complete range of cars in the '70s and '80s and undoubtedly inspired BMW to broaden the 3 series massively and the 5 Series just slightly.

Sorry if that history of the W123 came across as mostly a specification roll call, but honest, all the really boring bits were taken out. Unfortunately, I never found it a particularly inspiring car, just a reliable and efficient one. I never came across many W123s as part exchanges. It was as if the owners wanted to keep hold of them and you really couldn't blame them. These were not cars that set the pulse racing in any way, in fact they would be a great cure for insomnia, simply count the number in the queue at an imaginary infinite taxi rank. Much more effective than sheep. Even so, M535i apart, the 5 Series wasn't much more interesting. BMW had to bring that model into the '80s. So how did they do it?

BMW E12 5 Series & Mercedes W123 & Audi 100 vs The Rest

Austin Princess – Originally badged as the 18-22 Series, also there were Morris versions and an upmarket Wolseley. Hydragas suspension and wedge styling with a roomy interior, it should have been an upmarket Cortina alternative. Although comfy and practical, BL build quality and a confused image let it down.

Citroen CX – Proper mad Citroen, many say the very last one. All the usual tubes and valves and fluids that go into the unique hydraulic system, which means a sublime, floaty big car experience. Massive estate version. For the true individual who didn't mind the odd breakdown.

Ford Granada – From 1977 fashionably sharp styling and it came with German build quality as standard, because it was made in Germany. Great V6 engines and a ton of kit fitted to the Ghia.

Lancia Gamma – Huge saloon, which like the Austin Princess had hatchback styling. Front-wheel drive too and characterful flat engine. Killed by Lancia's reputation for rotting on the spot so stood no chance really.

Lancia Beta – Oh yes there was another Lancia too and this was closely related to Fiats. Quite smart, nice to drive and also quite rusty.

Opel Rekord/Vauxhall Carlton – Granada alternative, but not as stylish. Yes it was boring.

Rover 3500 SD1 – In theory it should have wiped the floor with the staid 5 and W123s. Ferrari styled front end, practical hatchback package and that lovely V8. Unfortunately it was underdeveloped and almost chucked together. Lots of executives stranded on the side of the M1 did not help matters.

Renault 30 – Gallic attempt to capture the executive high ground with this giant hatchback. Soft suspension and seating not to everyone's taste and the charisma free badging impressed no one except French VIPs. Better than contemporary Peugeots, Volvos and anything big and Italian but not in the same league as any BMW.

Saab 900 – Rock solid saloons and hatchbacks. Masses of room and reputation for toughness, however styling a bit too 'out-there' compared to a staid and sensible Mercedes. So bought by unconventional, well off middle classes.

Triumph 2000 – The Michelotti connection (designer for **BMW** too) makes this the Brit 5 Series in style and intent. Nearing the end of its life and would be replaced by the rubbish small-engined Rover SD1s. An opportunity squandered.

Volvo 240 – Tank styling and demeanour. Better to look at and more justifiable to own as the estate car. A big hit for the Swedes as so many wanted an uncomplicated big brute of a car and could not afford a Mercedes. VW diesels were under the bonnet you know.

In the Cassette Deck ...

 **Heaven 17 – Penthouse and Pavement** Most of us got the irony, but still liked wearing the double breasted suits anyway, although most drew the line at a pony tail (please see the cover). Lots of fairly heavy industrial funk offset with dour Yorkshire vocals. We didn't need that 'Fascist Groove Thing' of course. It was possible to confuse a student, or TUC member, by playing this at full volume in an S-Class.

7 Doors go 'chonk', Cd's drop and they even smell quick

German saloons come of age and go like stink. BMW E28, E34, Mercedes W124 and Audi 100.

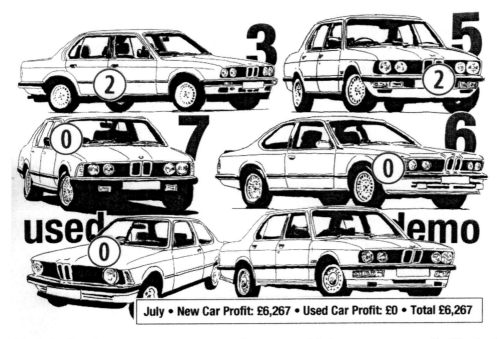

July • New Car Profit: £6,267 • Used Car Profit: £0 • Total £6,267

My 3 Series demonstrator was a popular car and it is was easy to sell. The lucky customer though had to wait for our time together to come to an end and that would mean four months before he got his hands on it. So what would I get next? Well obviously it wasn't up to me, however I would have a say if I was doing really well.

A demonstrator and its specification sheet was an excellent way of motivating, punishing and generally keeping sales staff on their toes. Get into management or be consistently number one and you could start playing around with the specification lists and colour charts to order your demo (within reason) on a factory build sheet.

The 'hierarchy of the demo' was quickly apparent. From what I could see the Managing Director had a 735iASE, plus a highly specced 323iASE for Mrs Managing Director at home. Then the Sales Manager had a 635iASE followed by the two assistant Sales Managers with lesser Sevens, 728i or 732i. The finance and insurance bloke had a lower 7, leaving the salesmen with the worst selling model in the entire range, and that would be the 5 Series.

Although there was the odd 3 Series floating around, like my 316i, mostly it was 520i, unless you had done something really wrong then it was the original uninjected 518. The 520i were ordered with a couple of extras, central locking and a manual sunroof as the bare minimum to make them saleable when the demo period was up. Obviously the 5 would have something more than basic radio preparation unless you had been especially naughty. There was sometimes a teeny bit of negotiation around just what sound system you might have. I do remember a salesman begging for something more than a bog standard radio on account of having a longer than average journey into the West End. He really, really wanted a hole in which to post his cassettes. He was made to really squirm.

Imagine my surprise then when I was handed the keys to my new demo. Obviously it was a 5 Series, but it was also a 525i automatic with all round electric windows, electric sunroof, a really decent in car entertainment system which was wasn't a Blaupunkt for once, but a bright silver Alpine which was very unusual. It was just waiting for me to post some of my cassettes inside it and start rocking. Or in the case of Sade, pseudo Jazzing.

I could spot it easily in the underground car park among the other 5s for a number of reasons. Firstly it was the only one with a spoiler, a big black wodge of rubber glued to the top of the boot lid. On a 5 that was a bit like your dad wearing a trendy hat. Then there was a number plate which was devilishly distinctive, more on that later. This fairly exuberant 5 was all topped off with a double side stripe along the flanks in black against the Sapphire Blue bodywork. We charged £50 for that and the bloke who did it for us in the underground car park only invoiced us a tenner, so we were always well up on the deal. You would not believe how many customers went for all manner of fifty quid side stripes and there were many other designs that I have deliberately obliterated from my memory. Although the stripery was questionable, the only truly naff bit of the 525i originated in the factory, and that was the wheel trims. Effectively they were pizza plates and described as much by everyone simply because they were flat, silver, quite boring and only truly useful as a base for eating a thin crust. Its plainness was justified on the grounds that it was more aerodynamically efficient, but they probably boosted the mpg figure by .00001. A set of alloys would have been perfect, but hey, I could hardly complain and only speculate on just what I had done to deserve it.

Well, nothing really. Presumably I was being incentivised and you know what, it worked. In the fourth month of the New Year I was finishing in the top three and my sales manager, assistant sales manger and the general sales manager seemed rather pleased. I really didn't think that I had been doing anything that special. Just getting on with the business of selling cars which was a lot more fun than trying to shift photocopiers and of course selling BMWs was far less stressful than trying to flog Austin Rovers. So I knew I had the best job in the world.

One day as I pulled up outside the underground car park and waited for the barrier to lift, the general sales manager who would boot me out with some relish a year later, made a comment on my extreme good fortune when it came to demonstrators. "You've done very well haven't you?" he said only slightly menacingly. Well it cost a bit more in petrol than a 520i but I really didn't care too much about that. It really was the sexiest car I'd owned and I can't begin to tell you the shenanigans I got up to in that vehicle. A666 UHX where are you now?

For me the 5 was a great car, even though it was a bit on the large and, it has to be said, staid side for a bloke in his early twenties. For the executive with a family it was perfect. So why on earth were they proving so difficult to sell?

Well it's hip to be square. Huey Lewis ('70s/'80s American pop rocker who looked like your dad) said that, so it must be true. And you won't see more right angles than on the second generation 5 Series, which had the internal model number, E28. It might have looked square, but the 518 apart, the model line-up could not have been more eclectic or exciting. Six smooth cylinders defined the range of course, but there was also the ultra economical 5, the 5 that was essentially a supercar and the 5 with the factory body kit. No one else had a line-up that included the 525e, M5 and M535, not to mention the middle order 520i, 525i and 528i.

The original 5 Series that first broke cover in 1972 had instantly repositioned BMW as purveyors of quality medium sized saloons. Like the New Class before it, the E12 broke some moulds, raised expectations and set some standards of its own. BMW were now building a real alternative to the W114 series Mercedes. BMW took their time and only began work on a replacement for the E12 in 1975. Eventually unveiled in 1981 the new middle-sized BMW saloon was underwhelming. It looked as though the design department had decided that they would only use rules and set squares for an entire decade as a bet. So the E28 resembled a mid life makeover rather than an all-new car, in contrast to Audi's groundbreaking 100.

It could have been so different, indeed the E28 could have been front wheel driven. BMW had been surprised at the success of the new Audi 100, which debuted in 1975 and unlike the Mercedes and BMW the driven wheels were at the front. The engineers even went as far as taking the 2.0 litre M60 engine and re-engineering it for transverse installation and operation. Indeed, several prototypes were made. BMW could not have been impressed, so stuck with the tried and tested rear wheel drive format, pretty much like the design of the bodywork then.

Building an E28 really, really carefully.

Conservatism. That's the main reason why the E28s struggled for attention, blink and you missed the difference between the old and new 5 Series. Whereas Mercedes were expected to deliver more of the same, buyers wanted something different from BMW. Also the closest competition for the 5 Series wasn't even Mercedes or Audi, it actually came from other BMWs. Customers could choose a cutting edge, handy sized 3 series with 4-cylinder engines that could easily cope with prevailing traffic conditions. Alternatively they could go for the bigger sixes that behaved really sportily and all for less money. Plus there was a similar amount of room inside. Why buy a big dull saloon when there was something sexier on offer in the same showroom? That meant the 5 Series was pretty much the only model we were allowed to discount. The 518 appealed to no one, few were sold or even tolerated as demo cars. The 520i shifted in reasonable numbers as an alternative Granada Ghia, for those who wanted the badge and not the toys that a GLX or Ghia enjoyed. The 525i in particular and the 528i really struggled at the upper end and that's when we saw buyers walk away and buy a 280E Mercedes. It was hard to disagree as they could get an established model with a good reputation that would not depreciate nearly as quickly as the 5. As for the 525e, or eh? No customers could ever grasp the concept and would simply shrug their shoulders and grunt "Eh?" when we espoused the finer points of the economical 5. Overall though customers struggled to find anything really new about the fairly old looking 5.

The E28 had similar dimensions to the old E12 although it was half an inch shorter and the same measurement wider. It had also lost some weight, at around 200 pounds (90.7 kilos). Weight savings were made everywhere from the interior to the drive train, in the engine bay and even by the use of lighter panels. That smoother body was also more aerodynamic than before as the drag coefficient dropped from 0.445 to 0.382. An engine undertray, standard spoiler, higher bootline and other styling tricks made the new 5 a much more fuel-efficient package and BMW took this concept to its logical conclusion with what was officially described as the 525eta.

BMW paid more attention than most manufacturers to the 1973–74 energy crisis. The vital US marketplace introduced the Energy Conservation Act in 1978 that insisted on average fuel consumption targets or manufacturers would be liable for penalties. The 525e or eta, (badged as a 528e in just about every other market outside the UK) that's the Greek letter which is the mathematical symbol engineers use to denote efficiency, was the response and it arrived on the European market in 1983.

Using the big block M60 6-cylinder engine which was radically reworked with just four main bearings rather than seven, bored and stroked so that it displaced 2693cc, the maximum output was just 125 bhp. However, peak torque of 177lbs/ft was delivered at 3250 rpm and this model was the first to get a new 4-speed automatic gearbox (with lockup torque converter) as standard. This was low rev, high efficiency unit that was almost ticking over at motorway speeds at just over 2000 rpm. It returned 40 mpg at 56 mph and over 20 mpg on the urban cycle and 35mpg overall, yet the acceleration was brisk enough, with 0–60 mph arriving in under 10 seconds, whilst mid range grunt would see it out drag a 635, well for a while anyway. It ran on skinny 175HR/14 tyres too. Despite BMW head office led indoctrination and reminders to us salesmen that away from the lights it was quicker than many sports cars, those who could afford a 5 were not obsessed by economy. Twenty years later they would of course buy a diesel without a second thought. At that time diesels were taxis and certainly not executive cars. The 525eh? was clearly the right car at the wrong time and completely misunderstood.

5 Series sideways on. Smart but not very exciting.

Compared to the 525e rather more buyers wanted the 518, not because it was so wonderful, or that it did almost 30mpg, but mostly so they could get a large four door BMW for £9435. The four-cylinder 105 bhp was slow, struggling to 60 mph in over 12 seconds and even the later installation of fuel injection didn't help much.

In September 1984 the entire sales force for the UK were told to show up at the National Exhibition Centre (NEC) in Birmingham on a Sunday. That was our day of rest, but we did as we were told especially as hotel accommodation was thrown in. Then in the NEC car park we all pointed and cheered when we saw the legendary James Burke taking a suitcase out of a 6 series.

A lead presenter of the BBC's science programme Tomorrow's World *and also the unofficial explainer of scientific matters to the people, Burke was a clever dick but a wonderfully passionate one. I loved his TV shows and particularly remember the 'Connections' one where he seemed to connect Stone Age man to Concorde in half a dozen easy stages.*

Anyway, a few hours later there was James Burke on stage at a packed NEC presenting the 518i to us. It wasn't a vehicle that seemed to warrant this much fuss, because they certainly never gave this much exposure to the M5, or M635. The thing is for BMW, the 518i looked like a ground floor entry into the fleet market. So instead of a Sierra Ghia, why not get a BMW? That was the reasoning anyway and BMW expected us to break into this lucrative market. The thing is though company car buyers would much prefer a basic specification 316i. Also if anyone was going to buy a basic medium sized saloon with a prestige badge then that automatically meant Mercedes. So we were on a hiding to nothing even though there was the MD of BMW UK telling dealers that some of them had to "shape up, or ship out". Not that it was going to affect us.

We were attending mob handed and it was brought home to me just how small some dealers were by comparison to Park Lane. Some had never seen, let alone sold, a 6 Series and just occasionally they might sell a manual 7 Series to a farmer. As we stayed in the bar until the early hours ordering Champagne, the last person to leave who didn't work in our showroom, said, "You win". Everybody hated us and I didn't blame them one bit.

The next morning we were all supposed to team up and drive the cars. Four of us climbed aboard a red 518i, but we were then joined at the last minute by a salesman from another dealership who rapidly regretted his decision. Our driver was handy to say the least. Every corner involved getting alarmingly sideways. Every gear was tested to the limits of, well, the rev limiter. It was a tyre screeching hooligan half hour at which point the bloke from the unknown dealership asked us to stop. By this time he was very green and when he got out was immediately unwell, poor chap. It was down to the newest salesman at Park Lane to drive the car back down the M1, as he was the lucky new owner.

518i sales limped along, but it was never a best seller for us. The true entry level was the 520i, which at least had six cylinders, although the standard specification didn't pick up until the arrival of the Lux pack models in the later '80s. Of course the 525i was a mid-market compromise of smoothness and a reasonable turn of speed, rich people who wanted to stay subtle would go for the 184 bhp 528i.

Indeed, I briefly borrowed a part exchanged 528iSE which had belonged to a High Court judge and nestling in the divide between the front seats where a cassette dispenser could optionally be fitted, was the first 'in car' mobile phone I'd ever seen. So I made a point of borrowing the 528iSE for the weekend and although the judge had wisely had what was then called a radiophone, disconnected, it still looked cool. At the traffic lights putting the receiver to your ear was not then illegal and guaranteed to get a reaction from those around you. Other drivers and pedestrians never thought you were a prat, as they would within a decade, many either admired the fact you had several thousand quid to splash out on a phone, or thought you were a real life member of C15, as depicted in the all action TV show The Professionals. *I pretended I was Bodie. That was a very good weekend.*

And a quick point about mobile phones, the only ones in the first half of the '80s, or even in the '60s and '70s were the radiophones, that required you to say "over" and press a button as if you were in a Lancaster bomber, or on a trawler. They cost a fortune and even the super rich car traders didn't bother because they never owned cars, just bought and sold them. What they did have though were pagers. These seemed impossibly high tech gadgets that clipped onto the belts of the jeans or corduroys, depending on how posh they were, and beeped. All it meant was "phone the Mrs back in the office".

The only interesting bits of an M535, even though the engine is standard.

Clearly what buyers really wanted were 5s that stirred the soul and the first truly thrilling model did not arrive until 1984 when **BMW** unveiled the M535. This was a straightforward engine transplant from the 635 coupé, combined with the 528i's gearbox and running gear with some uprated suspension springs and dampers. Not really very 'M' for Motorsport as critics pointed out at the time but the subtle positioning of the M at the front of the full nomenclature was supposed to be the clue that this was not the ultimate 5. They did throw the M-Technic catalogue of dressing up bits and pieces at it with fairly patchy results. Most would regard it as overstated and unsubtle, two things that **BMW** didn't usually do. The wider wheels were almost the alloy equivalent of the 525i pizza plates and were featureless and just odd. The bodykit was far from being a good idea and just added to the impression that someone's teenage son in the Motorsport department had been asked to sex up a 5 Series. Consequently the bodykit didn't look like a carefully designed piece of automotive sculpture that integrated with the design of the car. No, the slab sided design of the E28 did not help matters and the M535 simply had what looked like big old lumps of plastic glued to the lower third of the car.

Inside there were sports seats and a slightly funky leathery steering wheel with the M Sport stripes. At least it would do over 140 mph and get to 60 mph in less than 8 seconds and keep up with all those naughty little hot hatches that were breaking out all over the 1980s. However, for those who were offended by the sight of a **BMW** breaking out in a rash of bad taste there was another option. All they had to do was buy a standard issue 535i. Here was an M535i, but without the M fripperies which cost £800 less and came with the much better looking standard alloys. Then again, they could have wished upon a star that **BMW** would take the brand new, proper Motorsport tuned 3.5 litre engine and stick that in a 5 Series. Well, prayers were answered and **BMW** did just that in 1985.

BMW M5. Subtle, but deadly.

The M5 was no cosmetic outing; Motorsport dropped in the full house 286 bhp engine first seen in the M1. To help the E28 chassis cope it also gained the M535's mods with uprated springs and Bilstein gas dampers, plus a Track-link rear suspension set up. There was high speed steering, a reinforced Getrag 5 speed gearbox and the heavy-duty 90-amp battery, which was repositioned in the boot for weight distribution purposes. Helping it to stop were reinforced discs, larger calipers and a revamped ABS system. The M5 ran on BBS cross spoke alloys and the lack of body kit, just a deeper front spoiler, meant that the shed like aerodynamic Cd figure was a considerable 0.38. Luckily that didn't slow it down very much.

Inside, there was some quality velour, M5 kick plates, M-Technic steering wheel and on the majority of the 177 UK spec right-hand drive cars, leather and air conditioning. Never mind the spec, it was the speed that really astounded. 150 mph plus, 0–60 mph in a fraction over 6 seconds, clearly the M5 never hung about. In super saloon terms only the Cosworth tuned Mercedes 190 and the fine value Sierra Sapphire came close. Trouble was you could see their body kits coming and that was the great thing about the M5, it looked so ordinary, yet it was so extraordinary.

My involvement with E28s continued throughout my short selling career. After the 525i I was downgraded to a manual 520i with a radio, electric windows and manual sunroof, so I was really slumming it. For me the worst thing about it was the white colour scheme. Apart from socks and T-Shirts with Wham or Frankie Says! on them, white was starting to fall out of favour as a vehicle colour. At least the 520i had those funky fifty quid black stripes, plus right at the back balanced on the boot lid was another rubber spoiler. After the white one came the blue one. Arctic Blue was a lovely deep metallic colour and by this time I was beginning to get a slight amount of say about what I got. Invited inside the sales manager's office I was asked if I wanted manual or automatic? I was slightly overwhelmed and obviously being a young man it had to be manual. However, I had a slog in from East London and getting over the Bow flyover before 7am was a priority. But the traffic was always rubbish, so I said no, make mine an auto. If I wanted a manual I could always borrow one. So far so good, except for the bodywork.

As I was the youngest salesman I think he thought he was doing me a favour by fitting side skirts, a colour keyed rear spoiler and a fairly deep front one. There was method in this madness of course because we sold accessories and being able to point to the products was important. Actually I wouldn't have minded all the body kittery as it would have looked a bit like an M535i, except that it had a set of wheels even worse than the alloys which were fitted to the real M535i, this one sat on steel wheels. It was truly awful. Silver steel wheels with a chrome hubcap in the middle. To call the 520i under wheeled was an understatement. It looked like I had parked on the wrong side of town without locking wheel nuts and then come back to find that my Bimmer was on bricks. So to save time, I'd bought a set of ordinary profile tyres and steel wheels to get me home, but then forgotten to take them off. With the hubcaps missing it might have looked slightly cool, but I wasn't allowed to do that. Frankly it was embarrassing.

The right E28 was always a very good car indeed and for many the original M5 is the very best of that breed whilst the 518 was no more than a Munich quality control blip. For many the 525e was a technical dead end, though very good to drive. The old 'square-rigger' E28 as some people called it was fun for a lot of people like me who regularly set sail in her. The thing is though the very best 5 Series was yet to come and sadly I wasn't around to sell them.

However, before we get on to the E34, it is worth taking the time to look at BMW's brand new executive car rivals. Because if the old 5 was one of the squarest saloons to come out of the '80s then the Audi 100 (or C3 as absolutely no one has ever called it) was definitely the slipperiest.

The 100 doing its slippery stuff.

There was an easy explanation for that slipperiness which was the many hours that Audi engineers had spent in the wind tunnel, or rather wind tunnels. With an obsessive devotion to secrecy and detail, there were engineering teams scattered around Europe operating in five tunnels, neither of which knew what the other was doing. That seemed pretty strange, but the intention was to keep the whole slipperiness thing secret from rival manufacturers.

What they came up with certainly bore more than a passing resemblance to the NSU Ro80, but was even less of a drag. That's because it was long, wide and with sides that bowed slightly like a barrel. The airflow was designed to move efficiently around the engine bay and also underneath the car. It also helped that the windows were flush fitting which was a world first. This was achieved by turning the channels that held the glass by 90 degrees to face outwards which were then held in place by lugs in the corners of each window. Actually the flush fitting windows did not make a huge amount of difference to the airflow, it was just Audi's clever way of showing potential customers that it was serious about aerodynamics. Interestingly, Audi had paid a lot of attention to the oil crisis and felt the direct effects when Ro80 sales fell through the floor and ended up with a car that looked remarkably like it, but with flush windows and an engine that actually worked.

Classic '80s cheesy press picture to prove that the 100 was a lightweight. However, some of those German birds had biceps as big as their hair. Well done, from left to right, Helga and Heidi.

The 100 was designed to be lightweight as well, which also made it more fuel-efficient. Audi went even further and made the jack, for changing the wheel, from aluminium rather than steel just to save weight. Yes this was the car that explained the whole concept of Cd (drag coefficient) to the world. As I think I may have already explained this is the measurement of how aerodynamic a car is. The most efficient and narrow tyred 100 scored an impressive 0.30 and Audi was so proud of that fact there was even a little sticker on the rear quarter window, which said 0.30. As result it was very fuel efficient for such a large car. Hartmutt Warkuss got the credit for the air cheating design although plenty of appreciation should also go to teams working in the five wind tunnels and Ferdinand Piech. Piech was Audi's chief engineer and a member of the family that owned Porsche, who believed that high technology was essential for the manufacturer to get noticed. Indeed, the 100 caught the attention of all the right people which resulted in the 1983 Car of the Year title, just sneaking ahead of the equally slippery looking Ford Sierra. However, whilst one looked like a great big stupid jelly mould, the other was sophisticated, sexy and most likely to get you to the beach before the Germans.

Although Vorsprung durch Technic as a catchphrase had been around for some time it finally came into its own in the early '80s when the wonderfully lugubrious Geoffrey Palmer provided the voiceover. Suddenly the Audi was being taken seriously and became an alternative to a 5 or Mercedes. It was the estate Avant which made the biggest impact in the UK. Despite the sloping rear window, which looked good, but robbed it of some practicality, the Avant still had a pretty huge load bay. It was also far less boring, conventional and predictable than the 'Gerry and Margot, Good Life' (middle class next door neighbours in the BBC TV sitcom) Volvo 245 estate. Golden Labradors had never been transported in such smart surroundings. Then again, some very lucky hounds may well have been tethered in the back of a W124T.

Always first to the sun lounger, apparently.

Ah yes, the W124 from 1985 which raised the executive car stakes to a height that would inspire BMW to respond in the only way they knew possible, by designing an E34.

Incredibly the W124 had a lot in common with the W201, which is probably far better known as the 190. So the new mid sized Mercedes had the same suspension set up front and rear, although it was obviously modified to cope with the extra weight, girth and gravitas of the new car. Even so, it was fairly light-weight for a car of that size, again because it was so closely related to the smaller car. Indeed, without going all smoothie to become an Audi 100 clone, Mercedes managed to get the drag co-efficient right down to 0.29 and 0.30 Cd depending on the model. So without feeling any need to put a little sticker on the rear quarter window it became the slipperiest car in the world. There were though a lot of clever innovations such as a plastic tray underneath the engine, which smoothed the airflow around the vehicle.

As well as sharing the engines, the W124 looked like the 190's older brother, with a more laid back grille whilst at the back the boot opening had a more pronounced vee shape along with restyled tail lamps. Inside, Mercedes were finally waking up to the fact that customers wanted a bit of pampering and a less austere environment. So seats were reshaped, there were bits of wood scattered around the cabin and the fascia was based on the S-Class. Technically the W124 became the most advanced Mercedes as it benefited from a whole raft of meaningful acronyms (ASD, ASR, 4-Matic), designed to stop it falling off the road.

So just in case you wondered what they all meant, ASD (Anti Slip Differential) improved handling when moving off on a road surface, which is slippery on one side. What happens is that the locking differential is immediately disengaged when the brakes are applied, so that the ABS braking function is unaffected. Oh yes while we are here, let's demystify ABS, which actually stands for the Anti-Blockier System, in German. This stopped the wheels from locking under braking and allows the driver to maintain control. Then there was ASR (Acceleration Skid Control), which helps the wheel to regain sufficient traction. It does this using the same sensor signals as ABS, but to detect wheel spin rather than wheel lock. It actually brakes the spinning wheel and reduces engine speed to stabilize the vehicle. Finally 4-Matic, is quite simply Mercedes' own version of four-wheel drive.

The new W124. A collective sigh of relief from the world's taxi drivers.

As these systems were introduced to the W124 it was also a glimpse into the future when one day all cars would be a blizzard of acronyms with black boxes controlling virtually every area of the car's operation. Some may see this as a slippery slope towards complication and built in obsolescence. They may well be right, but whatever they built the black boxes out of back then, or ECUs (Electronic Control Units) to throw another acronym at you, they seemed to be a lot tougher. Yes Mercedes broke down a lot less back then simply because they were better built.

The four-cylinder engines (200, 230E) were familiar enough, but there were some new six-cylinder ones (260E, 300E) and Mercedes switched from aluminium to cast iron block construction. This seemed like a backward step, but actually it meant far more robust engines and also quieter ones too, as they did not generate so much noise. Also the latest computer aided design techniques meant that these engines could also be smaller and lighter. Engineers could also appreciate that a single overhead camshaft saved weight and that four bearings reduced friction, but did not compromise on the refinement that customers expected from a six-cylinder engine.

As well as the petrol engines there were of course the increasingly important diesel units, which effectively fell into the three main customer groups. The 200D was perfect for the taxi driver, 250D for the family buyer and 300D for the upmarket, money not so much of an object, business investor. Beyond that there was a 300D Turbo for the American market.

S124T. Shifting stuff, mostly children and dogs, for middle class families.

The W124 may have looked broadly the same over the decade it was around, but there were constant improvements and 1988 was a very significant year. On the outside panels were stuck to the lower part of the doors, which looked better than it now sounds. There was rather more shiny stuff like chrome strips, door handles and wood inlays.

More than 200,000 of the W123T estate (which Mercedes anoraks will tell you is technically an S124) had been built so it was inevitable that a W124 version would be reintroduced. The difference from the saloons, apart from the styling, was a raft of measures to make it more of a load lugger. So that resulted in revised gearing, reinforced suspension, self-levelling rear suspension and bigger rear brakes. It looked good of course and like the saloon had an excellent drag coefficient at a time when carmakers were interested in things like that. Certainly 0.34 for an estate car was impressive. Clever touches like the rear wiper switching on when reverse was engaged and detachable crossbars that turned the roof rails in a huge roof rack set it apart from all the other more mortal estate cars. Like the W123s, sorry S123s, the S124 will be around for the long haul despite the inclusion of those troublesome black boxes.

If you thought the saloon was handsome, here's the gorgeous C124 coupé.

Then there was the coupé, which while we are being pedantic, was actually a C124. It was not announced until two years after the saloon in 1987. As before it looked like the saloon but with fewer doors, which were pillarless, but ahead of the 1988 facelift to the other models, it already had those lower side panels in place. Yet again the coupé had the pick of the engines going for the bigger four-cylinder 230E and the six-cylinder 300CE (the 24 valve model from 1989) with diesel versions going to America.

Perhaps the most significant new W124 spin off though, was the carbriolet, which did not debut until 1991. Like a lot of other manufacturers they had abandoned full size, four seat open cars because of rumoured stringent roll over regulations in the US, which were never implemented. So having developed the SL specifically for America they used many of the lessons in the building of the C124. While the SL got an amazing pop-up roll bar the 124 made do with rigid head restraints that went upwards if the car should roll over.

The cabriolet did not have much in common with the coupé when it came to body panels as so many had to be modified. This pushed up the weight of course, but it was worth it, because unlike contemporary cabriolets it felt as rigid as the coupé. What piled on the pounds were things like the heated and tinted glass rear window, whilst many other cars made do with scratched up Perspex, or plastic that would simply discolour and split. Mercedes had thought it through, their customers demanded quality and rather than tug at the roof like civilians they would pay extra for the power roof option. Even so they would have to get a man to lock and unlock those latches that attached it to the header screen.

As well as keeping the rich happy and making their lives easier, Mercedes were now having to react to the more overtly sporting BMWs so they changed the gearing to improve acceleration and top speeds. An optional Sportline package meant lowered and stiffened suspension, wider tyres and more responsive steering. Sports seats, smaller sports steering wheel and a leather-covered steering wheel completed the Sportline picture inside. Although that was largely cosmetic, a new 24-valve version of the 3-litre 300 engine (the 300E-24) certainly wasn't and could reach 150 mph, which was thrilling enough. However, Mercedes were prepared to go all out and build some proper four-door supercars.

500E. It's a supercar, but with four doors and a proper boot.

Although strictly out of the time line of this book, in 1990 Mercedes took the four camshaft, 32-valve 5-litre V8 from the 500SL and put it into a W124. Obviously it was not as simple as that because that engine would not fit under the bonnet and neither would the exhaust system. A comprehensive re-engineering programme was required, so all the wings were changed for more subtle flared ones, while underneath the floor pan was altered so much that there was no longer any room for a centre rear passenger. Much of the SL's suspension and running gear was also adapted to fit, along with a lower ride height, wider tyres and distinctive eight spoke 16-inch alloy wheels.

Effectively this was like constructing an all new car, except that the numbers planned to be built would be no more than 2,400 a year, just a handful by Mercedes' own mass market standards. A good job then that Porsche who had lots of experience of building low volume sports cars found space on one of their production lines at Zuffenhausen, after production of the 959 supercar finished. This meant that W124 bodyshells were taken from Mercedes at Sindelfingen and then sent to Porsche to be converted before being returned so that the corrosion

proofing and paintwork could be applied. The finished shell was then sent yet
again to Porsche to be fitted out with all the important go faster gear.

All this activity created the 500E, which most significantly had a limited
top speed of 156 mph, and in a much less uptight, unrestricted world would have
reached 178 mph, but at least it would still accelerate to 60 mph in under six
seconds. That made it quicker than a BMW M5. Job pretty much done then.
Over to you BMW.

In the middle '80s the 3 Series was undisputed king of the compact executives. BMW had effectively invented, and then defined, that marketplace with the
3. Not only that, the E32 7 was comprehensively the emperor of the luxury car
high ground. However, it was the middle market executive crown that still eluded
them. The E28 was good, but not good enough. It may have only been a few
years old, but the shape was dated and the image was frumpy. M5s apart, the 5
Series did not have the sportiness that BMW were famed for, or the cosseting
that the average company director demanded. Customers who wanted that simply
bought a new E Class Mercedes. It's a good job then that the E34 5 Series was
launched in 1988. The world of classy company cars would never be the same
again and BMWs ruled in every important upmarket sector of the new car
market.

The E34, the 5 Series matures into a superb executive express.

In many ways the all-new 5 Series when it was first shown at the Detroit Motor
Show in 1988 was a compact. A compact version of the 7 Series. According to a
senior product engineer at the time who said, "We may lose the odd 7 Series
customer to the smaller car, but when you actually park them next to each other it
becomes obvious that they belong to different classes." He was right, the E34 wasn't
simply a downsized 7. For a start it had wedgier styling and dimensionally it really

was more compact. Plenty of glass in the passenger area and keeping overhangs to a minimum front and rear with a high boxy tail, all helped. It looked aggressive and purposeful unlike the old E28 'square rigger'. The designer Claus Luthe was also responsible for the 7 Series and had an impressive track record of great shapes that included the NSU Ro80, so it was another cracker.

Not only did the E34 look good, it went well too with a wind tunnel honed shape that saw models score from 0.30 to 0.32 Cd, which was 18% more slippery than the previous 'square rigger' E28 5. There was 50% less lift as the new 5 stayed pressed to the tarmac and bonding in the windscreen was also a big help, allowing the E34 to carve through the air.

The new 5 was bigger, at 100mm (4 inches) longer and 51mm (2 inches) wider, though just 3mm lower. More significantly the wheelbase was 136mm (just over 5 inches) longer which meant better interior packaging and niftier handling. However, all that hard work making the 5 Series more aerodynamically efficient was almost wiped out by the fact that it tipped the scales at anything from 3080lb (1.39kg) as a 520I manual to 3400lb (1.54kg) as a 535I automatic. By comparison a Mercedes 300E was a slim 2950lb (1.33kg) and the Audi 200 Turbo an almost feather-light 2860lb (1.29kg). That was the price you had to pay for torsional rigidity up 70% on the old model and if like BMW you believed in building a high quality, no compromise product.

Yep, what you got with the new 5 Series was quality. Quality with a capital C as the doors shut with a reassuring and very final 'chonk'. Inside there were no moans, creaks or vibrations to be heard anywhere. Indeed tyre roar, wind noise and general mechanical cacophony were kept to the bare minimum. Triple window and door seals obviously helped, as did 44lbs (19.9kg) more insulation but the 5 Series was also choc full of clever and innovative details that made living with it a pleasure.

The windscreen wipers were concealed, the door mirrors could be folded away and cunning drip rails meant no wet seat scenario when you opened the door. As for safety, an impact absorbing fuel tank was mounted on top of the rear axle. Meanwhile, lower speed encounters were taken care of by flexible bumpers that bounced back into shape whilst so called impact boxes cold cope with collisions below 9 mph with the minimum of damage. Corrosion resistance was impressive too as 45% of all the sheet metal was zinc plated, as the 5 Series was a car intended for the long haul.

The 5 may have been just 2.8 inches (7.1cm) shorter in the wheelbase than the 7 Series, but rear head and legroom were only ever adequate. Even the boot volume remained the same as the E28 at 16.2 cubic feet. Where it really mattered though, in the cockpit, drivers knew that they were piloting the ultimate driving machine. Ergonomically the 5 was faultless. All round visibility was good, every control angled towards the driver and the worst that any nit picking car test could say was that the seats were a bit too firm.

Despite what BMW were saying publicly the new 5 owed much to the 7 Series. The suspension set-up was essentially the same, because at the front lived a double-joint spring strut axle with gas pressure shocks and an anti roll bar. The new 5 also owed a lot to the old 5 Series when it came to powerplants. Coincidentally there were five models available: 520i, 525i, 530i, 535i and 524td came direct from the old E28 5 Series. Only the 528i was replaced with a 530i, which had 188 bhp. Yet the new 5 Series felt very different and so much quieter than the old one. That brand new and very sophisticated chassis helped, as did the rubber bushes and hydraulic drivetrain mounts, but these old six-cylinder engines had clearly been tweaked. There were new intake silencers, stronger manifold supports and an ultra quiet oil pump. Certainly with the 535I you could notice that the redesigned free-flow intake and exhaust manifolds, and optimised combustion chambers had all made a big difference. Also there was revised digital engine management, semi-sequential fuel injection for three cylinders at a time, computerised ignition and adaptive idle speed control.

Not surprisingly everyone wanted the E34 and sales hit the million mark in 1993. Indeed the E34 was an impressive franchise that would be stretched to a whole variety of models and that even explains the 518i. An export market special the UK was keen buyer of the M40 engined car that slipped into more user chooser budgets on the company car list. Unlike the previous E28 it even sold in decent numbers as a saloon and a Touring. So if anything was missing from the launch line-up it had to be a performance model. The 535I was fast on paper, although refined yet slightly sluggish on the road. Enthusiasts needed something to get really excited about.

The rather understated but very exciting M5.

They did not have to wait long. Rocketing towards them from the horizon just two months after the E34 went on sale was the all-new M5. Under the bonnet was the familiar M88 engine from the M1. However it had a longer stroke and the 3535cc engine produced 315 bhp, a massive 55 bhp more than the E28 version. Motorsport had to change the E34 to cope with this power upgrade by fitting thicker, larger diameter brake discs, lower ride height, revised spring rates, new dampers and beefy anti roll bars as part of the package. Not only that, self-levelling rear suspension was a huge help and pointing it all in the right direction was Servotronic steering with a special low ratio.

Like the E28 before it the new M5 was all about subtlety. You might just notice the front spoiler extension, the rear apron and side skirts and the M-Technic alloys, but those were the only clues. Confirmation came when 60 mph arrived in 6.4 seconds and the rev limiter maxed at 155 mph. Subtlety was good by the early '90s. A recession was on and flaunting performance cars was not a good idea. Owning a four-door supercar though certainly was and the E34 got even better in 1991. In response to Alpina's impressive B10 Bi-Turbo and also Mercedes starting to muscle in on their territory with the 326 bhp 500E, in came the 3.8 litre M5. The revised engine now produced 340 bhp and the 0–60 mph time dropped well below 6 seconds. Clever devices like Adaptive M-Technic suspension and even a 'Nürburgring' package of wider wheels, bigger anti roll bar, revised suspension and Servotronic settings were there to tempt the passionate buyer. M5s though, even when they came in 'practical' Touring form, were just ultra low volume, hand finished image builders. Sales figures were tiny. BMW's bread and butter was always going to be the standard E34 saloons.

BMW never forgot about the cars that really earned the money and that their powerplants were getting old. In 1990 it was time to overhaul the six-cylinder units with the introduction of the 24 valve M50 engines. They delivered more power, better acceleration, but less refinement. As the slow selling 530i went out of production so only the 520i and 525i received the engine whilst the 535I soldiered on for another two years. The next significant engine development was in 1991 when the 524td diesel was replaced with a 525tds. Not that the UK market would realise, because we never had the opportunity to own any oil burning Bimmers until 1993, but at least we got one of the best. This new M51 six-cylinder diesel engine pumped out an impressive 143 bhp and kept the company accountant happy too.

The true successor to the 530i came in 1992 with the M60 V8s, which were fitted to the E32 7s from that year and were later announced as part of the 5 Series line-up. It was no surprise because the engine was light, compact and brought a whole new dimension to E34 motoring. Suddenly the reasons for buying a 7 Series seemed few and far between once the 530i and 540i arrived. Powerful and smooth the 540i was particularly impressive, launching itself to 60 mph in just in under 7 seconds. If the V8s kept senior management happy then at the other end of the scale the area rep was pleased that the 518i was going to be upgraded with the latest M43 four cylinder. There seemed no end as to how far the E34 could be stretched.

E34 Touring. An estate in all but name.

And stretched it was in 1992. Instead of the usual bodge that can disfigure an elegant car, the BMW was different, because it was a Touring not an estate. The name suited BMW and set it apart from the load luggers. The Touring was different, capacious enough and clever. The sloping tailgate hinged from the roof but the twist was that the glass section could be opened separately to allow easy access to the load area. Electrically assisted catches for the window and tailgate, detachable wiper motor and hidden panel mounted washer jet were very clever touches. In practical terms there were four retractable luggage-securing latches, an additional storage compartment underneath the floor and a split rear seat. There was also general rejoicing around the country as aspirational estate buyers with a lifestyle to flaunt no longer had to make do with mundane Mercedes T, or a clichéd Volvo. Even better the Touring went four-wheel drive with the 525iX, but there was a less convincing case for the saloon. Sales were tiny for both models in the UK and the system was expensive.

The really interesting 5 Series variant was an M5 Convertible. Complete with two large doors and seating for five it would have met the Mercedes E cabriolet head on. Due to be announced in 1989 at the Geneva Motor Show, it was shelved when BMW realised that everyone would want one and not necessarily with the M5 engine. The 3 Series cabriolet would have inevitably suffered a sales dip too, so sadly a topless 5 was never to be.

From 1995 the E39 refined the E34 concept even further, emphasising the model's strength and heightening the car's desirability. In just seven years the E34 had helped BMW dominate the whole executive car market. Without doubt the E34 established the whole 5 Series range as the finest executive car you could buy. It probably still is.

BMW 5 Series vs The Rest

Alfa Romeo 164 – Euro co-operation made metal, also related to the Fiat Croma, Saab 9000 and Lancia and with its pretty Pininfarina styling best placed to take on BMW. Front-wheel drive, lovely V6 engine and quite a lot of fun. Seriously quirky inside compared to the Germans. Worth just a few Lira after a few years so not the sensible buy for business owners.

Citroen XM – Luxury car from another planet. Lots of buttons and eventually not all of them would work. Magnificently wedgey styling.

Fiat Croma – As 164, very roomy, but the Fiat badge always looks out of place on anything bigger than an Uno. Turbo quite exciting though.

Ford Granada 2.9 Scorpio Automatic – Sierra, after a blow out meal, styling. ABS brakes were a nice safe touch, but this was a big fleet favourite, which rewarded regional managers and made them feel important. About as important as a mini cab driver.

Lancia Thema – Yet another variation on the 164 and like the Croma fairly pointless. However, the 8.32 had a Ferrari engine for goodness sake, it was still no M5 or E500 though.

Peugeot 605 – A giant version of the 405 which is a good thing. Good diesel and petrol engines plus a 200 bhp V6. Like most larger French cars of the period, largely ignored.

Rover 827 Sterling – Better than the 825 although that is not saying very much. Attempt at BMW-like nomenclature did not work either. Narrow, but quite comfy, fairly quick and very well equipped, but build quality a long way off the Bavarian benchmark. Possible future curiosity.

Saab 9000 – The most successful of the related 164/Croma/Thema with body by Giugiaro, so it sort of looks like a big Golf. Saloons, hatches and masses of space, plus Turbo engines and loads of spec. Purists hate it as not a proper Saab, but actually the best alternative BMW/Merc/Audi of the lot.

Vauxhall Carlton – It's also an Opel Rekord of course and unlike many other big cars it has proper rear-wheel drive like BMW and Mercedes. Built in Germany too and the GSi and Lotus Carlton kept it all interesting. Best budget German car of the '80s.

In the Cassette Deck . . .

 Spandau Ballet – Parade My abiding memory of the '80s is seeing the Ballet at Wembley Arena and not being the only person who went straight from work with a plastic Samonsite briefcase. There were rows of us, I bet I was the only one with a 525i though. Meanwhile this was the summer of '84 soundtrack confirming that they were no longer new romantic, but old softies. However, 'Only When You Leave' was no 'Gold' though. Or even 'Musclebound' for that matter.

8 A Beetle but a bit quicker?
The legend of the 911.
Plus the Cult of the Quattro

All about Porsche (911, 924, 944, 928), oh and the Quattro Turbo ...

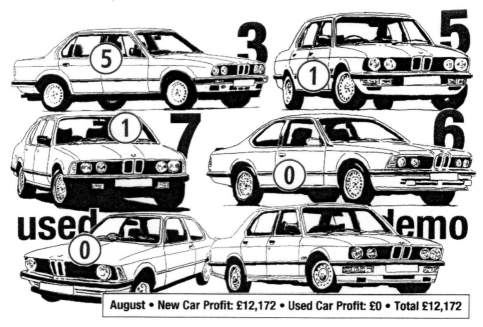

August • New Car Profit: £12,172 • Used Car Profit: £0 • Total £12,172

I suppose the real subtitle ought to be, how did a car that was so wrong, get so much right and still become a legend? Certainly the only Porsche that ever mattered was the 911. I soon found this out early when one evening someone borrowed my little 316 for demonstration purpose. I needed to get home and of course we would never use public transport when there was an underground car park brim full of cars. We were always encouraged to take out part exchanges so we knew what our rivals had to offer. The salesman who borrowed my 316 tossed me some keys with a Porsche fob on the end. That seemed like a good thing to me, but he added, "Don't get too excited, it's only a 924."

Once I'd opened the door though, I climbed down into it, just like a proper sports car and when I headed down Piccadilly I pushed open the sunroof so that I could hear the traffic and settled down to a very enjoyable drive home. I liked the chequered seats, and I really didn't care that the engine was in the wrong, or rather right end. A proper Porsche would have the engine not just behind the driver's shoulder like many sports cars; say a Ferrari or Lamborghini, but actually in the boot. This had all sorts of implications that we will come to later.

I had the headlamps on so they were popped up and that signalled to me that it was a proper sports car. It was easy to drive and very comfortable, the appeal was obvious, not least because it was relatively cheap too. For me there wasn't a lot wrong with the 924 unless you wanted to go very fast and then crash backwards into the scenery in which case I'd have been driving a 911.

Obviously purists hated the very existence of the 924 along with the fact that at one point it could well have been badged as an Audi. Actually the 924 was an early recognition by Porsche that they had one of the most desirable automotive brands in the world. To that end they could convince some buyers and particularly new customers that a Porsche could be much more affordable and accessible. Compared to an old MGB, or even a Capri, it really was a class apart and likely to be more fun to drive, better built and be much more of a hip and happening set of sporty wheels down at a 1980s' wine bar.

So at Park Lane the facts were that no one would ever part exchange a 911, certainly not for a 6 Series or any other Series BMW. However, 924s and 928s were an entirely different matter. But before we get stuck into the '80s Porsche and examining just what made the most profitable car company in the world tick, it is worth finding out exactly where Porsche came from and about the man behind the name.

How Porsches used to look, an all electric vehicle for Lohner.

Dr Ingo chi Ferdinand Porsche was born (just plain Ferdinand) on 3 September 1875 in Maffersdorf, in what was then Bohemia, later to become the Czech Republic. After moving to Vienna and taking on an apprenticeship, he attended night classes at Vienna Technical University, but that was the end of his formal education. By 1900 he had built an electric car for coach building company Lohner, with marginal success. It was very clever and putting the motors in the hubs on the wheel meant there was no need for a complicated gearbox.

Porsche moved on in 1905 to Austro-Daimler, actually replacing Paul Daimler, son of Gottlieb, when the former returned to Mercedes in Stuttgart. Porsche designed a very successful small racing car called the Sascha and became technical director of Daimler in Stuttgart. He was responsible for the huge proto supercars in the shape of the SSK and SSKL models, which were products of the new alliance of Mercedes-Benz in 1926. This was also the year that Porsche first met Adolf Hitler, invited by Daimler-Benz management to a race meeting. Their paths would cross again, as Porsche proposed a small, more aerodynamic and affordable car than the big Berthas that Mercedes were building at the time.

Mercedes didn't fancy the concept and after 23 years Porsche flounced off to rivals Steyr in 1929. It was bad timing on his part because it coincided with the Depression and Steyr ended up sacking Porsche. At 55 years old the prospects did not look good. Instead he decided it was time to set up on his own. Using the Honorary Degree from his old university to create an engineering consultancy, to this day the company's official name remains Dr Ing hc Porsche AG and was established with money loaned by his Jewish friend, Adolf Rosenberger, who had been a Mercedes racing driver.

The company struggled despite an open invitation to take control of the fledgling Russian car industry. However, Germany now had a brand new Chancellor who wanted a German team to compete in the latest Grand Prix Formula for cars weighing up to 750kg. The prize fund was 500,000 Reichmarks and with it came the honour of representing the entire German nation. Porsche's old employers Daimler-Benz won the contract which upset Auto Union (a recent amalgamation of Audi, DKW, Horch and Wanderer) no end. The Chairman of Auto Union, Baron Klaus von Oertzen, got a private meeting with Hitler and asked Porsche to join him. Hitler remembered Porsche, admired his work with Daimler and no doubt liked to think he was a fellow Austrian. Porsche had drawings of a V16 racing engine he had designed and persuaded Hitler that two world class racing teams would be better than one.

So it came to pass that the V16 engine was a crucial part of the 1934 Auto Union Grand Prix car and unusually for a racing car of that time it was positioned right behind the driver. Just as unusually the frame of the car was made from tubing and covered in a light aluminium skin. The suspension comprised rear swing axles and torsion beam frontal systems that would occur again in the future on Beetles and Porsches with interesting results. Auto Unions got off to a winning start at the German Grand Prix putting Mercedes firmly in second place. Porsche also got the contract to build Hitler's pet project.

Spot the difference. Original Beetle and the Tatra V570. Guess which one is which.

At its simplest Hitler wanted a family vehicle, something for a couple of adults and a brace of blonde kids that could cruise at 60 mph on his newly constructed autobahns and cost just 1000 Reichmarks. That's about what a Wallace and Gromit type motorcycle and sidecar combination would have sold for. Hitler apparently said it should also look a bit like Beetle, but rather more clumsily called it 'der Kdf' (Kraft durch Freude)-Wagen, short for 'the Strength-through-Joy Car' which was a terrible model name for anything. It was also a terrible car as none of them ever made it to the people who paid for them. The only Kdf-Wagens that were delivered were used by Nazi Party officials as staff cars and adapted for war as the four-wheel drive Kommandeurwagen and amphibious Schwimmwagen. Fittingly, non-driver Hitler's last journey was in a Kommandeurwagen, which had a roller at the front to push almost anything out of the way. At least nothing could stop him killing himself.

The Beetle though had not been all Porsche's own work. Josef Popp from BMW was also involved for a time and most infamously Hans Ledwinka from Tatra. He had designed a large very streamlined rear engined, air-cooled V8 saloon. Hitler was a big fan and had used Tatras to tour Germany, even though his favourite car had been the Mercedes-Benz, particularly the 7.7 litre Super-charged Grosser model. Hitler regularly spoke to Ledwinka who was a lot more Austrian than Porsche, having been born there. Despite that, he was regarded as a Czech (which of course is what Porsche actually was) being based in Moravia, which was not good. Especially as relations between the countries deteriorated in the run up to the war. Even so, Hitler kept in touch and at one point Ledwinka had given him detailed drawings about a prototype car he had built some years before which was called the V570. These were apparently passed on to Porsche. This V570 certainly looked Beetley with its sloped rear end containing an air-cooled engine and even more prominent bug eyed headlamps at the front.

When the Beetle, sorry Kdf-Wagen, was revealed Ledwinka began legal proceedings but the war soon stopped all that. After the war though Ledwinka had to cope with imprisonment and accusations of collaboration before seeking exile in his native Austria. He always believed that BMW and Mercedes had played a significant part in his downfall. Meanwhile he was sidelined as Tatra who stopped building cars and had their patents confiscated during wartime. Eventually compensation (three million Deutschmarks) was paid to Tatra by Volkswagen in 1961 rather than to Ledwinka, over the Beetle issue and the company remain touchy about the subject to this day. Ledwinka died in 1967, completely forgotten, yet he was one of the foremost automotive engineers of the twentieth century with the part he played in the Porsche and Volkswagen stories officially obliterated.

Porsche also encountered some local difficulties after the war. He had never joined the Nazi Party, although slave workers were used in the factories that made the military projects he was involved with. Safely relocated to rural Gmund in Austria, he just got on with engineering projects in Stuttgart and Wolfsburg. So imagine his delight when the French invited him to tea at their headquarters in Baden Baden near Stuttgart to chat about work. All they wanted to know was whether he would be interested in making a less German version of the Beetle for Renault and calling it the 4CV.

However, it all went pear shaped very quickly as Porsche was denounced as a war criminal and imprisoned along with his son Ferry and brother-in-law Anton Piech. Although Ferry Porsche was released his father wasn't, effectively being held to ransom, although he was never charged with any crime. So Ferry set about restablishing the company, designing a four-wheel drive Grand Prix car for Cisitalia in Italy, and generated enough money to post bail for his father and Piech. Porsche the car company was back in business. It was now 1947.

Porsche himself had not just proposed a sports car based on the Beetle he even built three Volkswagen Type 64s in 1939 specifically to compete in a fascist dictatorship capital to capital competition, also known as the Berlin–Rome race. Postponed, due to hostilities, the car was streamlined with all the wheels shrouded and was a classic teardrop shape. Despite the VW badges these were effectively the first Porsches.

Ferry Porsche was now firmly in charge and produced working drawings of what would become the 356. The first car, no 001, was to be their test bed and competition hack, as early on the company decided that racing was the best way to market a sports car and it duly won its first race in 1948. That car was soon sold to bring in vital Swiss Francs and the buyer was Mr R von Senger from Zurich who was one of the company's original backers. However making one-off specials was no way to build a sports car company. Constructing a space frame chassis was complicated and putting the engine in the middle of the car may have been perfect for handling purposes, but it caused all sorts of packaging issues when it came to passengers, their luggage and easy maintenance.

His and hers 356s, she has a 1955 Speedster, he's got a 1956 356A Coupé.

Redesigned, the 356 now had an engine at the back and a steel floor pan with torsion bar suspension, the whole thing stiffened by box sections whilst the bodywork comprised of hand finished aluminium. At this early stage Volkswagen saw an opportunity to associate themselves with a small specialist company and offered to supply parts, give access to their fledgling sales and service network and to use them as consultants and appoint them as distributors for Austria. Porsche was now financially secure.

Ferdinand Porsche whose health was failing after imprisonment had a stroke and died on 30 January 1951. However by then he had been able to approve the 356 and see it become a sales success as production moved from the disused timber mill in Gmund to the much more industrial surroundings of Zuffenhausen, Stuttgart. Also, just months later a Porsche won its first major international racing victory in the 1100cc class in the Le Mans 24 hours.

With the 356 the template had been set. Effectively this was a light and aerodynamic Beetle special with the engine tuned to produce 40 bhp rather than the standard 25 bhp. Obviously the engine was in the boot with the gearbox just ahead of the rear wheels. Torsion bar spring suspension was part of the steel platform chassis, with trailing links at the front and swing axles at the rear. Here was a sports car that could grip the road very tenaciously, but it could also bite back if the driver was not too careful.

Coupés were joined by cabriolets as the engine size and output was increased. Indeed, a batch of twenty lightweight roadsters were sent to America to compete and led directly to the very funky looking Speedster with a lower windscreen and a basic cockpit. James Dean had one for a while although the one he is most associated with and died in, was a Type 550 Spyder which was essentially a track car that was road legal, which he called 'lil bastard'.

It would be something of a bast**d to detail the differences between the 356, 356A, 356B and 356C with Carrera 2 variants before fast forwarding to the

911. However, it would be worth upsetting the Porsche faithful by insisting that the early cars really were just Beetle specials, if rather handsome ones. However, they did become less VW reliant with each incarnation and far more wieldy and quicker. Certainly the Carrera deserves a special mention not least because it had a more powerful overhead camshaft engine. It would though be wrong to overlook one of the most important technical advancements that made motorists lives easier and just a bit quieter.

Synchromesh revolutionised changing gear. This meant drivers did not have to rev the engine to match the speed for the next gear. Porsche designed a system that included a cone which spun the next gear up to the right speed, otherwise you would hear an almighty crunch. Porsche fitted it to the 356 from 1953 and got a royalty every time it was used by other manufacturers. So money was rolling in and was not going to be an issue. However, naming their new car would be.

Butzi Porsche with the 901, soon to become the 911.

The 901 certainly had a nice ring to it. Already Porsche had used 904 for their limited production track racer in 1963. 901 was the designation used when the car announced at the 1963 Frankfurt Motor Show. Peugeot had apparently trademarked all the numbers that began with nine and had a zero in the middle, hence the change to 911, which actually has an even nicer ring to it.

Now having said all those slightly negative things about the 356 it should come as no surprise that the new 911 in 1964 was not unlike the old 356 in so many ways. The gearbox was ahead of the rear wheels, the engine out back behind them and suspension provided by torsion bars. However, there were important changes when MacPherson struts were added at the front and the old swing axle at the rear replaced by a trailing arm set-up. Not only that, the separate floorpan was replaced by a monocoque body. However, the body was almost two and half inches narrower yet even more spacious inside so that you could actually get four bodies on board. Styling was courtesy of a third generation family member Butzi Porsche, who created one of the most recognisable and enduring profiles in motoring history. By comparison the 356 looked like an ugly dumpling.

The 911 didn't just look good, it went harder and faster than ever. In the boot was a brand new engine, which was just like the Beetle's flat four air cooled, except that it had two more cylinders, produced 130 bhp and used a five-speed gearbox. Rack and pinion steering and all round disc brakes helped the handling and the stopping no end. Porsche were now where they wanted to be and that was at the sports car top table where their cars would be considered in the same bracket as a Ferrari or Aston Martin.

It was of course hard for Porsche to leave its Volkswagen roots entirely behind. There was still room for an entry level Porsche to replace the cheapest 356, hence the 912. Essentially buyers got a pretty good deal, which amounted to the 911 body, combined with the old 1600cc Volkswagen derived engine. With a lower level of trim and a four-speed gearbox as standard it did a job and was only phased out in 1969 when the 914 arrived.

Here's VW's 914, it looks just like Porsche's 916. Or is it a 916?

Badged as both a VW and a Porsche depending on which engine was fitted, here was the first public admission that the two companies worked closely together. The styling of the 914/916 was the same, a low square cut Targa roofed body with pop up headlamps that looked very much of its time, 1969. Volkswagen's 914 had a 1795cc engine from the less than exciting or pretty 411 saloon. However, it did have disc brakes on all four wheels and a five-speed gearbox plus Sportmatic (automatic) as an option. A higher performance 1971cc SC model still didn't make it a Porsche.

The Porsche had a six-cylinder engine from a 911T and actually handled better than the model that donated it being seriously nifty with a top speed of 125 mph and a get to 60 mph time of just over 8 seconds. Unfortunately apart from the wheels and badging it was identical to the VW version. Not only that it cost almost as much as a pretty 911, so buyers didn't see the point and just 3350 were sold. VW did better managing 78,640 but had demonstrated the absolute limits of how far you could stretch a brand as strong as Porsche before it broke and buyers rebelled. In America the fuel injected 912E was added to the price lists in 1976 and became the face of the cheap Porsche, until the 924 arrived. More on that later.

Back to the 911, where the letter S meant a high compression engine and ventilated disc brakes for 1966. Two years later fuel injection boosted the power to 170 bhp and a top speed of 137 mph with 60 mph arriving in 8 seconds. The 911 was getting serious especially when the wheelbase was lengthened by just over 2 inches and the wheel arches flared. The engine kept on growing throughout the '60s to 2.2 and then 2.4.

The standard cooking 2.0 litre 911 had the letter T from 1967 with a carburettor and its engine size grew along with the S, but obviously its power output was just 110/130 bhp. Then again there was another letter, this time E, which in 1968 was the middle order model with fuel injection and uniquely, a self-levelling suspension system for a few seasons.

Ferry Porsche with the 2.0 911.

Overall the 911 range evolved as the coupé was joined in 1967 by a so-called Targa top whereby you could pop out the centre roof section and leave the rear screen and B pillars in place without a hint of scuttle shake that could spoil the enjoyment of so many contemporary open top sports cars. The drivers also avoided the sheer fiddly nonsense involved in putting up a folding roof. Although there had briefly been a zip out plastic rear window, which was not that clever, managing to leak both water and engine noise into the cabin. A one-piece wrap-around rear window was the obvious fix. A year later the Sportmatic gearbox meant clutch free changes as all the driver had to do was press a micro-switch on the gear lever. Porsche had identified another important group of customers who didn't want the stress of pumping their left foot up and down.

Hood missing? That would be the 911 Targa.

In 1972 the Carrera name was re-introduced. Carrera was first used in 1956 for the most powerful model in the 356 range, recalling a class victory in the Carrera Panamerica Mexico. Carrera means race and the Panamerica could not have been tougher, being contested on unmade roads. So the fastest Porsche whether for race or track was often named Carrera. In this case they took the shell from the S model and made it even less so by stripping everything out so that the whole car weighed just 900 kilos (1984lbs). The diet involved junking all the soundproofing, underseal, carpets and rear seats. Even the glove box lid, coat hooks and door trim were removed in the interests of weight saving, plus the engine cover was moulded from glassfibre. The engine itself was uprated and enlarged to 2.7 litres so that it produced 210 bhp. A combination of low weight and high power meant it got to 60 mph in under 6 seconds and would go on to 150 mph. To get all that power down the rear wheels were wider with seven-inch rims meaning that the rear arches were flared to accommodate them.

Can you guess what it is yet?

The Carrera was ripe for competition so at least 500 were scheduled to be built and homologated for racing in the GT category. In all 1600 were made and most of them (1036) were true lightweights whilst the remaining got the full road going and much more comfortable, S specification.

You could not miss a Carrera due to the large red or blue script on the flanks. The RS version also featured a prominent rear spoiler quickly nicknamed 'duck's tail'. It might have looked daft to some but it really did work cutting down lift and improving road holding. Meanwhile, an even more track focused 315 bhp RSR took all the racing honours.

The 1970s is when the 911 came into its own and effectively grew up, well it certainly grew outwards and upwards slightly. For 1974 it no longer looked like the slightly delicate, fey racer and suddenly became a lot more brutal and businesslike courtesy of the low-speed impact protection bumpers demanded by US law. These were made from aluminium with a thick rubber centre section and mounted on collapsible alloy tubes. It also had a front spoiler. This was known as the G-series, eighth letter of the alphabet and the eighth update and by far the most significant so far.

911 with those new US friendly bumpers.

All 911s now had a 2.7 litre fuel injected engine. Suspension had been revised for better handling and inside the trim was smartened up with new seats, so-called 'tombstones' with integrated head restraints, and a large padded steering wheel for safety. Ventilation and heating were improved to make it even more driver friendly, whilst the big 3-litre engine built for the driver unfriendly new Turbo was adapted for a new 200 bhp Carrera. Perhaps the most significant development was rustproof steel being used for both the body and chassis. Thyssen steel had already been used on the underside and now the body was going to be zinc coated and offered with a six-year warranty. Rust was a big issue in the '70s and it would crucify several manufacturers and eventually lead to the complete retreat of Lancia from the British market.

One of the most significant Porsche models from this period was undoubtedly the Turbo, which arrived in a post energy crisis world. It could not have arrived at a worse time, but its iconic status and ultimate survival was assured and we will take a closer look at it in the Wundercar Chapter. Although times were hard and not everyone could run to a Turbo, Porsche buyers, or those who aspired to be Porsche owners, might just want to consider something affordable.

Now things may have looked good for Audi as the 1970s arrived but a recession was on the horizon and Volkswagen had an ancient model range with no replacement for the Beetle in sight. Money was therefore very tight. Ferdinand Piech who ultimately went on to lead Audi and the Volkswagen group was a nephew of Dr 'Ferry' Porsche and working on the research and development for the sports car company who had a long-term contract with VW. Piech was a victim of cutbacks and cancelled projects, but he ultimately found a job at Audi first developing the 5-cylinder engine and then the Quattro. At the time though there was also another project for Volkswagen codenamed EA425 which was scheduled as a replacement for the 914.

The full on Turbo version of the lightweight 924.

Porsche continued with their development, but as the fuel crisis deepened and with the Golf not yet launched to international acclaim, it looked less likely that Volkswagen would actually want two coupés in their line up. Because if someone wanted an affordable coupé in 1974 they could buy themselves a brand new Scirocco, so an Audi Coupé was looking less than likely. Although the EA425 design was signed off as a VW car in February 1974 it became a Porsche project. Indeed, it already had a Porsche designation which was 924, the 4 standing for four cylinders, everything else about it was very much VW/Audi as per the original brief. The power plant was the 1984cc LT28 as seen in Audi 100s, reworked by Porsche with fuel injection and a redesigned cylinder head to produce 125 instead of 95 bhp. The gearbox was Audi and so were the brakes. All that was missing was the four-ring badge on the bonnet. But at least they got to build it.

The almost bankrupt VW had overcapacity and some factories were set for closure, so Audi's former NSU plant at Neckarsulm took on the job. Cynical motoring hacks and snobby Porsche owners constantly took pot shots at the 924 as being not a real Porsche. They claimed it was a parts bin Audi, or worst of all a VW. Their loss was 135,000 buyers' gain, who all appreciated the neutral handling, reliability, practicality and performance of this entry level Porsche. After all, Porsches had started out as adapted VWs and now a member of the Porsche family had joined Audi and engineered an all-new coupé that would not only give the relatives a fright, it would also transform the company's image. That'll be the Quattro, a few pages on.

So yes there were quite a few reasons not to buy the bargain baby Porsche, mainly because it did seem like the cynical coming together of VW group bits. However, in the last iteration of the 924 in the shape of the S it was arguably the best and unarguably a proper Porsche. For some it may never have been anything more than an upmarket Capri, however the 924S has to be judged in context and by 1985 a 0–60 mph time of 8 seconds was hot hatch quick. The larger 2.5 engine was responsive and made the S feel usefully lively even though it was detuned from the 944. Many criticised the handling at the time as being a bit on the soft side, but then it was never meant to be a hardcore performer. By contrast the 924 Turbo was quicker, but far more complex and anyway most buyers preferred to trade up to a 944 for that sort of performance.

The 944 in full on Turbo form.

Ah yes the 944, which is for many, exactly what the 924 should have been all along. For a start it looked a lot more butch with flared wings and wheel arches covering wider alloy wheels and under that bonnet was a proper Porsche engine. The all-new aluminium 2479cc, 163 bhp fuel injected four cylinder was effectively one half of the 928's V8, see below. Porsche had considered making it even more Porsche like with a 6-cylinder version, but there just wasn't enough room under the bonnet. Initially in 1982 it was badged as a Lux and for the UK market it had electric windows, headlamp washers and tinted glass. A year later there was firmer sports suspension and then in 1984 power steering, electric heated door mirrors and revised interior.

By 1987 the standard 944 was no longer designated Lux and central locking standard, but rather more significantly by autumn of the following year the engine was increased in size to 2681cc and 165 bhp, with ABS brakes bringing it all to a halt.

The 944 was not just a better-looking 924 it was always a serious piece of performance kit. With a KKK Turbo and intercooler bolted on in 1985 it would produce 220 bhp, do 157 mph and get to 60 mph in 5.6 seconds, which was quicker than a 911 Carrera. As a performance plaything the Turbo is perfect. The landmarks are 1987 when ABS was standardised, and a 1988 power boost to 250 bhp along with uprated suspension, brakes and a limited slip differential.

If the turbo was a bit too full on then the short-lived 944S from 1986 had 16 valves and 190 bhp was an interesting compromise. Later was always better when it comes to Porsches as they had a habit of using run out models as test beds, and in this case the S2 in 1989 was the technical run through for the largely identical 968, which was launched in 1992. What you get here is a bigger engine and turbo uprates including the suspension, brakes and a slightly re-styled body. Perhaps the most significant model was the cabriolet, also available as both a standard and Turbo S2.

Both the 924 and 944 were referred to internally as 'Transaxle cars', (gearbox at the rear) and by the middle of 1989 production had topped 300,000 so despite the critics these had been incredibly profitable models. Meanwhile the core product, in the shape of the 911, kept on evolving. For 1976 the range was streamlined to feature just a standard 911, Carrera and Turbo. The Carrera now had a 2994cc engine producing 200 bhp. However, by 1978 the model range was reduced to a 911SC and the Turbo and then for the next few years general fiddling with the SC's engine output so that they could pass the stringent American emissions regulations.

Just in case you were getting a bit bored with all the incremental changes to the 911 to make it better, so was Porsche. They reckoned they had taken the 911 as far as they could so they decided to design the future and call it the 928. It was conceived as far back as 1972, a year before the oil crisis hit, which eventually delayed its development by two years. Even so it still looked like something from outer space when it was eventually launched in 1977 at the Geneva Motor Show. Then in 1978 it became the first sports car to win the International Car of the Year award.

A 928S. The future shape of Porsche, or so Porsche seriously believed.

As departures from the Porsche norm went, this was a complete Year Zero for Zuffenhausen. For a start it had an upright V8 engine with two more cylinders than usual. Not only that, it used that vital element water, rather than air to do the cooling. Oh yes and that great big, brand new engine was finally in the right place. Instead of being in the boot it was under the bonnet at the front. That certainly helped the weight distribution especially as the gearbox sat on the rear axle. Indeed that axle was a clever thing and used flexible rubber bushes to allow the suspension to almost steer itself, which meant far better cornering and improved stability under braking. Getting back to the important issue of 'weight distribution issues' that the 911 had plenty of, the 928 also had its plastic fuel tank and battery behind that fancy new axle. In fact that axle was so clever it won an award for safety.

That beautiful body had seemingly done away with the need for proper bumpers, but the deformable front and rear plastic sections were even coloured with a state of the art elastic paint that was resistant to impact. Apparently the sheer width of the 90-degree V8 engine plus the room required for the fat front wheels to turn lock to lock meant that there was a big featureless bonnet. So to make it look less like a big slab of metal, designer Tony Lapine didn't put pop up headlamps on top, he took the covers off to break up the huge expanse of metal. In fact, that metal was aluminium, which also made up the doors and front wings.

The first buyers in 1977 got themselves a front engined rear wheel drive Porsche and if that simple fact didn't astound them, the fuel injected single overhead camshaft 4.5 litre V8 engine delivering 240 bhp at 5500rpm certainly would. They had the choice of a rear mounted (transaxle) five-speed manual gearbox, or a three-speed automatic. Suspension was coil springs all round with double wishbones at the front and trailing arms at the rear. An S model from

1979 upped the engine output to 4.7 litre which produced a massive 300 bhp, a top speed of 152 mph and a 0–60 mph time of 6.2 seconds. The S2 version from 1984 upped the output to 310 bhp with a four-speed automatic gearbox courtesy of Mercedes-Benz. Oh yes and ABS brakes were now standard.

Although there was a Series 3 for the US market in 1984 with a double overhead camshaft, four valve, 5-litre version of the V8 with Bosch LH-Jetronic fuel injection and power at 288 bhp, Europe soon caught up. In 1986 the 928S Series 4 now with a 5-litre unit producing 320 bhp with a larger rear spoiler and revised 'smoother' front end. Leather trim and 4-speed automatic were standard and finally in 1989 there was a realisation that everyone wanted an automatic, so the manual option was discontinued. However, for the minority who wanted to be more involved with their 928, Porsche introduced a performance focused 928S GT. It had stiffer suspension, wider wheels, broader rear track and 326 bhp, oh yes and it would be manual transmission only. In 1990 modified engine management meant 330 bhp which clearly necessitated twin exhaust tailpipes. And finally in 1992 the GTS was a 32-valve 5.4-litre monster producing 340 bhp getting to 60 mph in 5.5 seconds and with a nominal top speed of 165 mph. Plus it had snazzy alloy 'cup' wheels which were 7.5J x 17" at the front and wider 9J x 17" at the rear. Sadly the 928 ran out of road in 1995 and it still looked more futuristic, exciting and innovative than any other car on sale.

However, the rear seats were fairly marginal and only good for children, and this was a deliberate policy as Porsche reckoned that a full four seater could provoke Mercedes and BMW into upping their game, so they stayed out of that market. Even so, with the rear seats folded this gave a really decent load bay and I absolutely loved it.

Yes we got 928s as part exchanges for some reason and I really couldn't understand why. By comparison a 6 Series was certainly more light and airy, but very old fashioned and clearly a product of the mid '70s. When I pulled the gear lever into drive on an original 3-speed 'box the response was instant. Inside it looked like a space capsule with swooping plastic mouldings and crazy magic eye pattern chequered door inserts, plus an entire dashboard binnacle that moved with the steering wheel as you adjusted it. I may have loved the 928, but Porsche buyers didn't and sales were disappointing despite it being the fastest, safest, most practical Porsche ever built. That's why I only saw part exchange 928s and not 911s. Things though had changed radically in the performance car world and in particular a brand new type of vehicle, which would cling to the road whatever the weather and must have set Porsche thinking.

Audi Quattro, the point at which sports cars changed for ever.

Quattro is derived from the Italian for number four and was coined by one of the Audi engineers working on the project. So although the Audi Quattro was the first mass-produced four-wheel drive vehicle in 1980, as so often happens the pioneers were plucky Brits. Between 1966 and 1971 the Jensen Interceptor FF blazed the 4 x 4 trail that no one else bothered to follow. In 1977 a part-time project amongst like-minded engineers was picked up and formalised as Audi saw the huge potential in offering four-wheel drive to the masses. They wanted permanent, rather than part time four-wheel drive that could cope with every road condition.

Dr. Ferdinand Piech is credited with taking the running gear from a VW Iitis military vehicle and adapting it to fit an Audi 80 bodyshell and the result was codenamed A1. After some impressive demonstrations, legend has it that a prototype on normal tyres (no snow chains) easily scaled a fire brigade sodden ski ramp with a 23% gradient at Turracherhohe in Austria before stunned Audi board members.

Approval was given for a coupé that when it arrived in March 1980 incorporated every technical trick in Audi's book. Under the bonnet was a turbo charged version of the fuel injected 2144cc five-cylinder engine from the Audi 100. Power went up from 136 bhp to 200 bhp and produced an astounding 210lb ft of torque at 3500 rpm. That meant the Quattro got to 60 mph in just under seven seconds and went on to an incredible 140 mph top speed. In the mid range the 50–70 mph overtaking zone took just four seconds. At the heart of the Quattro was the four wheel drive system that meant power was transferred to the road surface at all times and in all conditions. There was a five-speed gearbox with a normal front differential, which allowed differences in road speeds between the front and rear axles when cornering. To give additional traction both the centre and rear diffs could be locked via a console switch.

So the Quattro handled brilliantly, it also looked the part too. Flared wheel arches, sill extensions and larger spoilers, which all sat on 6-inch-wide 15-inch Ronal R8 alloy wheels, contributed to a fantastically aggressive stance. The bold 'quadring' decals on the doors and sundry quattro logos also meant that there was no doubt that this Audi meant business.

Using the standard coupé's B2 bodyshell, the original plan had been to build just the required 400 for motorsport homologation purposes. However the sensation it caused at the 1980 Geneva Motor Show, where it was voted car of the show, and customer demand meant that it went into full production. The ur-Quattro (ur is the German prefix for original as it has become fashionable to identify this car) figures were rapidly revised upwards to 3500. However, the Quattro was not simply a showroom phenomenon, in the real world of international rallying it rewrote the rule and record book. In its first year, 1981, the Quattro led every single race, won three and came third in the Championship.

Yes the Quattro was that good. Not only did it win prizes, more than any other Audi it changed the way the world thought about the company. It seemed appropriate that surely any future Audi coupé could only get better? Not necessarily. Certainly Audi as a company was growing up fast. The final integration occurred in 1985, when that mouthful, AUDI NSU AUTO UNION AG was transformed quite simply into AUDI AG, with the head offices transferred from Neckarsulm to Ingolstadt. An additional 943 million Deutschmarks were allocated to new investment, earmarked mainly for production technology and the all-new fully galvanised Audi 80, which was launched in the autumn of 1986. It provided the basis for Audi's new sports car.

A dumpy Audi Coupé.

It's 1988 and an all-new Audi Coupé made its debut, except that it wasn't exactly all new. Underneath the new high waisted body was the suspension of the outgoing 80/90 models. It floated and wavered, was a stranger to composure and only the Quattro system, when fitted, saved it from further embarrassment. Not only that, the five-cylinder engine in standard tune was not sufficiently fast or refined enough. Matters improved over the years but not by enough. The S2 version with a handy 230 bhp was meant to be a '90s Quattro Turbo, but although it had the 20 valve engine, the hard edge of the original was missing. The unthinkable had happened and the Audi Coupé had gone bland.

For the moment Audi ceased to be any sort of threat to Porsche. In turn Porsche had only been competing against itself and had given up on the 928. So the company had no choice but to keep on developing the 911 and in the 1980s they turned it into the must have sports car for the big bang generation. The year 1981 was the company's 50th anniversary as the 300,000 Porsche was built and 200,000 of those had been 911s. Not only that, the car the movers, shakers and bankers were waiting for had first been shown at the 1981 Frankfurt Motor Show as a concept. The 911SC Cabriolet was the first truly open 911 and such was the reaction that Porsche rushed it into production for the 1983 model year. What had changed at Porsche was the arrival of chairman Peter Schutz, a German speaking American who could see that what the world wanted was more 911s and much better 911s. The models duly arrived thick and very, very fast.

Cabriolet 911 also wearing the popular 'Turbo Look' kit.

The cabriolet was a great way to get attention and all it took was strengthening of the floor pan and designing an easy to operate cantilever roof. Many would have thought that this new model was the quickest way to kill off the Targa, but that never happened as the novelty of the cabriolet seemed to wear off and the Targa settled down to sell in even larger numbers. Things though were changing for the 911, which was about to celebrate its 20th birthday as the SC was phased out and the Carrera name came back for good.

Porsche said it was 80 per cent new although from the outside it was hard to tell as the bodywork and suspension were carried over from the SC. Most significantly the engine was enlarged to 3164cc and its output increased to 231 bhp, up from 205 bhp although its economy went up by 10 per cent. This was due in part to a new Bosch Motronic electronic engine management system which made the new Carrera almost as quick as a turbo with a top speed comfortably over 150 mph, plus it would get to 60 mph in just over 5 seconds. Not only was it almost as quick as a Turbo, one of the cleverest marketing tricks was to offer Carreras with different body options. Paying extra for the Sport meant that the car was now fitted with wider Fuchs alloy wheels, ultra low profile Pirelli P7 tyres, stiffer shock absorbers and those distinctive front and rear spoilers. However the 'Turbo Look' was undoubtedly the ultimate expression of Porscheupmanship.

So for the 1986 model year Carrera customers could order the Turbo's wide body, uprated suspension and brakes. Spacers were used to pack the wheel arches out although buyers could go for the Turbo's 16 inch alloys that were wider at the back (9J), than at the front (7J). In the UK, that package which included Turbo touches to the interior was called the Sport Equipment. If anything summed up the '80s it had to be that huge 'tea-tray' spoiler. Arrogant and ridiculous in equal parts, yet utterly indispensable if you wanted your 911 to be taken seriously.

However the Porsche party was about to come to an end. Prices had to rise in the wake of the mid '80s financial crisis. After currency devaluations and the stock market crash on 19th October 1987, Black Monday may have been bad enough for those 911 owners in the City, it was becoming a bleak year for Porsche. Retail prices went up by as much as 15% and that coincided with a drop in sales and Porsche's reliance on exports exposed them first to reduced profits and then losses. Even though Peter Schutz was asked to resign, it was impossible to stop his ambitious, expansionist plans. It was not as if Porsche had squandered all the money they had earned. There was now a brand new three storey factory just ready to come on stream and that meant more 911s.

So 1987 wasn't all doom and gloom as Porsche showed off the Carrera Club Sport, almost a throwback to the 1973 Carrera RS Sport. Out went non-essential items like soundproofing, electric seat adjustment, powered windows, the rear seats and even the passenger's sun visor. In the UK though, buyers were treated to a radio and underseal, vital to fight against the salt strewn roads. Despite engine modifications and engine management tweaks Porsche made no great claims for performance or even weight saving, not least because it was heavier than the old RS, but then it was a much more modern and solidly built car.

The groovy open top Speedster.

The Speedster was announced in 1987, though not launched for another year. Its name meant an awful lot, not least the fact that James Dean had a Type 540 Speedster in 1954. That sadly did not end well, but the new Speedster was very popular. Essentially it was a modified Cabriolet. There was a dinky raked back windscreen that taller drivers could see right over whilst the whole car weighed 70kg less than a proper Cabriolet. Incredibly that screen could be unbolted completely though why anyone would want to do that has never been properly explained. The bubble pack rear canopy replaced the rear seats and covered the basic soft-top mechanism. There was even a Club Sport model which had a lowered racing seat, a tubular steel roll over bar and a weird canopy that covered the front of the car and had a thin tinted plastic windscreen.

Now an all-new Porsche is always something of an event. An 87% new 911 was certainly cause enough for celebration in 1989 with the Carrera 4 and the Carrera 2 in 1990. The internally designated 964 was something that Porsche needed rather urgently as the brand went off the boil in the late '80s and sales started to dip.

The basis for the new model was Porsche's ubersupercar in the shape of the limited run 959 (please see the Wundercar Chapter for further details). New engine, brakes, suspension and transmission were at the heart of the new package. The fresh Carrera shape shared some of the 959's blunted beauty and the polyurethane bumper design cues from the 944 and 928. One of the defining features was the trick spoiler. Out went the '80s tea tray and in came the '90s high tech solution that automatically moved up into downforce mode at 50 mph rather than just lying there waiting to work.

The old torsion bar suspension, around since the 356 era, and responsible for many a 911 novice reversing through a hedge, went into the skip. In came coil springs at each corner, with MacPherson struts up front and at the back with dampers and familiar trailing arms. But it was the small irritating things that were changed and transformed the 911. These included the less infuriating and more efficient computer controlled heating/ventilation system. Also the handbrake was repositioned, the fascia seemingly unchanged since 1963 got a mild makeover whilst the pedals were conventionally hinged. Well maybe I should have mentioned this earlier but originally the pedals were mounted from the floor which many found odd. Now, they hung down from the bulkhead just like a normal car.

The 4's four-wheel drive system was computer controlled but not as rocket ship complex as the 959's. The central differential split the torque by delivering 31% to the front wheels and 69% to the back. It was heavy though and at 1450kg almost tipped the scales at the 959's fighting weight. The new engine was increased in size to 3600cc and the output raised to 250 bhp. That translated into a 0–60 mph time of just over 5 seconds and a top speed limited to 155 mph. It was fast, but most of all it was a proper all weather Porsche with a new power steering and ABS system all helping to boost driver confidence. The enthusiasts who wanted involvement had to wait for the Carrera 2.

The whole set of 911s as they looked by 1993, from left the Speedster, then the 30th Anniversary Coupé and the Cabriolet. Bringing up the rear is the Turbo.

The 2 shared the same bodywork, interior, engine brakes and gearbox as the 4 except that it was rear-wheel drive. However, the Carrera 2 was slightly lighter, marginally quicker and demonstrated what a giant leap forward this new 911 set-up was. There was no reason to be that frightened of a 911 on the limit any more. It was offered with both the five-speed and a new four-speed automatic Tiptronic transmission. Both the Carrera 2 and Carrera 4 were available in Coupe, Targa and Cabriolet. The other additions to the range included the stripped out 260 bhp Carrera RS in 1991, and in 1993 a Speedster body based on the 2, the 911 Celebration (30 years of 911) based on the 4 and a 300 bhp RS 3.8.

With its job of civilising the 911 done, the 964 range was retired in 1993.

So perhaps I should have gone off and sold those high profit Porsches then? Well the thing is that at Park Lane we already had an ex Porsche salesman who had jumped ship to BMW because there was always a waiting list for Porsches. That meant earning money was guaranteed but desperately slow in arriving and there wasn't much scope at all for improvising. At Porsche you were selling largely to one type of customer, but with a BMW you could get the family man or woman, company buyers, private buyers, old rich geezers who wanted a 7 Series, young thrusters who needed a 3, it was great.

So moving to Porsche was never an option as there was no way to make decent money. I did though see a 911 in the Park Lane underground car park over one long bank holiday weekend. This white cabriolet was part of a complicated series of swaps among sales managers. It was one of the few cars ever to provoke wolf whistles from cynical, seen it all, hard to impress car salesmen. That's why, as long as there is Porsche, there will always be a 911.

Porsche 911 vs The Rest

Alfa Romeo Montreal – Supercar made out of more humble Alfa parts with a great big V8 and lots of rust.

De Tomaso Pantera – American V8 in an Italian body. Looked good, very fast, very brutal. Elvis apparently shot his.

Lotus Esprit – Italian styling, sports car handling and mid engine. Not quite the perfect combination as Lotus build quality a bit flaky. James Bond sunk his.

TVR Turbo – 140 mph and 60 mph in under 6 seconds, a recipe for outrageous behaviour and spectacular breakdowns.

Ferrari 308 GTB – Pretty and pretty fragile, won't do the daily grind, but that's not the point.

Renault GTA Turbo – Very bloody quick indeed, 165 mph. Fairly pretty fibre-glass body and the handling wasn't half bad, just a shame about the badge really.

Porsche 924 vs The Rest

Alfa Romeo Alfasud Sprint – Very pretty indeed, great engines, but rust obviously.

Lancia Monte Carlo – Mid engined, not that quick, basically a big Fiat X1/9.

Fiat X1/9 – As above but smaller, rustier.

Nissan Sunny ZX – Ugly in all its bodykitted glory. Quite nifty, but the words Nissan and Sunny were never going to help. Follow up Silvia ZX only slightly better.

Toyota MR-2 – Cute, mid engined, pocket rocket. MG Midget for the new generation and a million times more entertaining and better built.

Porsche 944 vs The Rest

Alfa Romeo Alfetta GT/GTV – Yet another gorgeous shape and equally fine engines. Interior a bit of an ergonomic disaster, and there will always be rust.

Lancia Gamma Coupe – Handsome, but it's a Lancia, so rust and rubbish build quality.

Honda Prelude – Well-built, great engines, very dull to look at.

Mazda RX-7 – Wankel engined coupé that is good looking and makes a great turbine whine. Well built, quick, just a bit thirsty and lack of charismatic badge.

Mitsubishi Starion – Chunky and purposeful and not remotely handsome, but brutal turbo delivered performance aplenty.

Nissan 200SX – Anonymous styling, but turbo engine and rear-wheel drive a potent combination.

Toyota Celica GT – Excellent engine, good standard equipment and great value. Proof that the Japanese were the real threat.

TVR 350i/390i – The most wedge shaped coupé ever. Rover V8 makes a lovely sound. Cheap enough to compete with 944, though performance very 911.

Porsche 928 vs the Rest

Aston Martin Vantage – Proper old school and it has to be said old-fashioned supercar. 170 mph and all that. Old school charm of course.

Jaguar XJS – As cramped as a 928 inside, but original V12 would top 155 mph. Less than pretty styling and below average build quality.

Bristol 412 – British bruiser, as square as the 928 is rounded. Also, rather more expensive.

Lotus Eclat/Excel – Plastic, pretty, great to drive, but it is a Lotus. So build quality patchy, needs looking after.

Nissan 300ZX – Fairly awful Z cars by this stage. Cheap, fairly fast, managing 149 mph, but otherwise a big useless coupé.

Audi Quattro vs The Rest

Alfa Romeo 33 4 x 4 – Not a hardcore rally weapon, just useful when it is a bit muddy or snowy. Only 1.5 engine, so quite underwhelming.

Ford Sapphire RS Cosworth – Very late to the 4 x 4 party in 1990, but very practical and well built. Bodykit not for everyone and about as subtle as a 911.

Lancia Delta Integrale – Arguably the only true rival to the Quattro, which went on to win rallies too. Not as solid as Quattro obviously.

Subaru XT Coupe – Had all the right ingredients, Turbo and 4WD, but styling pretty awful, all right angles and plastic. Gimmick laden console didn't help it. Only mad people bought it.

Toyota Celica GT-Four – Another World Rally refugee and another turbo powered success. Expensive but worth it.

In the Cassette Deck ...

 Roxy Music – Avalon By the '80s you just referred to them as Roxy and the Music provided the background to countless middle class, dream home, dinner parties. In the car it was perfect too, helping you to steer a large BMW or Mercedes around the West End in a seriously smooth manner which always impressed the ladies. At least there was no fruity cassette cover to cause any distraction.

9 Der Panzerwagen, the Batmobile and Glaseratis

Heavy, comfy, indestructible and quick – how the Germans did coupés and convertibles.

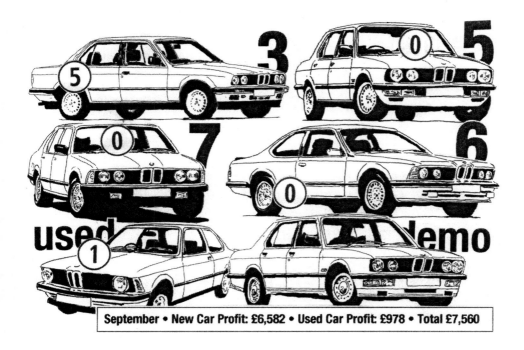

September • New Car Profit: £6,582 • Used Car Profit: £978 • Total £7,560

Selling a car was always a huge thrill. Of course it had an awful lot to do with the commission that I would earn and in a good month I'd get a bigger percentage of the profit. Salesman had a minimum wage, which was £6000 per annum. On top I would get 5% of the profit, but if you hit the monthly target then it would rise to 7.5% and on to a maximum of 10%. Plus I could get commission on aftermarket parts. The best one was air conditioning. We could charge factory money for it, because at Brentford there was a small insignificant bloke who was once pointed out to me as, 'the most important man in the company'. He had the tools and the skills to plumb in air con in a day, and we charged the full factory price, so it was a great payday for everyone.

Some sales were a bit more special and memorable than others and a 6 Series sale definitely fell into that category. There were never very many around, and they were not that easy to sell when you had customers measuring it against a 911. That's not to say that the 6 Series did not have a huge amount of raw appeal. The shape was dated, but it still looked purposeful and stylish enough. I can still remember driving a white 635CSi, with those £50 side stripes and rather more pricey red leather, to the middle of the City early one morning. It was warm and bright outside, inside it was all brand new creaking leather and ice-cold air conditioning. The bloke who bought it had been looking out of his office window and seen me arrive, then ran out of his Dolphin Square office in his red braces. He couldn't stop smiling. It was one of those moments that summed up the '80s for me.

Then there was someone who in the pre M635 era wanted a manual 635, but with the close ratio dogleg 'box. In case you wondered it meant that 1st gear was where 2nd usually was, so engaging the first meant across and down which looked a little bit like a line drawing of a dog's tail on top of the gear lever. Anyway, I had to take a substantial deposit for that one, as management would have kittens if he cancelled and it meant taking it into stock. He didn't let me down, paid the balance and screeched away from Park Lane to the delight of onlookers.

I couldn't forget a fairly scary Merchant seaman who desperately wanted a 6 Series. Luckily I had an ancient part exchanged 633i that would be within his budget. That was my first mistake as sorting out these '70s cars cost a fortune. Brakes, some paint, suspension, it seemed to go and on. But at least I had built all that expenditure into the price. Preparing the car seemed to go on forever and Captain Haddock had sailed the Seven Seas at least once by the time it was finally ready. There were lots of phone calls to Mrs Haddock and by the time he was back on shore leave, he was using some proper sailor language. If it wasn't ready he was definitely going to make me walk the plank. It's amazing what a set of very expensive sheepskin rugs can do to placate a customer who is about to kick off.

Perhaps my most memorable 6 Series encounter of all involved a gentleman called David Hart and a test drive of a 635CSi. Ah yes, test drives, these were interesting and sometimes very dangerous interludes that interrupted an otherwise profitable day. Where possible I would try and avoid the whole traumatic episode. "Do you really need to drive it, this is a BMW Sir/Madam." A surprising number agreed with me. For some it was their first time in a powerful car, and to mix that in with a damp Hyde Park Corner and rear wheel could be a recipe for disaster. Only once in a 3 Series did I have to stop a bloke from driving after he clipped a curb and missed a gear and almost made me revisit my breakfast. It was up to me to qualify each customer and make the decision as to whether they were serious enough to spend some quality time with me and one of my cars.

The way it was supposed to work is I would drive first to show how it should be done. Smooth gear changes, gentle braking and careful progress into the serene surroundings of Hyde Park. Once there I would stop the car and get out, remembering to take the keys with me, otherwise it was all too easy to lose the car as well as the customer. Then I would make sure they were comfy and the mirrors and seat in the right position before driving back to the underground car park. Usually the West End was so busy the rest of the journey was safe, slow and usually resulted in a signature at the bottom of the order form.

Mr Hart had a public school voice and a swanky address nearby in Knightsbridge which was a good enough excuse for me to take a 635 out of the garage and around to his place for a test drive. The terraced house was impressive and the door answered by a secretary. His office was full of books and papers with several telephones on his desk, one of which he was barking into. Hart looked exactly like he sounded, a sort of Lord Lucan alike with a bushy moustache and Brylcreemed-back hair. Once he saw me, he was keen to get outside and on with the drive and against convention I found him in the driving seat and was meekly handing him the keys.

When I asked what he did for living he was mysteriously vague. He said that he 'helped' the government and as I later discovered was right at the very centre of politics in the country. It was 1984 and this was his year. An Old Etonian he was then involved with helping rebel miners fight the year-long strike that had been called by the National Union of Mineworkers. His detractors and enemies accused him variously of being an agent of the CIA, the KGB and Mossad and quite possibly of all three. Many believed that he was possibly rather more Walter Mitty than 007, but as a member, for a time anyway, of Mrs Thatcher's inner circle his influence was very real. In my short time in his company Hart was an extreme force of nature, which was apparent the moment that the 635 reached a three-figure speed.

'Test Drive' was something that Mr Hart took literally in his search for a wide open stretch of road in the centre of London. He settled on The Mall, flicked the automatic gearbox down in second and then moved it up manually. As the revs screamed, I saw a hundred and something on the speedometer and Buckingham Palace growing larger in the windscreen.

I thought it was pointless to protest, but I genuinely thought that we were going to crash and die or at the very least be hunted down by the SPG (Special Patrol Group – the nearest thing we had to a paramilitary police force at the time) and shot. Perhaps Hart did have undue influence and he'd told Mrs T that he would be charging around around the W1 postal district in a BMW, so don't shoot. Well, after the high speed section where I had braced myself against the dashboard, it was now the handling part of the test drive around bits of Chelsea and Knightsbridge that I barely recognised as they became a blur. There was tyre smoke, audible screams from pedestrians and a fairly constant stream of badinage from Hart. I have to say, it really was quite a lot of fun. It sort of made up for not selling a 6 Series. I think that perhaps he had not much spying to do for an hour or so one afternoon and this was a way to fill it. Never mind, I am glad I met Hart and the world is probably a less interesting place for him no longer being in it as he passed away when I was finishing this book.

Almost anything to do with 6 Series was never less than interesting. That's because the art of the coupé is a very particular one and ideally they are special cars that should deliver a very unique experience. Not every company can do it, hence the Morris Marina. To really succeed it has to be stylish, eye catching and fairly quick. A good coupé has to be so much more than just a saloon with the rear doors welded up. It's something that BMW realised and when they launched the CS range it soon became one of the prettiest, fastest and greatest coupés of the last century and one of the finest BMWs ever.

Actually the original 2000CS wasn't in all honesty the most handsome of beasts, but it was developed into a legend after a restyle and 6-cylinder engines transformed its fortunes. Not only did the coupé look good, in CSL form it went on to dominate track racing in Europe and America. Batmobiles meant lightweight BMW coupés first and caped crusader transportation last. Certainly the CS never came cheap, but then it really did look and behave just like the competition whether it was Porsche, Jaguar, or Ferrari. Catch sight of BMW's '60s iconic shape and it reminds you just how beautiful, elegant and impressive these cars were. After the CS, BMW coupés always had a lot to live up to. In the very beginning there was the 503 Coupé which preceded the stunning and more muscular 507 both designed by Count Albrecht Goertz. The 503 was a large elegant coupé with 3168cc, 160 bhp V8 power built from '56 to '59, so more on these later.

However, BMW were torn between producing cars that would re-establish their performance reputation and those that would satisfy the practical demands of the marketplace. The 1955 Frankfurt Motor Show was perfect demonstration of this. On one part of the stand were the super sexy 507 and 503 sports models and on the other was the Bubble car, better known as the Isetta. So how did BMW get into this baffling position where they had the sublime 507 and the ridiculous, but useful Bubble?

Mercedes 190SL, expensive but profitable.

Blame Mercedes. In the early 1950s BMW Sales Manager Hanns Grewenig wanted to broaden the range with a sports car that would utilise the lightweight V8 used in the big Baroque saloon. What prompted BMW into action was Mercedes and in particular their spectacular gull wing 300SL aimed specifically at the American market. I've arbitrarily decided that the 300SL is a supercar so you will find that in the Wundercar chapter. However, just as BMW were showing their 507 and 503 models in 1955, Mercedes unexpectedly launched what was in effect a scaled down 300SL with a monocoque body. Like the 300SL it was based on a saloon car and in this case it was the 190 series. Not surprisingly the 190SL did look like a mini me 300SL, which was certainly a good thing, but obviously it was much slower with its 1897cc engine. That didn't matter, because this was a softer touring version of the grown up Mercedes, a sort of upmarket Triumph TR that wouldn't break down.

Available as both a coupé and open roadster, but they were one and the same. The Coupé just had a detachable hardtop with an optional soft roof so you could get the best of both worlds. The doors, boot lid and bonnet were all made from aluminium to save some weight. Discontinued in 1963 it was incredibly successful particularly in America and more than 25,800 were sold. That's rather more than the 412 and 253 that the 503 and 507 managed.

BMW 503. Big slow and expensive and not profitable.

It was Max Hoffman, an expatriate Austrian and probably the largest and most influential importer of cars to the USA, who brought a lot of influence to bear on the decision to go ahead with the project to build those BMWs. He also persuaded the Count to submit his designs to Munich. The 503 was based on the V8 powered 502 saloon, which was itself a big old barge of a car. Available as both a cabriolet and a coupé, what mostly counted against it was a high asking price and fairly ponderous performance.

BMW 507. Small, quick and expensive and still not profitable. But pretty.

By comparison the 507 seemed like a much better prospect. Certainly the designer Count Albrecht von Goertz was a very colourful character. Despite the title and an ancestral home in a 13th century pile in Hanover, Goertz was more of a 'free spirit' rather than a stuck up member of the aristocracy. Consequently he travelled first to England and then America where he worked on the West Coast. In fact, he was one of the original customisers building hot rods and specials. After serving in the American military during the war, his first real job in the motor industry was as an apprentice stylist with Studebaker. It did not take him long to go it alone though, and by 1952 had set up his own design studio in New York. That brings us to 1954 and the design brief from BMW which was essentially to capture the spirit of the legendary pre-war 328 roadsters and also be a measured response to the Mercedes 300SL.

The 507 succeeded in being beautiful, as well as much smaller and more wieldy than the 503. However, it was mechanically very similar to the bigger car, but there was much less bodywork, making it far more responsive (124 mph top speed and 60 mph arriving in 8.8 seconds). The muscular styling was very clever as the 507 could be ordered as a roadster or with a hardtop, and instead of looking like an afterthought the top integrated brilliantly with the rest of the car. It should have been a contender of course but like the 503, the 507 proved to be ferociously expensive. $9000 was an awful lot of money in the 1950s. BMW had miscalculated yet again and could only look enviously on as Mercedes made premium cabriolets and coupés that the world wanted to buy.

BMW wanted to be just like Mercedes with their desirable coupés and convertibles, and with perfect middle class couples buying them. This is a 250S from the mid 1960s.

Initially Mercedes had relied on the 220 with pre-war styling to re-establish the marque. From 1956 a modern monocoque chassis and a completely restyled 220S and 220SE were mid sized coupés and convertibles for the modern era. Mercedes also did luxury coupés and convertibles too with limited production 300s, which had slightly detuned 300SL engines so they didn't hang about. For 1961 the 300 had a complete makeover with the more contemporary squarer styling. It featured the engine of the 300S and SL and the chassis of the 220SE. The resulting 300SE had air suspension and a full rear seat and tapped into the very well off buyer who wanted practicality and comfort. The 220 sold in very decent numbers, the coupé more than 66,000 and the cabriolet almost 16,000. By contrast the 300 coupé managed over 1500 and cabriolet over 3100, but these were highly profitable sales and took the company through to 1965. Meanwhile BMW were still getting things wrong.

3200CS looked good, but sold poorly. Had strong bonnets though.

After the less than sparkling performance of the 503 and 507, BMW were determined to make use of the V8 engine and in 1962 it appeared in the 3200CS, the real forerunner of the next generation of coupés. The body designed by Nuccio Bertone was airy, rounded and pretty. Already the trademark C pillar dogleg kick was clearly visible. However, with bodies built in Turin and then trimmed in Munich this complicated and bespoke approach was at odds with the mass production success story of the New Class. Not surprisingly just 603 were sold.

Oddly that wasn't quite the end of the BMW V8 sports car. In 1967 they acquired a bankrupt sports car manufacturer called Glas. Like the 3200CS, Frua also designed these in Italy. They were nicknamed Glaseratis because (as you may have already guessed), of their resemblance to contemporary Maseratis. Once BMW took control they wore the distinctive blue and white roundel just in front of the bonnet, but the kidney grille was not incorporated. That's because BMW had other things, namely expansion, on their minds. So the Dinggolfing factory slowly stopped making any type of Glas when in 1969 they switched over full time to BMWs.

Glas V8, complete with BMW badge. A Glaserbimmerati then.

Meanwhile, Mercedes were concocting one of their most successful coupé/cabriolets ever when in 1965 they unveiled the SL to a stunned and very welcoming world. A classic from the day it was launched the SL carried on from where the old 190SL had left off and offered levels of refinement and comfort that customers were starting to expect. W113 was the model code and it didn't prove in the least bit unlucky.

Because the W113 was also expected to follow in the tyre tracks of the 300SL it was never going to be underpowered, but it was intended to be a very sophisticated package. The beautifully restrained and uncluttered lines were drawn by Paul Bracq. An optional hardtop with a concave roof gave the model its nickname, 'Pagoda'. This design was adopted to make the glass area bigger and the view out of the side windows better. Which is nice, but it does not look particularly Japanese or something you might want to put in your garden. Actually the SL was a car you really wanted to drive and it would even do 120 mph without any fuss.

Mercedes 230SL, Pagoda roof visible, but not the actual 'pagoda' bit.

Derived from the 220SE saloon the original 230SL had a larger engine and although it was never going to replace the hardcore 300SL it sort of filled the gap between that and the softer 190SL. The suspension was fully revised, technically it had a low pivot rear swing axle, which meant on the limit handling was excellent. This was surprising for what looked like the sort of car which would be more at home in the narrow, crowded but monied streets of Monaco showing off. In fact, racing drivers loved them, everyone from our own Stirling Moss, to Juan Fangio and Jack Brabham had them. The last two also ran Mercedes dealerships.

An interim 250SL had a 2.5 litre engine, followed in 1968 by the 280SL. Yes the SL was getting heavier, slower, at 114 mph, than the original 230SL. So was there a chance for BMW to steal back the initiative?

Just as the new SL was coming out in 1965 BMW turned their attention to their coupé range and the lines of the 3200CS were echoed, but not exactly followed with the 2000C and CS coupés. From the windscreen back it was fine, but that pig nosed snout was a design disaster. Heavier and much more expensive than the equivalent saloons the 2000C had just 100 bhp and a single Solex carburettor to help it along. Fortunately the twin carburettor CS developed a more respectable 120 bhp thanks to the 2000Ti's engine. Karmann's Osnabruck works produced 11,720 of them for BMW until 1968 when the CS coupé suddenly got handsome and a six-cylinder engine.

Yes the 2000C really was this ugly.

The new E9 (as it is only known to diehard fans) was the real thing. Essentially what buyers got was the basic rear two thirds of the earlier 2000C style with the front superstructure of the E3 saloon. So up front there were McPherson struts with a semi-trailing independent rear end. It was three inches longer, whilst the track was 4.5 inches wider. Gone was the pig's snout front end and in came the very distinctive quad headlamps and prominent kidney grille shark nose first seen on the E3 saloon.

Under that restyled bonnet was the powerful M30 6-cylinder engine. The 2788cc carburettor unit produced 170 bhp, had a top speed of 128 mph and could get to 60 mph in around 8.5 sec. Even so the 2800CSs was not perfect. For a start it was heavier than the saloons, there was a bus sized steering which made the handling feel a little less than quick and stopping could be a problem because the CS had to make do with rear drum brakes. Also, that beautiful body with its delightfully thin pillars was prone to just a degree or two of scuttle shake. And when it wasn't wobbling it was rusting. In common with all cars from that period, rustproofing and prevention was not really an issue, but on the UK's salt strewn roads it meant that the CS literally fell apart. Never mind, it was beautiful. However, the beautiful people who bought it still thought that a BMW ought to be faster.

3.0CS. Very pretty, fast and reassuringly expensive.

In March 1971 the 2.8CS was replaced by the 180 bhp 3.0CS which still relied on Zenith carburation, but delivered a 132 mph top speed and 60 mph in 8 seconds. Braking was now improved with the addition of 10.7-inch rear discs. Chassis tweaks and wider Michelin tyres certainly improved the handling. Getrag and Borg-Warner now supplied manual and automatic gearboxes. All this cost a staggering £5299. Back then it amounted to a substantial fortune and would have put a Porsche, Ferrari or Jaguar on your drive. Here was proof, if anyone needed it, that BMW had arrived as a premium brand because buyers were prepared to pay that much for something so elegant and capable. Then again it was also worth waiting a few months because something even more exciting was waiting to be launched.

Which brings us back to Mercedes. The SL had returned and it was bigger and arguably better than ever. It is worth reminding ourselves what SL actually stood for and that was 'sehr leicht' or 'very light'. The W113 may have been heartbreakingly pretty (and had several aluminium panels) but it had been piling on the pounds, 300lb (136kg) plus actually. Over the years as the engine size went up and an automatic gearbox became standard a 280SL would tip the scales at 3550lbs (1613kg) or so. For the most lucrative market in the world though, this was a good thing. The Americans really appreciated the scrumptious build quality, loved the creamy comfort and the icing on the SL shaped cake was of course its unfussy style. It was the perfect combination for the rich movers and shakers. Read the brilliant exposé of Hollywood in Julia Phillips' *You'll Never Eat Lunch in this Town Again* and the only cars that mattered on the West Coast in the '70s and '80s were SLs and SEs. Apart from a few mentions for a crappy but reliable Mazda when Phillips was at a low ebb, it is studio to soundstage or Wiltshire Boulevard to Sunset Strip, Mercs. So is it any wonder that they built an SL just for America?

The SL, perfect for the beautiful people in Hollywood, even if they had ugly habits.

In fact the SL had always been aimed at America from the 300SL onwards, but this new one was designed specifically with all the known North American regulations in mind. Over engineering had become a matter of pride and the internal nickname was 'der Panzerwagen' whereas the official designation was W107 (R107 for the SL).

It just meant armoured car and obviously being a Mercedes it had a safety cell, but there were no concessions to lightness as it was completely made of steel that was arranged to protect and serve. The 'hewn from solid' cliché started here as the huge doors were designed to withstand serious side impacts. Rather than door buttons there were pull handles to prevent them springing open on impact. The windscreen pillars were computer designed to cope with any roll over situation whilst rain channels incorporated into them directed water away from the screen.

If one of the styling themes was solid, the other was clearly rib. Although the lights had been ribbed for over a decade on the saloons the self-cleaning principle was taken a stage further by incorporating it into the lower bodywork. It too was supposed to deflect water and dirt and help keep the bodywork and side windows clean.

There was a lot of S-Class in the new SL including the modernized suspension, a semi-trailing arm rear end and the smaller V8s in 3.5 or 4.5 litre sizes. However, the coming fuel crisis led directly to the 2.8 litre six-cylinder making the mildly more economical 280SL. Oh yes and there wasn't just an SL, we had a whole new family of Mercedes cars to love. The SLC (C107) came as a proper coupé and not simply with a bolt on Pagoda roof, which was of course still an option on the SL.

Like the reg plate says it's a 350SLC.

With a wheelbase that was a substantial 14.1 inches (35.8cm) longer and 1.8 inches (4.6 cm) taller, the SLC now provided real rear seats. Not everyone liked the ribbed, or rather louvred rear pillar, which filled some of the gap where the rear side window should have been. But because it was Mercedes' tradition that these windows should be wound down to create a pillarless open expanse, the pesky rear wheel arch got in the way. So the compromise was the ribbed rear fillet that looked just a bit like a curtain, leaving room for a smaller window. That was the only criticism, which could realistically be made about the SLC. It was a very coherent design and looked all the better for being stretched into a coupé. Some commentators thought it had only been developed to compete in long distance rallies, which it did, and very successfully too; it won the Ivory Coast Rally you know. Another solid, sensible and profitable car from Mercedes.

BMW, however, were starting to move in the other direction and slowly developed a sporting range of coupés. The 200 bhp 3.0CSi with Bosch D-Jetronic fuel injection system was the first be used on a BMW in September 1971. A higher engine output and longer final drive meant 140 mph and 0–60 mph in 7.5 seconds. By 1975 3.0CSi had moved through the alphabet to the evolutionary 'L Jet' Bosch fuel injection. In the four years these models were to run, Karmann built 11,063 CS, and 8199 CSis. However, big engines were going out of fashion as the oil crisis began to bite in late '73. BMW's response in June 1974 was the 2.5CS. It probably didn't save much of the earth's resources (it could return 30mpg on a good day) and rejoiced in steel wheels, just 150 bhp and a despecified interior. Such a grim CS never made it to the UK. It's a good job then that the fuel crisis didn't arrive two years earlier or we would never have enjoyed the CSL.

A CSL in all its bewinged glory.

BMW produced 1,039 CSLs between 1971–75, just 1,000 were needed for homologation purposes. L stood for leicht (lightweight) and was the key to the car's improved performance with a top speed of around 135 mph and 0–60 mph took 7 seconds. The suspension was made stiffer with progressive rate coil springs and Bilstein gas-shocks. Lighter gauge steel, aluminium opening panels, manual Plexiglas side windows, lightweight Scheel bucket seats, no sound-deadening and with only one glassfibre bumper at the rear. So yes it was light. In the UK, the concessionaires could not be convinced that there were customers for such cars. UK CSLs (all 500 of them) had the 'City Pack' comprising power steering, bumpers, glass windows and soundproofing making them only 101kg lighter than the standard CSi.

Then in August 1972 the 3003cc 3.0CSL replaced the 2985cc 3.0CSL, with a larger bore and fuel injection. The big news though was in August '73 with the arrival of the 3153cc CSL, better known as the Batmobile. That's because all those wings and things had a purpose, well on the track anyway. That huge rear wing was usually sold in knock down form, so when customers bought it there was a self-assembly kit in the boot. Presumably this was so the buyer didn't feel so embarrassed about it. Two days in a wind tunnel helped ensure that that CSL stayed glued to the track and stopped shredding tyres. Hence the deep front spoiler, tiny fin 'splitters' on top of the front wings, and a roof-mounted scoop to divert air over an inverted wing on the boot. It apparently converted a 60kg rear end lift at 124 mph into a down force of 30kg.

With or without wings, though, the CSL was a great car, but it was never very cheap. In 1972 it cost a substantial £6,400 and anyone who stumped up for a Batmobile in 1974 paid around £9,000. In all, just 44,254 CS coupés were made and despite their beauty and power rust proved that they were fallible, almost mortal. That makes the CS and the CSL in particular so rare and so desirable.

I never got to drive a CSL, but I did get to see one very close up. At Park Lane's Brentford based service centre there was a multi-storey car park which comprised four floors of what looked like hundreds of RSJs welded together to make a small-scale model of an unfinished tower block, but with ramps. As space was always at a premium it was an ideal place to store cars, especially those waiting for a service or a bit of long-term fettling. One day I had to pick something up from the tower and on one of the middle floors I found myself in the presence of a true legend. Unfortunately something terrible had happened.

The usually handsome front end of a CSL had been cruelly disfigured. It was a tangle of bright silver paint and black bodywork stripes carelessly wrapped in blue tarpaulin. It was like a beautiful woman who had quite a night out and as the make-up ran she was clutching her little blue number to protect her modesty. It was a sight to make a grown man cry, especially one who appreciated a fine car, even when it was bashed up a bit.

I asked for the full back-story and it was a simple one. Bloke crashes CSL. Bloke then gets the bill for repairs. Bloke has sharp intake of breath. Apparently it would have involved rebuilding the car and they had suggested around £9000ish which would have bought you a new one back in 1974 and ten years later would fund a decently turned out 318i. Not something the insurance company involved was willing to consider. As I tried to tug the door open to look inside, I wondered what it would cost to buy. I was gently reminded that there were also storage charges to take into account and the clock had been ticking for several months. Not only that, I still had a Mini Cooper without an MOT. Whereas a CSL without a hand crafted front end was an entirely different financial matter altogether. I'd like to think that the CSL is still there and I'm the only one who remembers and that I could still go and rescue it, but it was probably broken for parts. Well, the few intact parts that were left, like the rear wing, deconstructed and returned to its resting position in the boot.

Getting back to both the E9 CS coupés and E3 saloons, both had done their job by the mid '70s and that was re-establishing BMW as a luxury brand. In particular the CS set the high standard that every subsequent BMW coupé has often struggled to live up to.

Over at Mercedes the SL wasn't getting any smaller or much lighter. 1977's 450SLC 5.0, which despite having a bigger engine was actually a lightweight design, aimed at making it a bit more emissions and mpg friendly. Apart from the engine it looked slightly different with the lower ribbed panels finished in a dark colour, plus a front spoiler and another on the boot. Apparently the drag factor was reduced by 9%, which always helped economy. To add to the lightness, alloy wheels were standardised, and both bonnets and boot lids were alloy too. All this delivered 16 mpg, which was regarded as rather good at the time. That was the least of their worries because the SL, or more accurately the SLC, now had some rather more serious competition.

The sharkish 6 Series certainly had a lot to live up to following on from the stunning and successful CS and lightweight CSL models. However, the circa '68 Wilhelm Hofmeister styling had grown old and the interior was getting dated too on those models. Something fresh was needed for the cutting edge '70s executive who wanted to arrive fresh for their pan European meeting after a blast from the other end of the autobahn.

630CSi. Simple, elegant and airy design.

Sechs, six, and indeed 6 may be the number of the beast, but there was nothing beastly about BMW's new 6 Series coupé. It was stylish, comfortable and quick and had 24 as its very own E number. Any real beastliness would come much later on when Motorsport awarded the coupé the coveted M prefix. No, the 6 Series was born in the smoothy Cinzano era, rapidly made its mark and then positively flourished into the '80s. It was handy on the track too.

Work had started in 1973 on an all-new coupé first by product development guru Bernhard Osswald; it was then completed by his successor Karlheinz Rader-macher. Unveiled at the Geneva show in March 1976 the 6 was longer, lower and wider than the CS series. Paul Bracq who had designed so many Mercedes was responsible for the taut and clean lines. All the traditional BMW styling cues were there, kidney grille, wide bonnet, big boot and greenhouse cabin. Karmann continued to build the beautiful body, but final assembly was at BMW's new Dingolfing factory because Karmann could not guarantee quality standards. Underneath the body was the contemporary 5 Series, with a fractionally shorter wheelbase. That made the 6 series a 2 + 2, rather than a full four seater. Although the legroom was tight and kept rear passengers' flares from flapping, they never really felt claustrophobic, thanks to the airy cabin.

Up front the driver got to play with some interesting gadgetry. The Active Check Control system comprised an impressive display of warning lights, which looked very Star Trek back then. These were just little lights that came on when the engine was started; apply the footbrake and they went out unless anything was wrong. It was simple, quite sweet and made you feel a bit like you were in the cockpit of Concorde and was clearly the shape of on board diagnostic technology to come.

There were three versions. A carburettored 630 CS with the familiar 3.0CS engine pumping out 185 bhp while the US got an L-Jetronic fuel injected model, which produced 176 bhp. At the top of the range was the 633CSi with a 3210cc block producing a handy 200 bhp. A four-speed Getrag gearbox was the standard transmission, or an optional three-speed. Underneath it all was the 5 Series floorpan, chosen to save weight, but the new 6 was 260lbs (118kg) heavier than the old CS and didn't feel any quicker.

635CSi in the snow, which must have been huge fun.

Apparently, BMW boss Eberhard von Kuenheim was keen to outdo Mercedes when it came to quick coupés and the result was the 635CSi. Whilst the Mercedes 450 SLC 5.0 could out-drag the 633Csi, taking the 3.5 litre M90 engine, adding spoilers and wider rims along with beefed up suspension and a 5-speed gearbox meant 140 mph. BMW claimed it was the fastest 4-seat coupé you could buy in 1978. Porsche could have argued that their 928 was swifter, but the rear accommodation in that model was even more marginal.

So at the end of the '70s the 635i was the Crown Prince of European coupés, however the best was yet to come and a new King was going to be crowned, with an M. The M635CSi, which was first shown at the Frankfurt Motor Show in 1983, was very much a track car for the road. Find out more about the M cars in the Wundercar chapter.

Surprisingly not all 6 Series were as brilliant as the M635. According to marketing departments it is always a nice idea to have an entry level model that looks like the real faster, more expensive thing, but is more insurance group or car tax friendly and maybe a bit more economical. None of that applied to the 628i which was rated in group 9 like the 635. Launched in 1979 dealers would register them as demonstrators so they could be sold on the basis of being cheaper than a brand new one. Even so it wasn't actually that cheap and was listed at over £20,000, not that much less (well about £4400 in the early '80s) than a 635. Not only that it was slow, or at least felt slow, it took 9 seconds to

60 mph and would officially do 130 mph. Also it didn't have ABS until '84 and was deficient in the luxury trimmings area.

I actually sold one in 1984 to a girl on the basis that she could get insurance for it. That was fun because she was a student with a fresh driving licence, perhaps the worst combination of all. It took a while to find a company to provide that cover, but it pleased the Finance and Insurance man who organised these things no end, resulting in a great deal of commission based joy. The girl's dad had to cough up a substantial £3000 to cover the premium. At the time a Fiat Panda cost £2098 and that probably would have been a better first car, and cheaper to insure.

The 628i was a special order from 1987, but I don't think anyone actually bothered to buy one after that.

Clearly the M635 CSi was the most exciting thing to happen to the 6 Series during its lifetime. However, the 6 Series was a model that improved when it really needed to. By far the biggest revamp occurred for the 1983 model year when it was completely re-engineered as it was now based on the E28 5 Series. Inside the dashboard looked even better and shared 5 Series style instrumentation. At the front was the 7 Series double-pivot geometry. At the back the angle of the rear semi-trailing arms was reduced from 20 to 13 degrees, all the better to accommodate the clever Trac-Link set-up which transformed the handling. A rear anti roll bar helped and lift off oversteer (that thing where you stop accelerating in a corner and the back end decides to swap places with the front) was greatly reduced with much less roll in corners. Oh yes and it got self-levelling suspension in 1988.

However, by 1989 the 6 Series was looking a little bit past it. The economy was overheating as interest rates soared and anyone who had bought a classic car like a Jaguar E-type as an investment was about to get their fingers seriously burnt. The party was over for the 6 and the final fling was the suitably high specification Highline. That is what manufacturers do when they really, really want you to buy their car. Not because it is cutting edge, or stylish, but because they have thrown the kitchen sink at it. In the Highline's case this amounted to full leather, air conditioning, green tinted glass and memory electric front seats. Now who wouldn't want all that?

Against the SL the 6 Series had a major disadvantage in that the roof was a permanent fixture so it couldn't really compete at all, which was just as well because the SL went from strength to strength. No other company was building a car that came anywhere near it for quality, style or sheer arrogance. You had to admire a car company that kept on adding bigger engines and seeing their sales spiral upwards as a result. For example the SL range was revamped in 1980 with the 500SL leading the big-engined V8 charge (even though these were now lightweight aluminium), which were later joined by 380, 420 and 560 units. It was the biggest 5.6-litre 227 bhp model which found almost 50,000 new homes making it the best seller by some margin. Oh yes and there was also a 6-cylinder 300SL which didn't sell in nearly as many numbers (around 13,700 apparently).

Overall the basic design and structure of the SL was one of the most enduring and even for Mercedes an eighteen-year production run was a very long time. Here was conclusive proof that when it came to stylish open tops, the rich, famous and purely fictional (the Ewing family in the long running soap, *Dallas*) knew that there was only one car for them.

SEC, huge, pillarless and arrogantly impressive.

We haven't mentioned the SLC for a bit and that's because it did not make it past 1981. At this point then it is time to introduce the SEC, effectively a two door S-Class that was probably the real rival to the 6 Series, except that it wasn't of course. Mercedes had done some research. The customers for their models wanted comfort and high technological sophistication rather than all out sportiness, or the latest shape. In effect then they were simply following standard practice whereby they took a luxury saloon and then made a high quality coupé out of it and charged handsomely for the privilege. So the SEC model was designed at the same time as the W126 S-Class, except that its designation was of course, C126.

Although the Mercedes engineers were not that fussed about the sportiness they had to be prepared for it, as the implication of having a two door is that it probably would be driven a lot harder than a big lazy S-Class. Consequently its steering was a bit sharper, but otherwise when it came to engines and transmissions it was all very much S-Class. That meant the first models were badged 380SEC and 500SEC. However the dimensions were different, being an inch and half (3.8cm) lower and almost three and half inches (8.9cm) shorter, but otherwise it was a proper four-seater and any lack of rear legroom wasn't that noticeable because getting in and out through the massive doors was easy, giving access to individual rear seats.

For such a massive coupé it was a handsome beast. The stylists working under Bruno Sacco had produced a car that was unmistakably a Mercedes, although it really wasn't an S with doors missing, as neither model shared any body parts. It had been planned to fit the S-Class bonnet, grille, headlamps and spoilers, but after some prototypes were made it was thought that the wide grille would be better. So although not intended as a sporty car, it did need the full width sport grille as seen on the SLs to give the car its own distinct identity. Like the saloon based coupés of the past the pillarless look when all the windows were lowered meant it had a timeless profile. Mercedes also managed to overcome the problem of where to mount the front seatbelt, which would normally sit patiently two-thirds of the way up a B pillar. Their brilliant solution was to install a telescopic arm that moved out of a plastic cowling and presented the front seat occupants with the buckle of the seat belt. This only happened once the ignition key was turned and a sensor could tell whether there was a passenger in the seat. It was slightly creepy, a bit like having an ever-present manservant in the back seat. So for most SEC buyers it would have felt just like being at home. In America though it was the only way to make sure that they would wear a belt at all.

Like all Mercedes saloons of the time it was designed to be aerodynamic with the windscreen wipers parked out of the slipstream below the bonnet line. The steeply raked windscreen and clever design of the door pillars and guttering meant excess water went up and over the roof instead of clinging to the side windows. This resulted in a drag factor of 0.34, .002 ahead of the saloons. Nevertheless, the mpg figures were not much to write home about, especially as they only weighed 10kg (22lbs) less than the four door. However, 15.7 mpg for the 500SEC hardly put off buyers as this model was an instant success worldwide with an 18-month waiting list for most models. So apart from mild specification tweaks in line with the saloon and larger capacity V8 engines (450 and 560), not much happened until it was replaced in 1991 by the W140 coupé.

BMW had no response to the SEC until that is the 8 Series came along as the decade ended. It seemed to be the right car at the wrong time. Complicated, a bit pretentious and lacking any real charm. Whereas the 6 defined its era, the 8 series was already out of date. But before we sign off with the 8 Series and where BMW were starting to go wrong, at just about the same time Mercedes had prepared a brand new SL that was going to tackle the '90s head on.

After eighteen years of the same shape it was time for a change with the new SL. It was elegant yet brutal, a velvet trimmed knuckle-duster riding on very fat wheels, from its clean shovel front end to the dismissively high rear deck. As always work had started almost a lifetime before it was launched way back in 1981. The engineers certainly put in the hours and it paid off.

An SL in its natural habitat, the Golf Club car park.

Probably the most significant thing about the SL was that all it took to lower the soft-top was the press of a button. 30 seconds of whirring, clicking and snicking followed and in eight easy stages the roof was down. First the windows would drop, then the roll hoop folded back, as the rear lid opened, the hood would raise, its lid shut and finally the roof would tighten as the windows raised. Very majestic. *Car* magazine had a Jaguar XJS as part of a comparison test in their December 1989 issue and its hood was a lot more involved. First two latches were released, then a switch pressed, followed by several minutes of electrical activity topped off with some physical jerks as the driver hid the furled hood beneath a cover involving 14 press-studs, straps, hooks and eyes. Meanwhile the SL's hood had long been stowed beneath a flush fitting steel panel and the driver was well on his or her way. The SL though needed 58 sensors and computers, 89 electric motors and 1.4 miles of wiring to make its particular kind of hood magic happen.

The tricks did not end there because once the driver had locked the doors then every internal compartment from the glove box to the cover over the cassette storage rack was also clamped shut. Now that is attention to detail.

Like every previous Mercedes the SL was built to be rock solid, but with the roof missing it had to be more so. The secret behind the stiffer shell and reduced vibration were two struts each fitted with its own damper, linked to the front suspension carrier and the door sills. Another pair of struts then linked the sills to the spare wheel recess. Even the seats were very impressive structures on their own, cast in one piece of magnesium they were effectively an integral part of the structure. Mercedes built each seat belt into the seat itself allowing the upper mounting point to adjust with the electrically operated head restraint. There was a padded roll hoop, but it was folded well out of sight and would only stand to attention in a third of a second if the sensor believed that the SL was about to topple over. Or as several owners and motor hacks discovered, all four wheels left contact with the road for any reason. Returning the roll hoop into the down position often involved a dealer visit.

An SL still in the golf club car park but with its metal lid on.

Keeping the SL firmly on the road was the ASR anti-slip device, which worked through the ABS sensors so when it detected slip it would first cut the speed by reducing the throttle opening. Then it would gently apply the most appropriate brake. After all, it was easy enough to get into trouble if you exploited the full power available. The engine at the heart of the original, the 500 V8, was a 32-valve development of the S-Class's 5.0 litre producing 326 bhp but with the top speed limited to 155 mph. It would get to 60 mph in 6 seconds without really trying too hard and of course the 4-speed automatic gearbox helped make it all seem so effortless. Certainly the fat eight-inch alloy rims with massive Dunlop D40 225/55ZR16 tyres could put the power down very easily. Soon other engines joined the range, from the 300SL, which had 188 bhp and a 300SL-24 with double the number of valves producing 288 bhp. To top it all though was the frankly outrageous SL600 which improbably had a V12 underneath the bonnet.

Was there anything wrong with the new SL? Well inside the all-black fascia was a bit grim, but no change there really. Also some of the controls were less than satisfactory as the column mounted stalk controlled far too many functions, while the tiny keyboard used to operate the air conditioning was just daft, almost as daft as the teeny tiny air vents. Also, no one outside of the West Coast of America would ever get on with the foot operated parking brake.

It was hard to escape the simple fact that the 500SL was ferociously expensive in 1989 priced at £58,045. At the time you could have the rather more old fashioned V12 Jaguar XJS for that money, plus several brand new spare cars, such as BMW 316i for the other half and even a Metro for the au pair. Tellingly that sort of money didn't put buyers off because even at launch the waiting list stretched into years.

An 8 Series in a field.

So what were BMW thinking of when they launched the E31 8 Series? On the surface it was an '80s mindset convinced that bigger was better. Greed was also good and being grosser than the nearest Mercedes was also a great idea too. The problem was, that no one had properly decided whether this new coupe' was going to be a luxury, or a sports car. Consequently it was neither and not everyone was happy about that, especially when it was more expensive and considerably porkier than the old 6 Series. BMW seemed to admit they had got it slightly wrong when at the 1989 unveiling, Project Manager Peter Weisbarth explained away the fact that this 300 bhp 850i might be the fastest BMW ever built, "We have a social responsibility. Somebody has to stop this nonsense. We have to stop the horsepower race." Well at least the top speed was limited to a highly responsible 155 mph and it still rocketed to 60 mph in under 7 seconds.

So the 8 Series wasn't that bad after all. Indeed with hindsight the 8 Series ought to be regarded as one of the very best things BMW have ever built. A no compromise, no expense spared, over engineered coupé. It was purposeful and if not pretty, then brutish like a Mercedes SEC, though possibly a bit meaner.

The 8 Series had a lot to live up to and that was the problem. Firstly it was no outrageous super car in the mould of the M1. It wasn't even in the same league as the focused M635 and was a world and a crash diet apart from the CSL. In fact, there was no clear link at all with the 507 or even the pre-war 328. The bloodline was definitely biased towards the bulkier and more comfy 327, 503; those Bertone bodied CS coupés and also the standard 635CSi. However, the closest in spirit to the 8 Series was not any BMW past or present, but the massive Mercedes 560 SEC, so the 850 was never really going to be a sports car.

Blame Wolfgang Reitzle. He was BMW's chief engineer. It was his baby, and indeed he realised just what the 850 should have been which explains why he had a custom model built by BMW's own Individual Division. He redesigned the interior and it was powered by a supercharged V12, which was engineered by BMW Motorsport's engine supremo Paul Rosche. So he clearly envisaged some sort of M car and certainly the 8 could have handled lots more power.

Reitzle was especially proud of the rear integral axle. A costly five-link set-up which had a degree of passive rear steer, here was the proof that the 8 Series was a no-compromise engineer's car. It was also the first BMW available with EDC III damper-control. Developed with Boge, MBB and Novotechnik the dampers could be either 30% harder or softer. So intelligent shock absorbers, five sensors and a black box meant that any adjustments could be made in milliseconds to respond to any inputs from the driver or road conditions. Oh yes and there was the option of Servotronic power steering. That was all very clever but there was plenty about the 850 that certainly wasn't.

The 850 was a big car and obviously it had a usefully big boot at 12.7 cubic feet, though not as big as the SEC's 17.8 cubic feet. At least there was room for four in the SEC, because there was naff all knee room in the back of an 850i. Chief Project Engineer Herbert Dormier was quoted at the launch as saying "There is barely enough room in the back for grown-ups, but it's okay for children." Indeed, BMW realised that the token back seats only added weight, mass and length. That meant they rethought a projected convertible strictly as a two-seater, but that was the least of their worries.

Inside an 8 Series. Sumptiously comfy.

At launch there was just the one engine, the 300 bhp 5.0 litre V12 familiar to owners of 750is. On paper the 850i was not as exciting as it ought to have been, taking 7.4 seconds to get to 62 mph in automatic format. By comparison the Porsche 928 S4 auto achieved the same in 6.3 seconds whilst the Mercedes 560SEC auto clocked in at 7.2 seconds. However, the six-speeder 850i, which we never got in the UK until '91, managed the sprint in 6.8 seconds, whereas Porsche's V8 did it in 5.9 seconds and even BMW's M5 managed the charge in

6.3 seconds. Suddenly the 850i seemed like nothing more than a 750i with fewer doors. Weighing in at 4000lbs was always going to be a problem and meant that although the handling was safe, that big mass certainly heaved, floated and drifted around in a very un-BMW manner.

At least the 8 Series looked good. The shape was a slippery 0.29 Cd. The lights were not meant to pop-up as the designers had planned to incorporate the headlamps into the front bumper until legislation ruled that out. However, the side windows were fully retractable, just like an SEC and just like the SEC the absence of B-posts meant that there was perfect cross-flow ventilation and very elegant side profile. Special seals gripped the glass like a solid frame to keep wind noise right down. The main novelty or party trick was casual side window drop when the door was opened followed by automatic closure.

So the 8 Series was clever, but did it get any better? Let's time travel into the 1990s to find out.

It was rebadged in September 1992 as the 850Ci and actually became more practical as the rear seats folded, even more luxurious as the hide trim spread to more panels, and it became even safer when side impact protection beams were installed into the doors. By January 1993 the 850Ci got a tad more capable with the addition of the Active Driving Package. If you are interested, that meant active rear axle Kinematics, electronic damper control III and Servotonic power steering. In the wheels and tyres department, M Technic cross spoke 17-inch split rims were the order of the day with 8Js up front and wider 9Js at the rear plus 235/45ZR and 265/40ZR rubber.

June 1993 was the watershed year, as the 850 became even more powerful with the installation of the 5.6 litre 380 bhp V12. This CSi had Motorsport alloys, limited slip differential and even an electric rear window blind. Rather more important though was the introduction of the 840Ci which took the place of the old 850, but with a 4.0 litre V8 producing 286 bhp and linked up to a five-speed automatic gearbox which would reach an unrestricted 156 mph. Who really wanted, or needed, a V12 now? The answer was not many. So it was no surprise that in September 1994 the 850 Ci was dropped. March 1996 saw the 840Ci's engine upgraded with the 740's 4.4 litre unit and a six-speed manual gearbox became standard.

In January 1997 another 8 Series reshuffle occurred. Now buyers could choose between two models, the 840Ci and Sport. The 'standard' 840Ci came fitted with the five-speed automatic gearbox. The Sport added M system II alloys, M sport suspension, sports seats, steering wheel (which was air bagged), plus an M body kit, which meant spoilers front and rear, plus M-style door mirrors. In many ways this was the sort of coupé that BMW should have built all along. It wasn't perfect, but it did at least have a bit of hard charging attitude about it rather than being a big soft GT.

The 8 Series was supposed to be a big happy family of coupés. Unfortunately the recession in the early '90s meant that all the really exciting versions would never get past the prototype stage. So the cabriolet planned for 1992 was canned. A 230 bhp, 32 valve 3.0 litre 830i was abandoned after 13 prototypes were made. There was even a 400 bhp 5.4 litre version. What we did get in the UK was 585 examples of the 850CSi with a six-speed manual gearbox powered by a 380 bhp 5.6 litre V12 with chassis modifications that were intended for the M8. Ahhh, M8, have I mentioned the M8?

Motorsport certainly had designs on the 8 coupé. A radical, lightweight monster with a four-cam V12 engine. The M8 had a variant of the 5.7 litre CSi engine, which was modified to operate with 48 valves producing 550 bhp. Apparently it was the very same engine which Gordon Murray dismissed when considering what to install in his McLaren F1. Just one M8 was built with a part Kevlar body, PVC windows and no pop up headlamps. It had a stripped out carbon fibre and racing seat equipped interior. It has been described as a Bavarian Ferrari F40. Unfortunately the BMW board couldn't see the point. According to Karl-Heinz Kalbfell at Motorsport, "We would have been proud to build some, we had enough signed blank cheques but it's now a closed business. This car will never be producted but it's good to know that our engineers can build such unique car with a perfect standard car finishing."

The Hockney 8 Series.

At least one 8 Series was a work of art. It joined a long line of BMW coupés that got the world famous contemporary artist treatment. "BMW gave me the model of the car and I kept looking at it and looking at it," said David Hockney in 1995. "And then, I must admit, I also looked at the other Art Cars. In the end I thought, probably it would be good to perhaps show the car so you could be looking inside it."

Several months later the inside out 8 Series emerged with stylised intake manifolds of the engine appearing on the bonnet, and the silhouette of the driver can be seen on the door. And you don't just see the inside of the car, but an abstract landscape. Because, said Hockney "Travelling around in a car means experiencing landscapes, which is one of the reasons why I chose green as a colour." Which is either pretentious boathooks or the nicest thing anyone has ever said about an 8 Series. So did it end well?

At the 8 Series launch in 1989 the production run was set at 10,000 to 12,000 a year and BMW claimed that they were sold out until 1993. Someone was telling porkies though because in its 10-year production run just 30,597 8 Series were made, in all there were 22,776 850s and 7,803 840s. The truth is that there were never enough people willing to pay £60,000 for a GT when there was a full on depression. However, they might have paid £60K for an M8 and maybe £40K for a smaller engined, stripped out 835i.

Essentially then the 8 Series was a 1980s hangover and its nemesis was the SEC. Then there was the 928, spiritually the closest to the 8 Series with a similar slightly remote driving experience, with just as little room in the back. BMW should have learnt from Porsche's mistake. What was crystal clear though is that for buyers who wanted a well built, classy coupé then there was only one country that could consistently supply them. So yes it was German coupés vs The Rest.

BMW 6 Series, Mercedes SL and SLC vs The Rest

Aston Martin V8 – Handbuilt in tiny numbers. Very special, very expensive and far more likely to break down than an SEC.

Aston Martin DBS – Granddad of all the '70s V8s and has dated badly unless you like that big, brutish kind of thing. Lots of power, but that was never officially revealed. It'll do around 160 mph though. Hand built and it'll cost a fortune to fix, just like all the other super '70s stuff.

Aston Martin Virage – Old school Aston meant thumping V8 up front but a more contemporary late '80s aluminium body style. Equally old school was the six-figure asking price. The nearest we Brits got to building an 8 Series. No high tech tricks but impressive handling and power.

Jaguar XJS – Seemed to be around forever and always squared up to the SL, SLC and the 6 Series as the value buy. Yes never mind the quality look at the spec.

Lotus Eclat/Excel – The most conventional models Lotus ever made. Great to drive, but never a day to day proposition like a BMW or Merc.

Nissan 300ZX – Japanese, so well built, otherwise nothing to recommend it apart from the kit list.

TVR 350i /390i – A plastic, wedge shaped coupé with a Rover V8 engine, so there is plenty to love. Brutal compared to the Germans with a distinct whiff of glue. Marvellous.

Renault GTA – A French Lotus which is not a bad thing. Better finished and more reliable too.

Ferrari Dino 308 GT4 – Effectively a Ferrari MPV with room for four, in theory anyway. Angular styling by Bertone not everyone's idea of how the Italian stallion should look. Strong transverse V8 and appropriately impressive top speed of 154 mph.

Ferrari 348 tb – Bigger and bulkier than the old 328, but it was the quintessential '80s Ferrari with a barely noticeable depreciation curve.

In the Cassette Deck ...

 ABC – Beauty Stab A bit of shock to anyone who had crooned along to the 'The Lexicon of Love' but this was harder and far better. I listened to 'SOS' in a 7 Series that pinged at me because it was sub zero outside. ABC were still cool, but they now had a jarring edge with guitars. Very much a 323i with a dogleg close ratio gearbox, subtle, but dangerous.

10 Wundercar – Yes that's right, Fritz invented the Supercar and perfected it.

Loads of letter and number combinations: 300SL, M1, 911 Turbo and C111s

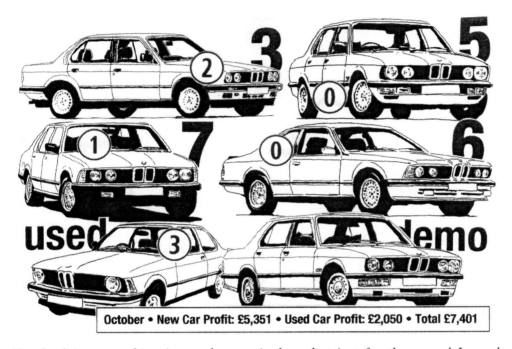

October • New Car Profit: £5,351 • Used Car Profit: £2,050 • Total £7,401

Nearly doing something is utterly meaningless, but just for the record I nearly did sell a supercar.

I once had a very small window of opportunity to try and flog one of the rarest BMWs ever, an M1. Acquired by the Leicester outpost of the Cooper Group it was then shipped down to Park Lane on account of the chances of selling a full-blown supercar were rather better where the density of ready money and shameless show offs was at its greatest.

Parked prominently in the middle of the showroom, the asking price was £50,000. As I remember the SIV, or stand in value – what it owed the company – was in the region of £38K which meant a very good pay day if we could sell it. Not only that, there was plenty of leeway to come to some agreement in the middle £40Ks if we were allowed.

I did have one hot prospect who asked all the right questions on the telephone and did actually turn up in person to take things a little bit further. In the flesh though he was a rather unremarkable person. Spectacles, a side parting, jacket and no tie. He was also English and didn't seem like the sort who was going to shell out that much money, for that sort of car. However, if I had learnt anything about rich people it's that most of them were fairly unremarkable. They just got on with the business of earning lots of money and then quietly spending it with the least possible fuss and drama. It was always the brash, boasting, showroom poseurs who usually had no money and no intention of signing the bottom of an order form.

I had also been taught that you treated everyone with respect until you discovered otherwise. That's why what appeared to be a scruffy hippy was given time to come with the readies for a coupé when he signed on the dotted line as Mike Oldfield. Tubular Bells and all that. A few years later a colleague spent rather a lot of time talking to a pretty, but faraway, girl who 'lived in a cottage with white gates'. Still, he managed to sell Kate Bush, Wuthering Heights and all that, a 3 series cabriolet and find out exactly where she lived.

My first instincts that he wasn't going to buy were proved right as his story changed to acting on behalf of someone else who wanted the M1 and then all contact petered out. At least he didn't muck me about too much and it allowed me to get inside an M1 and play with it for a bit. So I was grateful for the opportunity to get excited about possibly selling a supercar, but the question remains, what actually is a supercar?

Supercar is a relatively modern word coined by the great LJK Setright in *Car Magazine*. It has come to mean something that is incredibly fast with its engine behind the driver built without compromise and any budget in mind. And it would usually be Italian. On that basis the BMW M1 as we shall see would qualify on all those counts. Essentially a supercar is all those important things, fast, sexy, expensive, effectively a racing car for the road, but one that is officially for sale in the showroom.

As for the very first of the supercar breed, well that would be the Lamborghini Countach. It was beautiful, incredibly fast with the engine behind the driver and in 1966 there was nothing else like it, certainly not from the established maker of superfast, super expensive cars, Ferrari, which was Ferrucio Lamborghini's point. However Ford, makers of super practical and super good value cars did in 1964 build the GT40 in Slough. Also intended to smite Ferrari on the track rather than the road, Ford did nominally trim some out for general sale, so maybe that was the first supercar? Then again in the old days engines of very fast cars were up front under the bonnet. So forget about where the engine was because a Ferrari 250GTO would certainly be in the frame. So supercar is clearly a late twentieth century term referring to a brave new world of very fast cars. But just because they weren't referred to as supercars back at the dawn of motoring doesn't mean that they weren't super.

A Vauxhall 30/98 built up to 1922 could do 100 mph. Then there were the

'Blower' Bentleys that in racing trim dominated Le Mans as the Speed-Six and the 8-litre. The Mercedes SSK had a whopping 200 bhp and was possibly the ultimate vintage sports car, which also competed at the highest level in Grands Prix. Bugatti also had a brace of models such as the Type 55, which could power to 120 mph, and the beautiful Type 57, which also had 8 cylinders and similarly outrageous performance for the day. However, all of these very expensive cars were built in relatively small numbers, often just as chassis on which a coachbuilder would plonk whatever the customer ordered on top.

No, the first true supercar needed to be a fully formed model, designed completely by the manufacturer to be sold in the showroom and be road legal. That would be the Mercedes 300SL then.

A prototype racing car, the W194 appeared in 1952 using the 300S's six-cylinder fuel injected engine, which sat in a complex spaceframe chassis. It was a potent combination that went on to win Le Mans taking the top two places. The car was also tough enough to compete in and win the Carrera Panamerica. It didn't seem like the obvious thing to do, and Mercedes were still rebuilding the company after the war, but the decision was made to put this car on the market.

A set of gull wing doors with a 300SL attached. The very first supercar.

Launched in its prime market, North America, in 1954 the most distinctive feature of the W198 was the centre roof aluminium hinged doors. Not only did it look good, these doors which each included half of the roof, were vital to the structural integrity of the vehicle. Indeed, the sill that the driver and passenger slid over was as wide and accommodating as many sofas. I know this because a top of the range 5 Series customer had one in his garage. "Come and have a look at this," he said after I had delivered his new car. As the fluorescents flickered into life I saw his rather old car, a truly wonderful blue 300SL. Up went the door and in I went, it was wonderful. He knew I was a car-fixated life form and just sitting in an SL going nowhere was enough for me. It was definitely my first supercar and it wouldn't be my last.

The 300SL had a long and very low aluminium bonnet, which necessitated the engine being tilted over by 45 degrees to achieve this. The engine produced a substantial 240 bhp, which translated into 140 mph and 60 mph arriving in 8.8 seconds. Despite the breathtaking styling, which had an imposing physical presence with lots of muscular bumps and sinews, it had some serious flaws. The much criticised swing axle rear suspension was difficult to control especially for a novice. Also those who managed to park it upside down in a field then had the problem of just how they would extract themselves from the wreckage. Even in normal use the novelty of the gullwing doors soon wore off and fixing a crashed SL was a complicated and costly business.

300SL, the very first convertible supercar.

Consequently a new 300SL arrived in 1957 with a lot less roof, in fact it was a roadster. This had a so-called low pivot rear swing axle that was a lot more predictable. Being a roadster the doors were much more conventional push open and shut items, rather than the more complicated up and overs. The spaceframe was also simpler and so easier to repair. Also its hood folded neatly out of the way behind a sliding metal cover.

The open SL may not have been nearly as striking as the original model, but Mercedes upped the engine output, which put 150 mph within reach and also built 29 all-alloy models, which saw action as full blown racing cars. Otherwise Mercedes went back to normal with the next SL and all thoughts of gullwing doors were forgotten, well until 1969.

That's the year that the C111 came into my life. It may not actually qualify as a supercar under my rules, as it amounted to a concept car. Often a concept has no engine, is rarely made out of metal, so in no sense is it a proper usable vehicle. It is just a way for manufacturers to show off a bit and part of a plan to get some attention for the rest of their boring range. However, the C111 was different because it wasn't made out of balsa wood and sticky backed plastic, it actually worked and was effectively the test bed for lots of new ideas. To a 9 year old it was real because not only could you buy Corgi and Matchbox models, it was in The Observer's Book of Automobiles.

Up to the point when the C111 arrived, Mercedes had been amongst my more boring toys, such as a blue Husky 220 saloon which had lovely chrome bumpers and sills, but otherwise little to recommend it. I did love my 600 Dinky Toy which was impressive rather than exciting. By contrast the C111 was a big fat wedge of attitude and brought back those brilliantly attention grabbing gullwing doors. To me it looked like the future and if this is what Mercedes were going to look like, then I was going to start saving right there and then.

C111s – More than pretty prototypes these are fully functioning supercars.

Apparently I wasn't the only one to think that Mercedes were going to base racing cars, or maybe their next SL on the C111. Grown-ups did too, ones who wrote for newspapers and magazines. But it wasn't to be and perhaps the engine it used had something to do with it.

Back in 1961 Mercedes took out a licence to make the Wankel rotary engine. There were three rotors, which in conventional engine terms amounted to a size of 3.6 litres and sending its power through a five-speed transaxle. This was carefully positioned in the middle of the car. It was surrounded by a wind cheating, lightweight glass fibre bodywork, which was bonded and riveted to a combined steel frame and floor unit. It produced stunning statistics, a top speed of over 160 mph and it would get to 60 mph in around 5 seconds, comfortably quicker than anything other than a fully prepared racing car. Indeed this was no one off and Mercedes had produced an upgraded C111 within six months, which had even more aerodynamic bodywork with improved all round visibility. More importantly it added yet another rotor to the engine which was now the equivalent of 4.8 litres in size that made it even quicker. More C111s were built, but Mercedes were starting to discover that the Wankel had its drawbacks. Reliability was obviously an issue as NSU with their Ro80 were discovering, but it was the low speed responsiveness that was so disappointing for Mercedes.

As a result the C111 was quietly pushed into a shed and no element of its design or technology seemed to find its way into any Mercedes production model. However the C111 did break cover one more time when in 1976 it was used as the sexy outer covering for the company's new 5-cylinder diesel engine and tuned to 190 bhp it did some record breaking runs at the Nardo test track in Italy. At the time putting a diesel engine in anything but a taxi would have been viewed as highly eccentric. In the twenty-first century it could be seen as highly prescient. Yes the C111 was ahead of its time in using alternative propulsion and fuel systems in what was clearly one of the most super special of supercars, that you couldn't actually buy.

Although the Supercar 1970s might still seem to be largely Italian, with the Lamborghini Countach, Maserati Bora and Ferrari Berlinetta Boxer, there was one old German from the previous decade that still had something to prove, the 911.

Fat arches, fat wheels, flat rear spoiler, yep it's a 911 Turbo.

Now September 1974 was not an especially good time to launch the fastest road going 911 ever. That's because the world had endured an almost cataclysmic energy crisis; luckily enough this car was good enough to ride out that storm. Known internally as the 930 the 911 Turbo had a real purpose and that was to homologate (qualify) for motor racing. Porsche had been here before of course, but with the stripped down, almost hair shirt 2.7 RS Carrera. However the world's first turbocharged sportscar was going to be a five star experience. Porsche chairman Ernst Furhrmann had insisted on creature comforts such as air conditioning, electric windows, electric sunroof and leather trim. Comfy on the inside, it was easy to spot on the outside with its wider wheels covered with massively flared arches, and 'tea tray' rear spoiler. Which wasn't all show of course as it dramatically reduced lift.

However, it wasn't all good news. The big 3.0 litre and 260 bhp provided a massive shove in the back seemingly all at once. When the turbo wasn't blowing hard (this is when drivers discovered something called turbo lag) the four-speed gearbox struggled, plus if the driver misjudged the situation in the wet, or forgot how marginal the brakes could be, then it sometimes ended in disaster. The 155 mph top speed and 0–60 mph in just over 5 seconds were what the buyers really wanted to hear.

In 1988 Porsche managed to fix many of the problems, firstly by installing a bigger engine as the 3.3 litre had 20% more power and reached an almost magical 300 bhp, whilst a new KKK Turbo improved responsiveness. The slightly heavier Turbo could now manage over 160 mph and get to 60 mph in just a tenth over 5 seconds. Many though were now describing this Turbo when compared to the original 930 as a complete Jekyll and Hyde. Obviously completely mad when all the power was being used, but otherwise when doing the daily commute just like a standard 911, it could not be easier to live with. This was despite the handling being ever more dicey when the engine was moved back even further to accommodate a larger clutch. Higher tyre pressures and an even more unmissable rear wing were all meant to help as was a four caliper, servo assisted, cross drilled brake set-up in bringing it all to a halt. What it didn't get though was a five-speed gearbox and customers had to wait until this version of the Turbo was sent for a well earned rest in 1989, before the extra cog arrived for a more relaxing motorway experience.

Porsche's 911 Turbo was a remarkable supercar because it sold in such massive numbers. The first flawed 930 managed to shift an impressive 3,227 which would be considerable for any truly special car, but it was the 3.3, with 17,425, which really put the supercar into the mainstream. For many, the fact that it was always a challenge to drive makes it truly special and the fact that you could see out properly and use it almost normally was a bonus.

Just as the 911 Turbo had been created by racing regulations, BMW's long overdue entry into the supercar field was dictated by the need for speed on the track. Indeed, if the 911 Turbo is here, surely the CSL should be? Well, that's been put somewhere else, it seemed to fit better with the coupés so we will park it there, leaving more room here to tell the story of the M1.

The 1972 Turbo powered concept that inspired the M1.

It is important to remember that even in the 1970s BMW were still a relatively small car manufacturer and they constantly looked for ways to raise their profile. Racing was always a good way of doing that and had clearly worked for Porsche. So when BMW developed a CSL turbo, which had a top speed of 185 mph that left the opposition standing, it was still unreliable enough for the opposition, mainly Porsche 911s and Ford Capris, to leave BMW by the side of the track with the bonnet up. It seemed to BMW that a lightweight rear mounted engined model like the 911 may be one answer.

Well, way back in 1972 BMW seemed to have such a car, because during the opening ceremony for the new four-cylinder building and adjacent museum, a radical new concept had garnered a lot of attention. This was a turbo powered, gull winged mid-engined supercar designed by Paul Bracq who was the styling director. The product chief Bernhard Osswald thought there was much that could be learned by taking this concept further so he got very involved.

At the heart of the car was a steel and aluminium body/chassis. It was powered by the 2002's own turbo engine mounted transversely behind the cockpit just like a proper Italian supercar and used a four-speed gearbox. The all-independent suspension consisted of MacPherson struts front and rear with coil springs surrounding the struts. This was no display only concept as the factory claimed. The engine would get the car to 100 mph in 15.7 seconds, just over 6 seconds to 60 mph and a top speed of 155 mph. However, the original plan was to put a 4.0 litre V12 engine in the concept supercar, which didn't yet exist, but was being considered for a luxury saloon.

M1 in proper PROCAR specification.

Everyone except BMW got excited about it. The E26 as it was officially called went into the museum and stayed there until 1976 when BMW realised that they could homologate a new car for Group 4 racing. There still wasn't a V12 but at least the very excellent 6-cylinder units could be massively modified. Designated the M-88 the 3.2 engine was increased in size to 3.5 litres. It was mounted longitudinally as it was too long to be transversely installed and anyway that meant it would be more reliable and efficient. Engineer Rosche took a four valve cylinder head that had been developed for the CSL and these were serviced by overhead camshafts. Fuel injection, dry sump lubrication and digital electronic ignition were all part of the propulsion package. This M-88 was produced in three stages of tune, a 277 bhp for the road, which could still get to 62 mph in 6 seconds and manage more than 160 mph top speed. The racing engines for Group 4 were modified to produce 470 bhp while Group 5 had the smaller 3.2 litre output and a KKK turbocharger, which resulted in an astonishing 800 to 850 bhp.

The Group 5 car was calculated as having a top speed of 217 mph. This was all very theoretical much like their entry into official competition. Unfortunately the M1 as it was designated so as to associate it with the Motorsport division, could not compete in Group 5 as they would need to build at least 400 within a 12-month period. Clearly the tiny Motorsport division stood no chance of producing such a large number of cars in such a short space of time. That task was given to Giugiaro and his Ital Design firm who were put in charge of the design and production of the fibreglass bodies. Not everyone liked the styling and some reckoned it was not as daring and interesting as the Paul Bracq Turbo on which it was based. Neither did it have the light purposeful stance of the 635. What we had here was a no-nonsense supercar with lots of vents, plus chunky and defined panel work that looked as though it meant business.

Meanwhile the chassis and engine assembly was trusted to supercar makers Lamborghini. They had spare capacity at the time and their contract called for a production rate of two a week and a total run of 800 cars. However, the Italian end of the operation was not a success and instead the bodies were shipped direct to BMW's coachbuilders Baur who fitted the chassis. These then went on to Motorsport who carried out the final assembly. It took until 1981 to finally build the 400 M1s required and by then it was too late to go racing. Except that it already had been used in anger on the track.

Back in 1979 BMW linked up with British racing car designers March who managed to put their version of the M1 together for competition. Having missed the minimum build requirements for Group 5 and an engine too large for Group 6, the head of March, Mr. Max Mosley, had a brilliant idea. He proposed that there should be a PROCAR series pitting Formula 1 drivers against privateers who all drove identically prepared M1s before the main event.

Appropriately it was the then double Formula One World Champion Niki Lauda who led on points and claimed the series with three outright wins and one second place. As well as a wodge of prize money, he also got an M1. One down, 456 more to sell and even I didn't help matters. This was the forgotten supercar and one of the most underrated.

Look, it's Formula One World Champion Nelson Piquet and an M635CSi.

In competition terms the 6 Series had taken a back seat to the M1, which had missed out on serious racing and only ended up as a pre-Formula 1 warm up act. However, the 6 Series had been turned into Group 2 racing cars in Switzerland producing a substantial 370 bhp. Even so, they were always trounced by Porsche. Luckily revised Group A regulations in 1983 meant that showroom specification was the norm and a host of tuners including Alpina and Schnitzer piled into the championship with their versions of the 6. Austrian Dieter Quester fought off the Tom Walkinshaw Jaguar XJS at the wheel of the Schnitzer prepared 635CSi. Covered in BMW parts sponsorship with distinctive 'see through' graphics, the car and driver convincingly won the European Touring Car Championship in 1983. That gave BMW a brilliant idea, why not build a race ready 635?

Badged as the M6 in the USA, the M635CSi was the result. A modified M-88 engine from the M1 was installed and produced 9 more horsepower at 286 bhp. Revised intake and exhaust systems, a 10.5:1 compression ratio and the latest Bosch Motronic II engine management system all helped. The maximum torque of 250lbs/ft was delivered at just 4500rpm and the claimed top speed was an astonishing 158 mph and 60 mph arrived in just 6 seconds. BMW had joined the supercar league and the 635 won the touring car championships yet again in 1986.

M1 and M635Csi, supercars that share the same powerplant.

Before the '80s ended it was time for Porsche to get serious about racing again and that gave them the excuse to create what is arguably the first truly modern supercar. It wasn't just about how fast it actually went and how macho you were to keep it on the road, no this was all about the technology, which actually made it easier to drive. Not quite the first supercar for rich wimps, but certainly the start of a trend.

Racing for Porsche this time didn't mean on the track, indeed the racing was very much off it. The 959 was a homologation special intended for Group B rallying and quickly proved its worth when a pre-production model won the 1986 Paris–Dakar event. If it could win the world's toughest rally obviously there were no limits to its potential, but what was the secret of its success?

Porsche 959, an even more super 911 Turbo.

Well, when it was unveiled at the Frankfurt Motor Show in 1985 the most unusual thing about the 959 was the four-wheel drive system, the first 911 to have it. Obviously Porsche were paying close attention to the Audi Quattro, but they went several stages further. Electronics would continually alter where the power went, whether to the front or rear wheels, to ensure neutral handling. Also the driver had the option to select dry road, rain, snow or off road options and then the computer would do the rest. The dampers stiffened as the speed increased, plus a manual adjuster meant that if they weren't hard enough then they could be stiffened even further. This was also the first car to have electronic monitoring of the tyre pressures.

Fitted with a competition type suspension set-up consisting of coil springs and double wishbones, driving a 959 was relatively easy with light controls and an easy to operate 6-speed gearbox. The engine was still air cooled as all 911s had been but the cylinders were specially water cooled. Its 911 Turbo engine delivered power (405 bhp) more smoothly because instead of just one Turbo an extra sequential one made all the difference. Top speed was a significant 197 mph while 60 mph arrived in just 3.7 seconds, oh yes and 100 mph in an astounding 8.3 seconds. The other significant fact is that they only made 200 of them.

Ground clearance could also be set to three different heights and once the 959 went above 94 mph then it would drop right down to hug the tarmac and get the maximum amount of grip. There was a so-called 'comfort' model which had novelties such as rear seats, air conditioning and extra sound deadening.

No other company had a car that was anywhere near as sophisticated and it pointed the way forward certainly for more commercial minded supercar manufacturers because their customers would find it a doddle to drive. Porsche though did not let all these technological advances go to waste. It would be used to radically overhaul the 911 range, which back in the early '80s had been scheduled for replacement. Indeed as the new Carrera 2 and 4 models were introduced the Turbo went away for a well-earned rest. It came back even stronger.

Making do with the old 3.3 engine the output went up by 20 bhp to 320 bhp. The treacherous torsion bars had gone in the bin replaced by coil springs at each corner, with MacPherson struts up front and at the back with dampers and familiar trailing arms. All the traction went to the rear and this became the most wieldy turbo ever. Some old problems remained though as at lower revs (under 3000rpm) getting the Turbo to do much within the widely spaced gear ratios was a challenge. At least the quality of the gearshift improved beyond recognition, with less baulk and a more positive snick. Getting to 60 mph in under 5 seconds and onwards towards 170 mph was now a pleasure.

It still wasn't perfect, but then you would never want it to be. There was still a touch of uncertainty on the limit and the power steered wheel would jump playfully about to the torque's tough tune. Best of all instead of the new automatic trick spoiler there was still a great big 'up yours' fixed tea tray job.

The 959 led directly to this, the next generation 911 Turbo.

German supercars were not the prettiest but they were some of the most competent and usable fast cars ever made. Compared to contemporary Lamborghinis and Ferraris they were far better built and would never leave you stranded. To some they may not have been so lovable as the temperamental Italians, but you had to respect them. Every German supercar significantly raised the stakes and we should all be grateful for that.

Porsche 911, BMW M1, Mercedes C111 vs The Rest

Aston Martin Vantage – We've mentioned this one before, not least because it would do 170 mph, what we failed to mention was the open top Volante version which would give you a very good, bad hair day.

Ferrari 365GT4BB/512BB – All Ferraris are effectively supercars but these had flat 12 racing car engines which the factory claimed would easily manage 175 mph.

Ferrari Testarossa – Spiritual successor to the above with an even bigger engine. Wide as a lorry, 78 inches (198cm) across the wonderfully scoopy air vents could suck in small pets and flambé them. Could manage a pulverising 181 mph.

Ferrari 288 GTO – Incredibly another Group B Rally spin-off which would have been amusing to watch. V8s and Turbos means 190 mph. Smaller, prettier and faster than a Testarossa.

Ferrari F40 – 40th birthday present to themselves this was a stripped out supercar with all sorts of exotic carbon fibre materials and a shamelessly big wing at the back. Noisy and for a time the fastest production car on the planet, promising 201 mph.

Jaguar XJR-S – Not really a supercar is it? More an ageing old girl teased up in a bodykit but it is so hard to overlook a 6.0 litre V12 engine. So downhill it would do 158 mph.

Lamborghini Countach – Scissor doors are just part of the attraction, the V12 helped as does the Jet Fighter styling. Early ones without wings are beautiful. Oh and 170 mph by the way.

Lamborghini Countach LP500S QV – This was the '80s one with a great big wing and stick on wheel arch extensions. However, the four valve cylinder heads meant 455 bhp and at least 178 mph, though real nutters would claim they saw 200 mph.

Maserati Bora – Giugiaro styled supercar that looks very aggressive. Not remotely boring especially when the 5.0 litre V8 engine can take it to 165 mph.

In the Cassette Deck ...

 Sade – Diamond Life Now routinely slagged off as Jazz-very lite, it sounded sensational at the time and was the perfect accompaniment to an evening spent with an attractive lady. There I said it. Played to breaking point on countless company car specified 316is, but always better suited to something large, shark like and automatic, such as a 635iA.

11 Master Race

Explaining just how and why German cars won all the prizes in the 1980s.

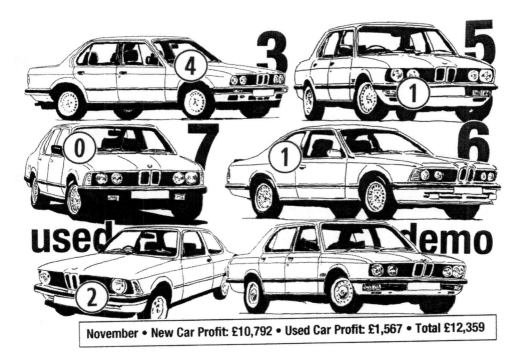

November • New Car Profit: £10,792 • Used Car Profit: £1,567 • Total £12,359

Motorsport didn't really figure much at Park Lane. The Cooper Group didn't appear to be sponsoring anyone, unlike BMW dealer Hexagon of Highgate who at one point were involved with Formula One and Sytner of Nottingham backed their boss Frank Sytner to the British Touring Car Title. Obviously there were a few customers who claimed to be very handy behind the wheel and always kept a helmet in the boot.

As you have probably forgotten by now back when I joined Park Lane I was given a book about the history of BMW. There were three to choose from, two straight histories and one about BMW going racing called The Ultimate *which had a full on Batmobile CSL bouncing over the kerb and heading straight for the reader. I chose the Batmobile.*

Good choice. An even better book was one published in January 1984 to celebrate the fact that BMW engines had won a stack of races powering bikes, cars and most celebrated of all, a Formula One title. Officially published by BMW and translated from German. That book is 630 Days to the Top. *It is all very 1980s album cover with big blocks of primary colours, over exposed pictures, highly pixelated ones and wholly inappropriate Max Headroom type treatment of amongst others, designer Gordon Murray. This book can induce epileptic fits or at the very least a severe migraine. Indeed, a short history of German cars in motorsport is not really possible. However, I will have a go and try not to give you a headache, by concentrating on the 1980s, which of course is what this book is about.*

So to start at the very beginning, why on earth do car manufacturers go to the bother of racing? Well, the obvious answer is that they have something to prove. They actually need to establish that their cars don't just work, but are better than other companies' cars. So those who chose to become motorists in the later part of the nineteenth century would also know which car to pick. In fact the first motor races were actually reliability trials and the French were taking an early lead. Even so, in 1903 when a factory fire burnt Mercedes racers to a crisp, they borrowed cars direct from their customers and duly won the Gordon Bennett Trophy in Ireland.

Mercedes go racing in 1914.

It was the French Grand Prix that became the must enter annual race, but when Mercedes won it in 1908 the French effectively sulked and didn't organise another until 1912. By the time of the 1914 event, racing had become highly professional rather than a jolly lark. Mercedes turned up with a large team of four spectacular looking racers finished in white. Already they had studied the 23-mile course and decided on which gear ratios would be best. Tactics and team orders rather than just pure wheel-to-wheel racing decided the outcome. Mercedes sent one car out to set a furious pace with the intention of tempting the French Peugeots to follow suit and then break down as a result of the extreme speeds. Even though a Peugeot led towards the close of the race the Mercedes pushed it all the way. After six hours of racing and just two laps from the end a Mercedes driven by Christian Lautenschlager took the lead. Frantically trying to keep up, the Peugeot's back axle broke in two.

Mercedes finished 1, 2 and 3 in an utterly convincing victory. The 4.5 litre engine that had propelled them were one month later powering the aircraft which were fighting in the skies over France in the first weeks of the First World War. Winning the race was a propaganda victory then and more than 20 years later the Germans were at it again.

Mercedes W125, in action.

As you will have read earlier in the Porsche chapter, not just one racing team but two went on to dominate racing in the 1930s. With speeds reaching 200 mph the Mercedes and Auto Unions were pegged back by new regulations that were designed to cut the maximum weight to 750 kilograms and reduce the speed. However, with a morbidly obese Third Reich piggy bank, it financed light alloy 600 bhp engines, revised suspension, tubular chassis that carried on from where the previous racers left off. The Mercedes W125 and Auto Unions were only occasionally interrupted by Alfa Romeo victories. In 1937, the last proper racing season, there were nine Mercedes victories to Audi's six, so no doubting who built the best racing cars, the rest sadly was going to be decided on the battlefield.

The start of a 2-litre race in 1938, the grid packed with 320s. No 10 won, No 19 has the evil insignia of the Waffen SS.

BMW had been operating at a lower, but no less impressive level. Their motorcycles did extremely well and from the start of building bikes in 1922 until 1925 they scored more than 100 race wins. When it came to four wheels the smallest Dixi, a rebadged Austin 7, won hillclimbs and rallies, and the team victory in the Alpine Rally of 1929 (at a breakneck average speed of 26 mph) as well as a class win in the Monte Carlo were the high points. With the more grown-up 328s BMW could be found winning numerous endurance races and class wins in prestigious events such as the 1938 Spa-Francorchamps and the 1939 Le Mans. In fact the victories were so numerous that even BMW's own official history does not list them all.

Post-war it was business as usual for Mercedes when they returned to the circuits in 1954. With the 300SL they had the tool to start and finish the job. On their first appearance in the French Grand Prix, the W196 Mercedes finished first and second. Its bodywork rather got in the way in the British Grand Prix and prevented the great Juan Manuel Fangio from claiming victory. Once redesigned the car was unbeatable and Fangio was now unfettered by the front bodywork that hampered his precise steering. The world championship was Fangio's in 1954 and in 1955 Stirling Moss took the Millie Miglia road race title.

For BMW the post war was a lot quieter as they waited until 1956 when motor-sport events were allowed to resume in Germany. Oddly it was the Isettas which proved to be incredibly successful, and the 600 version even won the Alpine Rally outright in 1959. The first proper small BMW in the shape of the 700 was fully factory backed and officially returned the company back to racing. It was nimble yet powerful and in 1960 won the National Hill Climb Championship outright followed in 1961 by the National Saloon Car Championship. This was valuable experience for the competitions department, which had a limited preparation area in the factory. Incredibly the little car went on winning right up until 1965.

Auto Union had a quiet time post war, mainly because they didn't exist. However, there was a new kid on the racing block, Porsche. The company started early when Porsche built 46 aluminium cars for customers to use in competition. Being lighter and fitted with better brakes they were faster and stopped quicker so it was no surprise that Porsche held four back. One of them won its class in the 1951 Le Mans and they were off. The 550 Spyder was becoming a legend and the design of a new engine, the type 547, a 4 overhead camshaft, flat four, which was used in a variety of racing applications. Sports cars, hill climb and Formula 2, Porsche could clearly compete and dominate at every level of motorsport.

Porsche leading from the front. A 956 in first and second at Le Mans.

At this point we really ought to fast forward to the '80s otherwise listing all their victories would fill up the rest of the book. Porsche sports cars dominated the long distance events whether factory backed or privately entered. In fact, Group 5 Racing ended in 1981 when Porsches were the only marques left that were competitive. At Le Mans the factory won yet again in 1981 with a 936 model driven by Jacky Ickx and Derek Bell.

From 1982 a new Group C World Endurance Championship meant that any manufacturer could compete with any design of car or size of engine, provided it didn't gulp more than 600 litres of fuel per 1000 kilometres. Although Ford, Aston Martin and Lancia entered the fray it was Porsche and the 956 model which won every single race in 1982. Factory backed with Rothmans sponsorship it also took the first three places at Le Mans. Porsche kept on winning interrupted only briefly by Jaguar. So although 1987 marked the seventh consecutive Le Mans victory Jaguar won the renamed Group C title (World Sports-Prototype Championship) and the 24 Hours title a year later.

Porsche also had plenty of successful engine projects to keep them busy. They designed, developed and prepared the 1.5 litre turbocharged V6 engines that powered the Marlboro McLaren team, which took Niki Lauda and Alain Prost to three consecutive Formula 1 titles from 1984 to 1986. They also designed an engine for the American CART racing series scoring one victory. However, the '80s didn't end well for Porsche. At the end of their contract with McLaren they went into partnership with the Footwork Grand Prix team. Unfortunately Porsche produced an overweight, underpowered engine that failed to do anything except embarrass its maker. At least there was still the 911 which in highly modified form competed at Le Mans and was a stalwart of club and international racing along with 944s, mainly in the hands of privateers.

The re-emergence of the Audi badge in the late '60s had resulted in the Super 90 and later 80 GTEs, both winning the European Touring Car Title, going back into competition, driven by privateers but often supported by Audi themselves. The company though was destined to change the world of rallying for ever when in 1982 Audi won the World Rally Championship. Out went those rear wheel drive Escorts and stripy jackets and in came all wheel drive sophistication and a girl who could drive.

Audi Quattro going about its business in 1982. This time driven by Hannu Mikkola and winning the Mintex Rally.

The Audi Quattro made its debut in Portugal in autumn 1980, but not in competition, it was a service car. However, on at least one stage of the rally the Finnish driver Hannu Mikkola used the car and drove so enthusiastically that he reached the finishing line half an hour ahead of the eventual winner. That was unofficial of course, but it was only a matter of time before the Quattro was pitched into full combat for the 1981 season. In that first season it won the Scandinavian, San Remo and RAC Rally. Indeed, the RAC was a significant event as the Quattro took a 90-degree bend too fast in Grizedale North and turned over in the mud. Incredibly they were 40 seconds ahead of the pack and managed to right the Quattro. Mikkola then went on to stay ahead of everyone else with never less than a minute to spare. The San Remo was also important for another reason being the first all female team (Michéle Mouton driving and Fabrizia Pons navigating) to win a World Championship event.

1982 was the year that the Audi won the Manufacturers World championship trophy, while Michéle Mouton as the runner-up in the drivers' championship. In 1983 it was the drivers' title that fell to Mikkola and runner-up in the Manufac- turer's Title for Audi. Following that there were thirteen national championships in Europe and worldwide which was capped in 1984 by the double, Audi taking the manufacturers' crown and Stig Blomqvist the drivers' title. Not surprisingly the car itself got a gong as it was named 'Motorsport Car of the Year'. In all, Quattro scored 23 victories in five years.

Quattro Sport in all its stubby glory.

Great as it was the Quattro was never an easy car to drive proving to be a bit of a handful especially on the tarmac stages. One answer was to build the stubby Quattro Sport, which was better able to compete with a new generation of mid-engined equally four-wheel driven rally cars. Aimed at the doomed Group B category a standard Quattro was taken off the production line and then reduced in length by 320mm (12.5 inches) from the front of the door backwards. All the metal panels were replaced by lightweight Kevlar ones. Being shorter meant that it was now easier to throw around, the vented bonnet helped to cool the turbo engine, whilst the flared arches contained even wider wheels. Oh yes and the rake of the windscreen was changed as drivers often complained it caught the sun which resulted in blinding reflections. All Audi did was install a more upright metal screen and doors from a humble Audi 80. Not cheap, but effective and actually a waste of time. It only won one rally, the Ivory Coast in 1984. They did though perform well in the unique Pike's Peak hillclimb in Colorado setting the fastest times in 1984 and 1985.

Quattros didn't just come as stubby racers, there was also a 200 version that won the Safari Rally in 1987 and the overall German Rally title. A team was also sent to the USA to contest the Trans Am series in 1988 and after just ten races they had pocketed the title. The following year there was the IMSA GTO series to contest and this time Audi came second. Then in 1990 the oddest Quattro of them all was sent onto the racetrack in the imposing shape of the V8 Quattro. It was a good decision too as the V8 won the German Touring Car Championship that year and the year after, the first manufacturer in the history of the event to successfully defend its title.

The success of the Quattro four-wheel drive system obviously encouraged Porsche to rethink its own racing programme. This explains why the 911 went back to World Rallying in 1984 when Rothmans decided to back a team. Here was the genesis of the 959 supercar, which you have read about previously. All Porsche had to do was build 200 four-wheel drive models, so that it could be homologated for Group B rallying in time for the 1985 season. The trouble was that Group B got cancelled because it was proving to be very dangerous for both drivers and spectators. That was due to the massively powerful 500 bhp engines the cars had, fairly lax regulations and a shockingly high death toll. However the 959 won the Paris–Dakar Rally, which is arguably the toughest race, so it wasn't a complete waste of time.

More conventional, yet still modified, 911s with the weight reduced to 960kg were sent out in Rothmans colours to compete at international level. A 911SC RS managed to finish an impressive second in the 1984 European Rally Championship.

Mercedes 450SLC wasn't just for the beautiful people, it was ugly enough to go rallying.

Mercedes meanwhile would seem to have nothing to prove. After leaving the top flight of motorsport in the 1950s after winning all the prizes, they only sporadically supported and dipped their toes in international competition. That explains how heavily prepared 450SLCs and 220 saloons would occasionally feature in the East African Safari to prove the toughness of their products. Competition was not a priority for the company and they preferred to spend money on research and development. However, in order to sell sporty cars, you need a sporty image. Not only that, Mercedes could not fail to notice just how well Audi and BMW were doing on the track and in the showrooms.

The decision to re-enter the world of motorsport was not taken until late in the decade, in December 1987, when Mercedes supported teams already running the 16-valve 190s in the European Touring Car Championship. The first fruits of that intention to compete wheel to wheel was the launch of the Evolution and Evolution II 190s. It was too late for any real impact to be made in the 1980s, and although the cars looked suitably up for it, no wins were recorded.

Even more ambitiously Mercedes resolved to develop sports racing cars in partnership with Sauber, to whom they already supplied 5-litre V8s. For the 1988 season the Sauber C9 was now badged as the Sauber-Mercedes C9. The silver sports car performed impressively and the twin turbo engine produced 700 bhp and propelled it into second place in the Championship behind Jaguar. Not really good enough for Mercedes so they reworked the engines and upped their involvement so that after six races they had enough points to win the Championship outright in 1989. An added bonus was victory at Le Mans with the rest of the team finishing second and fifth. By the 1990 season the Sauber name had disappeared altogether and it was rebadged as the C11, which had a longer wheelbase, a monocoque body made of lightweight carbonfibre and 730 bhp. The World Sports Car Championship was the result. It seemed as though Mercedes had hardly been away.

Overall the prize for the most improved sporting marque must go to BMW and the credit for this goes to the creation of BMW Motorsport GmbH in 1972 and the appointment of Jochen Neerpasch from Ford to manage the department. What followed was Batmobiles, defeated works Capris and overall victory in the European Touring Car Championship as well as an outright class win at Le Mans for the CSL. Yes BMW were getting serious about sport as their 2-litre engines were installed in a March Formula 2 car and domination of that class continued until 1982. Meanwhile Turbo powered CSLs were sent to America to take on Porsche 930s and spread the word that BMW were back in business.

To fully appreciate the CSL, you have to understand how it came to be built. The CS2800 was not a natural for the track. However, despite being overweight and under-braked and slow it had potential. Schnitzer the tuning firm were particularly good at teasing out extra power achieving 360 bhp by the early '70s. However, even these models were still roundly beaten by of all things – Ford Capris. It was so embarrassing that the factory put the CS on a diet.

A CSL up against the old enemy, Capris.

There is a UK connection here because Broadspeed got the first two light-weight bodies. The racer which was produced had big arches and a large front air dam with John Fitzpatrick at the wheel. It appeared just once on the track at Salzburgring and some ideas certainly found their way into the factory CSL. Importing Ford team manager Jochen Neerpasch in 1972 to head a new BMW competitions department was a smart first move. The 3.0 CSL racecars were the first to be developed under BMW Motorsport GmbH. They were also the first to sport the newly designated official colours of BMW Motorsport – red, blue and purple – and the first to use ABS. The Solex-fed 2985cc engine was increased to 3003cc so that it fell within the FIA's over 3 litre category. Eventually it was bored and stroked to 3.5 litres in the racers, giving up to 450 bhp with 24 valve heads. Then there was the 750 bhp Turbo in 1976.

The 3.0 CSL won 5 European Touring Car Championships between 1973 and 1979, as well as several national championships. So without versions built for the road the CSL could never have shone on the track.

Not the most obvious racing car the E12 5 Series never had official factory backing like the CSLs, but BMW did give limited support. In the UK the TWR group was partly founded on the back of racing 5 Series. In 1976 Tom Walkin-shaw approached BMW and suggested that the 5 Series might make a good racing prospect. Aimed at Group 1 saloon car racing in the UK, Belgium and France, BMW homologated the American specification 530i, which then produced around 250 bhp. Some class wins in Europe with strong performances in the UK and third place in the 1978 Spa 24 hours were the high points for a car that was never really at home on the track.

BMW Junior team tactics involved a bunch of 320is driving very closely together.

In racing track terms the E21 3 Series didn't quite have the success of the earlier 02s or later E30. One very exciting development was the creation of a three-car team of E21 320is. Stripped out, bespoilered and with bulging bodywork these cars were powered by Formula 2 engines and entered for the German Touring car series in 1977. Called the **BMW Junior Team**, the young drivers Eddie Cheever, Marc Surer and Manfred Winkelhock all went on to get Formula 1 drives. They were good value, but crashed a lot, often into each other and old hands like Ronnie Peterson and Hans Stuck were drafted into the driving seats. Attempts were made to turbocharge the 320, which were not successful despite producing up to 600 bhp, but they just could not be engineered to be fully reliable. However Schnitzer's 1.4 litre 320 Turbo developed a more usable and dependable 380 bhp and went on to win the German Touring Car Championship in 1978. The next stop for a development of that engine was Formula 1 glory.

No doubt as to which model would win. M1 go PROCAR.

We have already mentioned the M1 supercar programme which didn't exactly go as planned, but at least the car was driven in a rough and ready fashion by F1 drivers plus it was a lot of fun to watch. The M1 did have some genuine racing form though, because Nelson Piquet and Hans Stuck came third in the 1980 Nüburgring 1000km, which is probably the most meaningful result. Otherwise, it failed to impress in the American IMSA series and a French team even went rallying in one. Well at least they tried.

Brabham BT-52 with Nelson Piquet in the pilot's seat.

Motorsport developed a 1.5 litre 16-valve four-cylinder engine specifically to go racing and in 1979 after preliminary discussions with both McLaren and Ligier the British Brabham team agreed to test the engines. Initially it proved to be powerful but unreliable. From failing to qualify for the 1982 Watkins Glen (USA) round of the World Championship the BMW powered Brabham went on to win the Canadian Grand Prix just two weeks later.

By the opening round of the 1983 Championship the engine had been fully modified and installed into a brand new body made of carbon fibre and aluminium. It was called the BT-52 and in Nelson Piquet's skilful hands it won the Brazilian Grand Prix. From there it was on to second places at the French, Monaco and British Grands Prix. Teammate Ricardo Patrese took third in the German Grand Prix before Piquet regained form to finish third in Austria and then go on to win the Monza and European Grand Prix. It then all hinged on the final round at Kyalami in South Africa, with Renault's Alain Prost just two points ahead. A third place was enough to give Piquet victory in the drivers' championship and BMW perhaps their most significant title ever. The BT-52 was also the first ever turbocharged car to win the Championship.

BMW continued to supply engines to the Brabham team until 1987 and also to Arrows until 1988 plus you could also find them in the back of a Benettons, which increasingly outperformed the other more established teams.

Dieter Quester in his transparent 635 claims the European Touring Car Championship.

Touring Cars was where BMW had some history going all the way back to the tiny 700. In 1982 the 528i didn't seem particularly special or that powerful with just 240 bhp, but it still took the drivers' title. The following year the cats turned up in the shape of the V12 Jaguar XJS. That was the cue for BMW to bring back the 635CSi. Prepared by Schnitzer and driven by Austrian Dieter Quester, it won the European Touring Car for the fourth time, although Jaguar fought back the following year to claim the title. BMW's response in 1986 was a win at the Spa 24 Hours with another team car finishing third. Most important of all Roberto Ravaglia secured the drivers' title. The Italian had started racing in the traditional way in karts, before progressing to Formula 3 and now he was poised to get the drive of his career.

BMW built the M3 with a single purpose in mind: racing. However, the competition M3 was a very different beast from the road legal one. First of all it had been on a diet and weighed just 960kg (2116lb) compared with the road car's 1200kgs with a perfect 50/50 weight distribution. The engine capacity was upped to more than 2.3 litres with modified Motronics and typically pushed out 300 bhp, which steadily rose over the years. The racing transmission would have either short or long ratios depending on how it was going to be used. Out went the power steering and in came a quicker ratio rack. The semi-trailing arm suspension was reinforced, the anti-roll bars were fully adjustable and the Bilstein aluminium spring struts were modified with adjustable spring plates. It ran on new hubs and single nut three-piece 9 x 17 wheels, with a lower 40mm (1.6 inch) ride height. Racing regulations required a roll cage and a safety fuel tank.

With an M3 at his fingertips Ravaglia duly went off and won the inaugural World Touring Car title in 1987. The M3 also scooped that year's European Touring Car title amongst several other national gongs for touring cars and hillclimb events. The M3 even diversified into rallying and chalked up several wins in the World Rally Championship. In fact the roll call of M3 successes is long and impressive. Here are a few highlights: the European Touring Car

Championship in '88; the British Touring Car Title in '88 and '91; the Italia Superturismo Championship in '87, '89, '90 and '90; the Deutsche Tourenwagen Meisterschaft in '87 and '89, and the less tongue-twisting Australian Touring Car Championship in 1987. Oh and a string of endurance titles including five straight wins from 1989 in the Nüburgring 24 Hours and 4 wins in the Spa 24 Hours, Of course there was far more than that, and far more titles than any other manufacturer can shake a podium at for a single model. The E30 M3, a true legend.

M3 winning everything. The prizes are probably in the boot.

So there we have it. German cars were clearly the ones to beat in the most prestigious races in the 1980s. Sure, Jaguar were prodded from a 20 year slumber to get serious again about races and the Italians can always be relied upon to pop up in Lancias and Alfa Romeos to pull off the odd surprise result. Otherwise this is another decade that can be chalked up to the German car industry that won all the significant races and championships. Not only that they set the racing agenda. Quattro. M3. 930. Even Mercedes got their sporting groove back with the C11.

Did we forget Volkswagen? Well Audi was part of the VW Group of course, but the GTI did go rallying. At a time when there was a lot of uncertainty in the sport and Group B was cancelled, it was decided in 1986 to create a one-off World Championship for Group A cars. The GTI won this and then the following year another one-off competition, for two-wheel drive rally cars.

When these German carmakers put their minds to it and applied their usual engineering rigour, they could win just about anything. In the process they enhanced the appeal of their showroom products several thousand fold. Few buyers took Audi very seriously as a brand until the Quattro arrived. How could BMW use the ultimate driving machine as a mission statement if they weren't driving to victory? Porsche's utter domination of the sports car racing scene was the very least that their core customers demanded. Mercedes-Benz could seemingly at will set their sights on a racing prize and then go for it, hence a Le Mans victory to take them confidently into the next decade. Sporting success is a measure of a manufacturer's health and ongoing commitment to make their products get better. Race on Sunday, sell on Monday may be a cliché, but it is true. The person who buys a car that has been built purely to qualify for racing like an M3, Evolution, or a Carrera Club Sport is unlikely ever to use it on a race track or exploit a fraction of its abilities. That is irrelevant of course, because demand has been created for a limited edition work of engineering genius and customers are prepared to pay to be part of that exclusive club. Getting from the racing track to the showroom in just a few seconds was brilliantly clever.

When it came to racing, first past the finishing post was the German Car Industry who were clearly years ahead of everyone else.

German Racing Cars vs The Rest (too many vanquished marques to list . . .)

Lancia Integrale – Won six consecutive world rally titles up to 1992. Effectively carried on from where the Quattro left off.

Williams Formula 1 Car – They were the reigning World Champions with Keke Rosburg at the wheel in a normally aspirated Ford powered car. They switched to turbo power and Honda engines after the BMW turbo's success and they eventually won the title again 1987.

Jaguar XJS – Put together by TWR and producing 400 bhp this was part of Jaguar's mid '80s racing revival that saw a Touring car title in 1984. Sadly the old girl could not keep up after that.

In the Cassette Deck...

 Simple Minds – Sparkle in the Rain Uplifting arena rock before they ever played arenas. Atmospheric, bombastic and at the right volume it made a 520i and any diesel Mercedes saloon much, much faster. That's an engineering fact by the way. Excitingly, Nastassja Kinski is name checked in 'Up on the Catwalk' and it along with most other tracks, a great blokey chantalong experience.

12 Big Hair, Big Shoulders, Big Wings, Bigger Engines

How and why German cars got more difficult to miss and harder to keep up with.

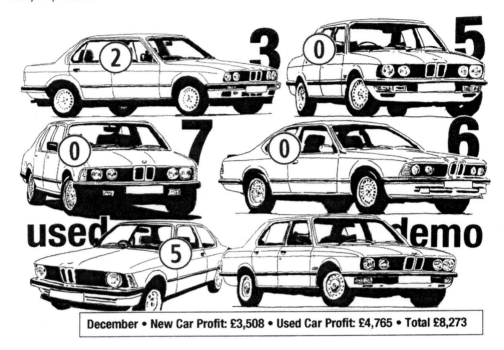

December • New Car Profit: £3,508 • Used Car Profit: £4,765 • Total £8,273

If 1980s German cars were automotive perfection, then how come there were so many individuals and companies keen to change the way they looked and the way they behaved? Well, there was good and bad. The bad was making cars look fashionable. The problem with that is the car will date really quickly. One good aspect though of interfering with a proven product is that they can be made to go faster and stop quicker. However, re-engineering a car that has already been so well designed seems like madness, but there was at least some method to it. However, when it came to changing the way a perfectly handsome car looked, now that was true madness.

At Park Lane we had an A4 folder with clear pockets which contained what would now be regarded as automotive sacrilege. Inside were exciting and extravagant adventures in leather, paint and plastic. Chrome, which had looked perfectly good as standard factory decoration for decades, was painted over, or to use the correct term, colour keyed. That meant it would now blend in better with its

Sapphire Blue, Henna Red or Bavarian Black surroundings, but then the Dulux colour chart, metalflake and fashionable two tones were all optional finishes. There was no end to what could be changed, whether it was choosing an alloy wheel that looked like a UFO, or a body kit that cloaked the bodywork in what looked like giant Lego pieces. Inside, animal hide could be applied to every available surface from the headlining to the dashboard. When that book came out Park Lane was no place for shrinking violets, or vegans.

Let me explain. Back when the Cooper Group were the importers for BMWs their depot was based in Dover, where they had a large facility to prepare the brand new cars. Once the concession was taken over by BMW, they switched to Daihatsus. Something had to be done with all that space and one activity they occupied themselves with was customisation. So if we had a customer looking for some isation, then we would get out the folder. This was a bit more than those £50 side stripes that could be done in the underground car park. These were full-on revamps involving paint, trim and major refits. It was good for us salesman because you got paid a commission. So without doing much, not that a car sales executive did that much anyway, here was an opportunity to earn extra money.

This is view inside the Dover workshop when Cooper was the official importers sometime in the early '70s. A decade later they would be changing the way BMWs looked both inside and out.

There were some mistakes of course. When a customer ordered an Arctic White 635i, they wanted the interior to be equally striking. So white leather of course inside, plus everything else had to turn white too. Headlining, door trims, and dashboard. However, the dashboard was a coat of paint too far. Once driven out of the underground car park and into the daylight it was blinding. Not just 'blinding' in a cockney geezer way, rather more blinding in a cockney gangster manner. The reflection from the top of the dashboard hit the windscreen and it was a total whiteout and that made the 635CSi utterly undriveable. Back to Dover then for a dash top respray in a more sombre black.

So who was the typical 'isation' type customer? Hard to say, it could just be someone who wanted leather trim and the car we had in stock didn't have it, but they were not going to wait three months for a factory fit order. Otherwise, the largest proportion of those who wanted to change the way that their new BMW looked often came from the Middle East, but not always. I remember a short banker with a long coat who seemed like a really nice chap ordering a perfectly agreeable 323i in metallic grey when he was suddenly gripped by a moment of madness. He wanted something 'different' at which point I pulled out the folder. To my horror he picked out a body kit and square headlamps. No really he did. There was nothing wrong with the front end of a 3 Series, but he was determined to change it. So he ticked the equally square headlamp box, plus an extensive programme of colour keying the chrome grey. As a car purist I was quietly horrified, as car salesman though I remembered the extra wedge I would earn and thought no more of it.

When I delivered the car the chap didn't come to his senses. He still loved it and presumably thought that I'd done the conversion and paintwork myself, which explains why he gave me a bottle of Bollinger Champagne in a box. It was very nice and at least he took the 323i away.

So Park Lane carried out these highly unofficial upgrades, then there was Alpina. We weren't allowed to sell Alpina BMWs, only the company with the concession Sytners in Nottingham could. However, the export department who shared our office were allowed to sell them because the models would leave the country permanently. So there were always Alpinas around for us to look at and drive. At one point we were informed that passing on Alpina enquiries that matured into a sale would result in money for us, which was nice to hear. In the morning meeting one day the sales manager said there was a 7 Series (Alpina B12) for us to enjoy.

With Alpina there is yet another batch of letter/number combinations to bone up on to truly understand their line up. However, the only numbers relevant that day was 5 blokes in a 7 in Hyde Park. If you have read this book in sequence then you will know that silly things were done in a 518i in the interests of youthful high jinks. Well much the same happened in this huge luxury car. It was all very juvenile and no animals, people, or other vehicles were harmed during its excursion, but there was a lot of screeching and burning rubber. It was a lovely car, so it is worth finding out just how go faster BMWs came about in Germany and came to their most receptive overseas market, the UK.

Not surprisingly the idea of making BMWs go faster all began in Germany. Just when the company had broken away from building bubble cars and the V8 baroque angels, several specialists helped BMW revive their sporting and performance car heritage. Two companies in particular led the way. Firstly there was Alpina. The company's founder Burkhard Bovensipen appropriated the family company's brand name (ironically they were a stationery company) previously used on typewriters, but he moved on to making Fiat 1500s, then new class BMW 1500s go faster. Indeed, a few pages on there is a more detailed explanation as to just how closely Alpina is associated with the UK. A country willing not just to embrace even faster BMWs but also to pay a lot more money for them.

For the moment though the significant date is 1963 when Alpina produced a tuning kit for the 1500. Modestly it consisted of two Webber twin barrel side draught carburettors on short intake manifolds and a large oil bathed air filter. A legend was born and these bolt on goodies suddenly became an option for the BMW enthusiast who could afford it.

The other major player though less well known in the UK was Schnitzer. Josef Schnitzer won the German Touring Car Championship in 1966 whilst steering 1800Tisa and 2000Tis. With his brother Herbert they developed their race bred components for civilian use. They also took the 2002's engine and gave it a 4 valve head, but in the early years the emphasis was on competition parts although the many racing components found their way onto road going BMWs. And then there was Hartge. Herbert Hartge was well known for tuning BMWs in the 1960s but did not incorporate Hartge GmbH until 1971.

These German tuners never made much impact initially in the UK. That's because BMWs were never cheap cars. A much less sexy 2000C in 1965 was £2958, that's a grand more than a Jaguar E-Type. Owners were not going to tinker with these cars which which may have been regarded as New Klasse, but they were old money and the cars even bore the old-fashioned Fraser Nash badge (the UK importers) in place of the BMW one. The mostly old boy owners network were going to leave well alone. However, the introduction of the 2002 changed all that, even though the Tii was still E-Type money. The appeal of the 2002 was to younger owners who were more open to making changes. Also as the '70s wore on it was the relative cheapness of corroded 02s that encouraged ordinary mortals to try and improve on Bavaria's finest. Bigger air filters and extra Weber carburettors were always the simple way forward back then. Perhaps the most obvious way of being different was to overhaul the exterior. In this respect BMW had already set its own mad standard of excess, which was almost impossible to better.

The CSL wasn't called the Batmobile for nothing. Wings and little aerodynamic things everywhere. Alternatively, in the 1970s you could mail order (old fashioned internet) Ripspeed for some Wolfrace Slot Mag alloys and Richard Grant Trans Am air dams at £15 and £14.25 for a boot spoiler. The finishing touch for that genuine Bob Marley and the Wailers (BMW geddit? ©1978) look were chrome covers over the already rusty wheel arches.

Initially the E21 3 Series was something of a disappointment in the performance department, but there was a whole load of tuning companies just waiting to prove what the new 3 Series was capable of. The model that launched the Alpina range was the B6. Effectively an E21 with a 628i engine from the smallest 6 Series coupé installed, although the 200 bhp that Alpina extracted made all the difference. The company quoted the 0–62 time as 7.2 seconds, although road testers could get below 7 seconds and the top speed was 140 mph. In late 1981 a new induction system saw the bhp rise to 218 bhp. Alpina also produced their own version of the 323i, badged the C1 it was teased to produce a useful 170 bhp. Yet sales of the B6 actually outstripped the C1.

Schnitzer's 323i Turbo going excitingly sideways.

Hartge and Schnitzer also got in on the E21 act principally with turbo versions of the 323i. However the award for the most outrageous E21 goes to United States Alpina importer Dietel. They specialised in the large 6-cylinder units such as the 2.8, 3.0, 3.3 and 3.5 in either standard or an enhanced state of tune. Their meister-werk was the Dietel-Alpina 345i, which as the name suggests incorporated the turbocharged 3.5 litre unit from the 745i into an unsuspecting US specification 320i. Obviously the suspension and brakes were uprated to cope and the E21 even sat on custom built **BBS** split rim alloys which were 15" x 9" at the front and 15" x 11" at the rear with the bodywork suitably modified to accommodate them.

British Griffin Motorsport 323i with modified engine, exhaust and suspension with a top speed of 162 mph.

In the 1980s though tuning finally came of age as both Alpina and Hartge were recognised as car builders in their own right in Germany. In the UK BMW went from interesting niche manufacturer to mainstream maker of prestige performance cars. Even though BMW still had their image intact the cars were becoming more ubiquitous and that meant owners wanted something different. That's why they bought cars converted by Alpina in Nottingham or Birds Garage in Buckinghamshire who would carry out Hartge uprates. There were even home grown BMW conversions from Griffin Motorsport. Bill Griffin a racer who won the Modified Saloon Car Championship offered 320i and 323is with an uprated cylinder head, performance camshaft and free flow exhaust, which delivered an extra 25 bhp. It could run on Griffin Sports suspension with lowered springs, Bilstein gas damper, anti roll bars and strut braces. They even offered a high ratio steering rack. Meanwhile in Scotland Fleming Thermo-dynamics pursued the supercharging option with a Sprintex unit they designed. These were exciting times for those who wanted to make their cars not just quicker, but more distinctive.

BMW realised what they were missing out on and although they were never going down the turbo route favoured by Alpina, Hartge and Schnitzer, the in house Motorsport division refined what BMWs were all about with the M series cars which you can read about elsewhere in this book. Alpina though had already established a strong foothold in the UK. Right from the early days the Brits could fully appreciate a finely tuned BMW when they drove one. So here is the previously untold story of how Alpina came to Britain and became one of the company's largest export markets.

In beginning there was Crayford. This Kent based company were best known for chopping the tops off Ford Capris and Corsairs and in fact anything else that wore the blue oval in the '60s and '70s. Starting in 1970 Crayford Auto Developments diversified by importing Alpina parts and put together a distinctive 2002 demo car which even had an Alpina branded bonnet scoop. The standard TI engine was given a new cylinder head with the compression ratio raised to 11.5:1 with special valve springs, uprated guides and gas flow for £250. Not cheap, also looking at the price list a 300-degree camshaft cost £38, but a wilder 324-degree job was just £2 more. A twin Weber set up cost £67. Also available was a 'sports chassis', which meant reinforced rear trailing arms, uprated rear dampers, stronger front hubs and bearings plus ventilated front discs, all for £139. Crayford would also quote for a full house Alpina race engine pumping out 180 bhp. It cost a staggering £850, which would buy a brand new small car at the time. Even then buyers also needed an exchange engine with no more than 5,000 miles on the clock. Here was conclusive proof that buying Alpina was never the budget performance option and that quality always costs.

By 1973 BMW Concessionaires GB Limited had realised that there was money to be made from persuading cars to go faster. They used that year's

Racing Car Show to launch their Sportpart subsidiary. Realising that the Alpina bits were on the pricey side they also offered tuning parts from Mangoletsi in Cheshire and Mathwall Engineering who prepared Group 1 racing BMWs. Orders could be placed through local dealers, but the actual fitting had to be performed at BMW's own workshops in Brentford so as not to invalidate the warranty.

Fast forward to 1975 and Alpina took the decision to set up authorised dealers throughout Europe. One of the first was in the UK and the man in charge was Tom Walkinshaw. Hardly a surprise that they should choose him as head of the fledgling TWR organisation; Walkinshaw was involved in Group 5 racing driving a factory prepared CSL. He soon became deeply involved with the preparation and homologation of 528s and 530s, which raced throughout Europe. B7 Turbos based on the E12 5 Series and E24 6 Series, then B6 3 Series from 1979 would have been the staple models from the period, but the actual UK imports were negligible. Something needed to be done especially as Alpina gained recognition as an automobile manufacturer from the German Federal Motor Vehicle Registration Agency in 1983.

Alpina approached BMW GB and asked who would be the best person to handle the franchise and they didn't hesitate. "Have a word with Frank Sytner," they said. So begins a uniquely British chapter in Alpina history as one part of Nottingham turned Bavarian. The trouble was that Sytner wanted around 60 to 80 cars to sell each year but Alpina were ticking along at just 200 annually. Clearly UK demand and Alpina supply were going to be a problem, until that is, the two companies came to a unique arrangement whereby right hand drive Alpinas would actually be made in Nottingham.

Created in Nottingham, the UK-only Alpine B.5.

It worked like this. Sytner would take out the engines from the standard BMWs, crate them up and pack them off to Germany. By return they would get a crate back from Alpina, which would be unpacked and the engine carefully installed. Not only that, Sytner would carry out all of the suspension and brake upgrades too. Plus on the early models they would trim the interiors as well, with unique sports seats and steering wheels. The models that made the biggest impression were the E28s, E34s and the 325i version of the E30, a.k.a. C2 2.5s. According to mechanics that worked at Sytner in the 1980s they basically built exactly what the customer wanted and that could even mean leaving things off, like an Alpina steering wheel as some buyers wanted to be very subtle. However, the one thing they would not do is put an Alpina badge on a standard car (see the B3.5 below), but on the whole almost every British built Alpina was different in some way.

The really interesting thing about Synter's involvement with Alpina is that they were given a free hand to create UK specific models, which is as big a complement as being allowed to build Alpinas. The B3.5 has been described by many as simply a 'BMW wearing an Alpina dress'. This was dressed up in a bodykit and ran on Alpina alloys, which satisfied a particular kind of customer who really didn't want the full house engine. Rarest of the lot were always the B11 and B12 6 and 7 series. However, Sytner cleverly made up for the fact that the 745i never made it to the UK market hence the creation of the 735i B10. As usual the hand built 261 bhp, 3.5 litre, 6-cylinder engines were delivered fully built from Germany and mated to a manual gearbox. Sytner fitted gas-filled Bilstein shock absorbers and progressive rate springs. It sat on 16in Alpina alloys and was finished off with Alpina front and rear spoilers. The car accelerated from 0–62 mph in around 7 seconds and it had a top speed of nearly 146 mph so it would actually outdrag a 745i. Just 22 were built. From the E34 B9 onwards the BMWs were fully built by Alpina and imported as such, which was the end of the Robin Hood BMWs.

BMWs are what fattened up my pay cheque each month and all I really cared about. However, there were dozens of companies based in Europe who put the kitsch into body kits and numerous conversions of seemingly unimprovable German cars. You could fill several books with daft pictures from the '80s and as fascinating as that might be let's just see what was on offer in the early '80s.

Founded by Alois Ruf in 1939, Auto RUF was a general garage which gradually expanded, becoming a bus operator and then appointed as main agents for both Porsche and BMW. In the 1970s they decided to start upgrading the 911, first in 1975 by enlarging the Turbo's engine to 3.3 litres long before the factory did. The 1980s is when the company came into its own and was designated as a manufacturer in its own right. In 1983 the RUF BTR now had a 3.4 litre turbo engine producing 374 bhp plus a five-speed transmission. It was available as a standard narrow body, or with the pumped up turbo one. By 1987 they were continuing to make the factory Porsches look almost pedestrian with the CTR. This had a 469 bhp twin turbo engine and was taken to the Nardo Racetrack where it topped 212 mph making it the fastest road car you could go into a showroom and buy. So there.

Buchman + Buchman made a Turbo Targa 911.

If Alpina were tuners by appointment to BMW, and RUF for Porsche, AMG also fulfilled the same sort of job for Mercedes. As often happens the company name was a combination of the founders' names Hans Werner Aufrecht and Erhard Melcher, with however the area where the firm was based, the Old Mill in Burgstall near Grossaspach for the G, which doesn't normally happen at all. The company was originally called 'Engineering office for the Design and Testing of Racing Engines' which was a bit of a mouthful and would look silly on the boot lid, so obviously AMG made more sense. They had started tuning Mercedes for motorsport and back in 1983 the top of their range was a 500SEL with a very uprated V8 engine. It had polished induction ports, new camshafts, valves rockers and springs, increasing output by 59 bhp and bringing the total to 290 bhp. Suspension was also uprated with shorter springs that lowered the car by 3cm and also helped out by gas filled dampers. The unique alloys were 7 inches wide wearing suitably impressive Pirelli P7s rubber that was 225/50VR 16 and that resulted in a 150 mph top speed and would cover a kilometre from a standing start in 28.3 seconds.

AMG also targeted perhaps the oddest and least satisfying Mercedes in the Tonka Toy shape of the G-Wagen. Customers could specify just about anything of course although an extra 25 bhp was on offer for the 280GE model, a ride height control, wide BBS alloy wheels and wheel arch extensions plus a traditional grille from an E Series saloon. It sounds awful and of course it was. A fairly pointless exercise as a customised G-Wagen was a bit like gift-wrapping a breezeblock.

Obviously AMG offered a whole range of spoilers and bodykits to fit across the entire Mercedes range and also high-end stereos (as radio/cassettes were called back then) as well as televisions and sports seats. These seats could be fitted front and rear and incorporated such jollities as electric remote controls, heating and lumbar support courtesy of three inflatable cushions. All this, long before Mercedes would offer similar fripperies belatedly realising that customers would be only too happy to pay. Interestingly Mercedes' head office could be irritated about who did what to their vehicles. Indeed, they would request that some companies actually remove the three-pointed star from their precious vehicle before it was delivered to their customer. That didn't happen with AMG, but there were plenty of other guilty parties.

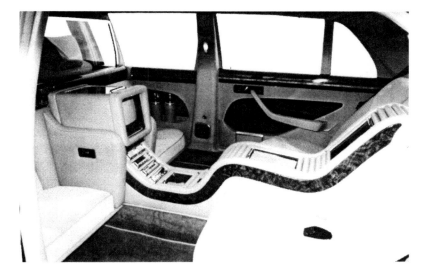

Inside a custom Mercedes 500SEL which had a telly and everything.

Duchatelet from Belgium were not known for their restraint. They concerned themselves with the cosmetics which had huge appeal in the parts of the world that didn't mind attracting attention. For instance they took a 500SEL and called it the Duchatelet Carat, attempting to make the connection between a diamond and their reworking of a luxury car. In my limited experience of precious stones a diamond is a simple, elegant and classy item, that may shine, but in isolation is never brash or vulgar. So what did Duchatelet do with the S-Class? Well first of all they did quite a nice thing, which was to simplify the bumpers and add some extra rubber to them, which looked fine. The alloy wheels lost their distinctive design and three-pointed star, but at least we know why. The low profile tyres had a set of surprisingly anonymous deep-dish items. What you could not miss though was the gold plated star on top of the grille, or the paint job. There would be up to 48 coats of opalescent blue paint, which meant that the colour changed depending on the angle that the car was viewed (through clenched fingers probably), becoming more luminous on some parts of the body.

Inside, it was the usual Middle Eastern kitchen sink specification. So there could be a TV, video player, roof mounted Hi Fi System, a radiotelephone, refrigerated drinks cupboard with solid silver Cartier goblets and gold cigarette lighter. They also came with a sophisticated anti-theft system, after all there was even a safe back there amongst the goblets and cigarettes. Apparently nefarious characters would get a spoken warning from a voice synthesizer before presumably being zapped by a laser. Indeed the talking car thing would seem to predate David Hasselhoff's KITT as the synthesized voice was part of a system check covering such remote functions as door and boot opening, engine starting and temperature control. Perhaps the most appropriate part of the specification according to the brochure was that the gear lever had the owner's initials engraved into the knob.

To give them their full title Sport Service Lorinser also stuck to the aerodynamic and cosmetic titivations to Mercedes cars. Although they supplied useful items such as ski racks, Lorinser would normally fit a whole host of inappropriate shovel fronted ends to perfectly good looking 200s, 380 and 500SECs.

Meanwhile Styling-Garage would take the roofs off the lowly 280CE and more substantial S-Class based 380 and 500SECs and put an electrically operated folding roof in its place. As well as all the usual tellies, fridges, cassettes, spoilers and wheel arch extensions they could make an S-Class 60 cm (23.6 inches) longer and call it the 600 SG5 5.0.

Also taking the roof off German cars was a company called Tropic, who mainly specialised in BMWs, strengthening the chassis of the 628, 633 and 635CSis and making a full four-seat convertible. They would fit an electronic hood, which uniquely had an automatic closing mechanism, which operated in response to a moisture sensitive micro switch. They could also uprate the suspension and fit a turbo, as well as doing the big spoiler thing.

Kamei wrapped a Golf Mark 2 in plastic, which seemed to make it go faster.

Yes there was no shortage of companies who could add various bits of plastic to mostly drastic effect. Kamei could restyle a Polo, a Golf or a Scirocco. Their so-called Golf X.1 went down the square headlamp route, a large vented grille and industrial strength spoiler. Plus the bonnet could be topped off with two big scoops leading to a spoiler on top of the hatch, which incorporated two extra stop lamps. Along with large plastic mouldings over the wheel arches and joined along the sill to make thick side skirts it looked very much like a Lego company car. Even so Kamei had spent quality time in the wind tunnel and claimed that there was a reduction of 9% in the car's drag coefficient (Cd), plus there was added stability at the rear of the car and a significant 3% decrease in fuel consumption. So there was method in this plastic madness. And yes there was an X.1 version of the Scirocco and Polo. In particular the lower Scirocco actually benefited from a 10% drop in Cd. With all models there was tick box list of extras from Recaro sports seats, through to Alcantara or leather trim, pearlescent paint and branded sound systems from Clarion and Bose.

Zender was another company at the forefront of plastic surgery and as well as the bits you could buy off the shelf to make the inside and outside of your German car look different they would also make their own versions of popular models. For instance a perfectly blameless BMW 323i was given a improving front spoiler, plus one on the boot lid and most importantly an Alpina suspension kit, helped out with 15 inch Pirelli P7 tyres. Inside there were Recaro seats and Alcantara trim as well as a full Hi Fi system that BMW always forgot to fit. So not a bad package then.

Zender also offered a slanted 935-style bonnet with pop up headlamps to fit a 911 Turbo, something the factory eventually offered on 911s as a special order. One of the oddest Zender makeovers was the Golf 'Stummelheck'. This involved extending the rear of the car by 7 inches. Obviously that meant there was more room in the back and what would have set it apart from say a more practical Passat which was a giant hatchback and didn't have all the wheel arch, spoiler and side skirt appendages.

Yet another concern that radically re-engineered German cars was b + b who routinely made Targa topped versions of 911 Turbos and 928s and even graft a 928 nose onto the front of a 911 to the irritation of Porsche. This is of course the tip of a rather large polycarbonate, colour keyed iceberg. I could go on, but I won't, as there are dozens and dozens of companies that interfered with varying degrees in success with German built cars. Perhaps the most important question to be asked at this point is why this happened?

The simple answer is that customising brand new cars has always occurred because at its most basic this is simply showing off. At the dawn of motoring rich people just bought the chassis and then they commissioned a coachbuilder to plonk something unique and often extravagant on top to outdo their friends and impress the lower orders.

Even though a 3 Series was not a common a sight in the earlier '80s customers were aware that they needed to set themselves apart. Once the novelty of the latest registration had worn off, and subject to getting another attention seeking device such as a personal registration number, some owners needed to be loved, or despised. The last thing they wanted was to be ignored. Maybe that's why so many buyers would ask in a slightly apologetic way for an extra Park Lane rear windscreen sticker for their Mini Metro.

Alpina BMWs, AMG Mercedes and all those modified Germans vs The Rest

Tickford Capri – The most exclusive Capri ever, just 100 were built, was the 205 bhp turbo charged Tickford model which was transformed by Aston Martin in 1983 and 1984. Finished in Essex Stiletto white with a body kit and colour coded alloy wheels it looks every bit the '80s custom car. Inside it was proper luxury with leather trim, walnut fascia and velour carpets.

Arden – They did a body kit for Jaguars, all the usual skirts and spoilers whilst claiming that the engine department would get a constant circulation of fresh air.

Lynx – Took the XJS and created the Eventer, which was the estate version and then took the roof off to create the Spyder, well ahead of the factory version, which also had an electric roof.

Lister – Using the name of Brian Lister, a famous racer from the '50s, XJS's were given 6-litre engines and the bodies heavily modified. They lost the controversial flying buttresses at the rear and the front end was modified, however the most important mod at the end of the '80s was under the bonnet. A 7-litre version of the V12 engine meant 500 bhp and 200 mph. Golly.

Covin – British based kit carmaker turned Volkswagens into something else. Their decision to modify a Type 3 Variant into a Porsche 911 was particularly successful. Porsche didn't like the idea and sued. Changes were made to the body panels, but it was still so easy to confuse these plastic Porkers with the real thing. Later on they used transversely mounted Ford XR2 and XR3i engines.

Eurosport – Not so brilliant was a body kit that turned an innocent Triumph TR7 into an unspeakably awful rendition of a Ferrari F40. So wrong on every level and every single detail. It didn't go much better in the United States when **Corson** took a Pontiac Fiero an changed it into something that looked slightly like a 512BB. The Fiero became the basis for numerous lookie likey Ferraris. Then there was the brilliantly named **Machiavelli Motors**, which used a Pontiac Trans Am which was turned then into a child's sketch idea of what a Ferrari might look like if you glued on scoops and spoilers and painted it red.

Nostalgia Cars – These flourished in the 1980s. Part of huge trend throughout Europe and America using modern cars as the underpinning to running boards, mud guards, upright grilles and big headlights. In most cases they aped the style and presence of the pre-war Mercedes Benz SSKs. There were countless companies at it all over the world. In Japan BUBK put a 1930s roadster on top of a Nissan 200SX. In America Clénet created a Mercedes 540K, which was made from a Lincoln Continental with a large V8 under the bonnet but amusingly a tiny MG Midget providing the cockpit, windscreen and doors. And finally the US Gullwing was as the name suggested a fibreglass copy of a Mercedes-Benz 300SL Gullwing.

Jankel – From the founder of Panther Westwinds (a company that through the '70s had made its own Nostalgia Cars aping Bugatti and Jaguars) Robert Jankel went on to build stretch limos and pricey convertibles like Le Marquis, which was a bespoke convertible, based on a Bentley Turbo R. Also available was the Le Marquis XJ40 Coupe was a turbocharged two door Jaguar XJ. All were ferociously expensive.

… Apologies to the millions of engineering companies, parts suppliers and chancers who rented something interesting for the weekend and then took papier mâché moulds off it before trying to flog body kits or complete cars off the back of that initiative.

In the Cassette Deck …

Prince – 1999 This was much more than a soundtrack for the '80s, as the title track future proofed it, but more than that obvious gimmick, it sounded like music being beamed back from the 21st century. That's because it brilliantly blurred all the usual soul/funk/dance/pop/rock lines and put them in 2 a melting pot of wonderfulness and invented text speak for U. Deserves to be experienced in the most futuristic car of the time, which is either an Audi 100, or an Audi Quattro.

13 Sauerkraut. Some German Cars were Rubbish ...

They weren't always precision engineered 911s and 3 Series and S-Classes you know. Here's a roll call of mistakes.

January • New Car Profit: £3,112 • Used Car Profit: £243 • Total £3,355

It is wrong to think that the German Industrial miracle ran without a hitch. In the summer of 1984 the German metalworkers went on strike for more pay, or better conditions, or more Sauerkraut or something. The knock-on effect was a shortfall in the raw material required to make BMWs and it got so serious that one day we ran out of 3 Series.

We looked in the system and it was bare. In the days before a system meant it was computer software, it was a very real piece of hardware. Comprising of metal racks that could be flicked back and forward like a giant Rolodex and from them hung T-shaped cards on which were written vehicle specifications, customer's name and, crucial to getting commission, my name. So the Park Lane cupboard was bare, well not exactly bare, but right out of saleable stock. There were no physical cars and all the others were backed up at the factory, but then came some good news. At Brentford, where the new cars were prepared, someone had found a 3 Series. I didn't know the precise circumstances, whether they had tripped over it, or moved a pair of fossilised Baroque Angels and discovered it in a corner, but I didn't care. It was over a ton's worth of protective wax covered commission. Once cleaned off, a job I had once done myself to speed up a delivery, it was revealed to be a Bronzit 320i 2 door. The announcement of its discovery was made at the morning sales meeting. Along with the added incentive of commission was a champagne and smoked salmon lunch. That was the reward for the entire team, it was just a case of which salesman on which team sold it first.

Now that was a nice lunch and I have to take the credit. I had a customer who was hot to trot and it turned into the easiest possible sale in the history of car sales. Where else was he going to go? Getting a yes is one thing, getting the money was quite another. In those days the next best thing to cold hard currency was a Telex of intent. Before facsimile machines, or fax, there was the good old-fashioned Telex machine. A sort of giant pre-Internet telephone line-based typewriter and only usually seen on the Saturday afternoon TV sports show called Grandstand, *delivering the football scores. So with the Telex in my hand and smoked salmon on my tongue I did start to wonder what we were going to do next.*

This was the first and last time that BMW ever let any of us down. In my relatively short time there, we never had any recalls, breakdowns or any relia-bility isue that shook our confidence in the product we were selling. But then we were selling BMWs in the 1980s. It certainly would have been harder work back in the '50s to sell some off the cars that wore the BMW badge. Although we can snigger at the BMW bubble car now it was crucial to their survival and a spring-board to greater things.

We have met the bubble a few times so far, but it is worth taking another look at what started life in 1953 as a tiny Italian Iso or Isetta four wheeler. BMW's commitment to engineering meant that they adapted it. For BMW it represented a quick way into the mass market and hopefully some mass profits. The first BMW-Isetta came off the production line in April 1955 and the 10,000th followed just eight months later. This was no joke, but a sure fire success. BMW got rid of the nasty Italian 2-stroke and put one of their own R-25 motorcycle engines in its place. It may have been called a Bubble in the UK, but in its homeland it was 'das rollende Ei', or the rolling egg. It was uprated with a larger engine, and a longer body and called the 600, which could seat four. BMW exported a three-wheel version to the UK to take advantage of the lower tax rates. A.F.N., the distributors for BMW, were soon selling over 500 a week. Apart from looking silly the only disadvantage was a lack of reverse gear. Potentially then you could park forward facing into a wall and not be able to open the door or reverse away. In reality that doesn't seem to have happened very often. That's because you could climb out via the sunroof, or passing children would hear your cries for help and happily lift the bubble up and turn it around to face the right way.

A few years after I left Park Lane I did get to sample a BMW Bubble car first hand in its home town of Munich. Jovial Scotsman George Halliday worked in the archive department at BMW and his everyday transport was a Bubble. This was no museum piece, it was a hard working commuter car with great lumps of plastic filler packing out the dents on the single front door. George bought it in 1974 for 300 Deutchmarks and buzzing around Munich with him was an immense amount of fun. Climbing in with my briefcase was a piece of luggage too far, but as a sort of pre inflated, solid plastic air bag it made me feel just a tad safer. For George though, ex-RAF, the experience of taking the Bubble car out and about was just like piloting a Gloucester Meteor jet aircraft. Well only he would know.

The whole post war Bubble car phenomenon was certainly kicked off by BMW and although the craze in the UK only lasted for a couple of years, without them Leonard Lord at the British Motor Corporation would never have told Alec Issigonis, 'God damn these bloody awful bubble cars. We must drive them out of the streets by designing a proper miniature car.' The result was the Mini. As for the other Bubbles and tiny invaders from Germany it may be a bit childish to point and laugh now, after all they were rebuilding their industry and for a time were making exactly what the public wanted. So here's a brief guide to the sublime and ridiculously small German cars before they went all grown up and serious on us.

Britain could never get enough of small cars. There had been the phenomenon of the cycle car that got the nation motoring in the '20s and '30s and in the austere '50s if cash strapped motorists could not find a second-hand Austin 7 then there were all these Germans queuing up to take them to work, shopping or on holiday.

On the left is the rather odd and over doored Zündapp Janus, then the rather funky Messerschmitt which looks like a lot of fun.

The three-wheeled Messerschmitt KR200 from 1953 was one of the most distinctive. Built by the former aircraft manufacturer the rumour always was that it was made from left over fighter aircraft canopies. At least that's what the bigger boys said in the playground. It certainly was very aircraft like as the whole canopy tilted to one side to let driver and passenger in and out, plus the steering was by handlebars, which closely resembled aircraft controls. Also there was a TG500 Tiger in 1958, which had four wheels, all the better to cope with the huge amount of power, all 20 bhp that propelled it to 75 mph, which must have been truly terrifying. This wingless ground hugging denuded fighter also came as a KR201 without a roof. Whilst on the subject of German ex-aircraft manufacturers flying on the ground there was also the Heinkel, which looked almost identical to the BMW Isetta, but it was a bit narrower, plus there were tiny seats in the back for kiddies. The Heinkel ended up being built in Brighton and badged as a Trojan from 1961.

The Zündapp Janus was another variation on the Isetta theme, but longer and with four properly spaced wheels. There was a door at the front and the back and on the offside so there was no shortage of entry and exit options. If that wasn't odd enough, probably the single most absurd vehicle to come out of Germany was the Brütsch Mopetta, or Rollera (depending on where you bought it) in 1957. Designed by a Mr Egon Brütsch it resembled a single seat bumper car and actually was far more ei (egg) like than the BMW Isetta. At just 67 inches (170cm) long it had a tiny 50cc engine, two wheels at the back and just the one up front.

A not at all ridiculous, Goggomobil T300

And finally, Glas was a company that BMW ended up buying to get their hands on the factory so they could expand. Originally Glas were a manufacturer of agricultural machinery before they moved on to making a scooter funkily entitled the Goggo. Inevitably the four wheel Goggomobil arrived and it is worth quoting the 1959 British Motor Show Guide to the T300, "Neat and nimble is this natty little German coupe in gay colours which make it a favourite second car with the ladies." Well you couldn't print that today except in this book, but you can't argue with the rest. "Twin cylinder air cooled engine, rear mounted, has only a tiny thirst and gears are changed by a flick of a switch on the optional electrically controlled gearbox. Simple to park and a stout hearted performer on the open road."

There was also a T700 listed which saw the company switch the engine to the front end and although it remained rear wheel drive it was bigger and more practical than the T300. Even so these were just the sort of cars which at £467 and £671 respectively would be swept away by the all-new Mini which had more wheels, more seats and cost just £497.

However, there was one car the Mini could not compete with and that was the Amphicar. At the time, 1961–1965, it was the only production amphibious passenger car in the world and it is easy to see how it stayed that way. If ever a car cried out to be made from fibreglass then the Amphicar was it. Unfortunately the 14-foot (4.3 metre) hull was made from steel, the sort of steel that rusts. If a combination of water and oxygen is bad enough, there were also sealant issues meaning constant leaks.

The man behind the Amphicar was Hans Trippell, best known as a designer of amphibious vehicles for the German Army during World War II. Trouble is it was no Volkswagen Schimmerwagen, the floating version of the Beetle. Being neither a car or boat meant that it wasn't particularly good at either task and the Triumph Herald engine struggled to get the weighty car to 65 mph on land and it putted along at just 7.5 knots once immersed.

That Herald engine linked up to a propeller at the back, while the front wheels acted as rudders. It wasn't cheap at £1275, so buying a proper Triumph Herald for £702, then a hull, trailer and outboard motor would have been the simpler and cheaper option. And when the Herald eventually died you would still have a boat to fall back on. Only 2500 were made and most were exported to an easily disappointed American market. Now though everyone wants one.

A half submerged Amphicar and happy couple shooting ducks. Well what else are going to do once you've driven into a lake?

Amphicar were lucky to last for that long as some German manufacturers didn't make it out of the '50s or '60s. Veritas was a very short-lived coming together of ex-BMW employees who wanted to build sports cars based on the old 328 design, which in 1948 was still pretty advanced. By 1950 they closed because of financial difficulties, but reopened and as they could not call themselves **BMW** had to settle for Veritas Nürburgring. They made tiny numbers of coupés, convertibles and pure track cars using initially the **BMW** engine, then a new one designed by Heinkel. Distributing the French Panhard in Germany gave the company the opportunity to produce their own car based on its chassis, but the company had run out of customers by 1953.

A Borgward Isabella. Named after Isabella Borgward.

Borgward had the distinction of producing the first all-new German car after the Second World War. Carl Borgward split his company into three separate entities to increase his allocation of raw materials, so as well as Borgward, Lloyd and Goliath were the other brands. The Borgward Hansa was a modern and very advanced looking vehicle when launched in 1949. A synchromesh gearbox, overhead valve engines and independent suspension all set the standard when other companies would simply reheat what they had sold back in the 1930s. Undoubtedly the most elegant and successful model was the beautiful Isabella. It was Borgward's wife's name, first used to hide a pre-production prototype's identity, but it stuck. Along with the more staid saloons, Borgward became a force to be reckoned with and rivalled Mercedes-Benz when it came to quality and sales. However, a clumsily designed saloon, the P100 was underdeveloped and underpowered and optionally could be fitted with air suspension. That pneumatic technology cost Borgward dear and the money started to run out and by 1961 the company was bankrupt. A broken hearted Carl Borgward died two years later.

A sad end to one chapter of the story but what about his other Borgward concerns? Well Lloyd were part of the economy car generation but managed to do without the Bubble designs and had a full complement of four wheels. The body panels were made from fabric stretched over a wooden frame, which made them light and cheap to run. However being faster than a Volkswagen Beetle was one thing, being more expensive was always going to be its undoing.

If Borgward was the premium line and Lloyd in the bargain basement then somewhere in the middle was Goliath. Starting with pre-war two-stroke, air-cooled engines with modern bodywork, a programme of modernisation ensued and led to the 1100 model which was eventually renamed the Hansa. This was powered by a water cooled four stroke, flat four engine and a synchromesh gearbox, plus coil spring suspension. That was a heady mixture in the late 1950s, but even high technology could not save Goliath, Lloyd or Borgward.

NSU had a complicated history and stuck to making motorcycles and mopeds until 1957 when they dived back into the car market with the rear engined NSU Prinz. Here was a small car, much like a German Hillman Imp in style and execution which sold in decent numbers but then in 1967 they got a bit too ambitious.

We have already met the NSU Ro80 and you will have read the whole sorry story in Chapter 6. This NSU succeeded when it came to design and theoretical technology, but failed in practice. The Ro80 now counts as a heroic failure, even if as an owner you would have been pretty hacked off when it went in for its ninth engine change. Interestingly the Audi 'design language', as designers are wont to say, came from the Ro80 and some of that bad luck seemed to rub off on another related product in another important marketplace, North America.

Audi 100/200 (5000 in the USA) was never a bad car, just a bullied one.

Audi's 100 had been rebranded as the 5000 and did reasonably well with strong sales of 74,000 vehicles until that is the model was branded as a killer. Popular American current affairs TV show *60 Minutes* claimed that drivers of the big Audi experienced an almost supernatural occurrence. As the brakes were applied it also coincided with the 'gas' pedal as Americans quaintly say, having a mind of its own. The clue as to what actually happened could easily have been found in the original police report, "Foot slipped off the brake pedal onto the gas pedal accelerating the auto."

That wasn't dramatic enough for the TV people and especially as the drivers of the Audis were convinced that they were the victims of so-called 'unintended acceleration' as their foot had been on the brake pedal the whole time. Viewers couldn't see the compressed air contraption that had been rigged up so that the Audi 5000 appeared to be operating entirely independently. They actually didn't need to go to that bother as every automatic car when in D will creep forward. However, the National Highway Traffic Safety Administration (NHTSA) issued a report in 1989 tackling what they described as the "sudden unintended acceleration problem". They cleared Audi pointing out that the pedal placement was "marginally closer to each other compared to American cars", as a result it might cause some drivers to mistakenly press the accelerator instead of the brake.

Incredibly and to their eternal credit Audi chose not to blame the drivers and watched as their sales dropped to just 12,000. Meanwhile in the early 1990s those who held on to to their 'killer' 5000s chose to launch a class action for the plunging resale values. And the moral is, be very careful when you sell cars in America. Something that Volkswagen should have been aware of.

Volkswagen may have been a byword in Europe for utter reliability, but the Beetle aside that reputation did not seem to travel across the Atlantic. Indeed Volkswagen's early attempts at replacing an icon did not go down very well. Known as squarebacks or fastbacks from 1966 they had a four cylinder air-cooled engines that lived under the floor at the back and suffered from both air and also oil starvation.

Then from 1973 the Dasher (Passat in Europe) introduced a VW with a water-cooled engine, which seemed to overheat in America. Perhaps many owners still thought the Dasher only needed fresh air. Even the Rabbit from 1975 (Golf in Europe) and the original Scirocco had problems again with cooling as well as exhaust and brakes. Meanwhile anyone who ordered a diesel found that it belched black smoke, but then all diesels did back in the 1970s. More seriously there were complete engine failures, broken crankshafts and cracked oil filters until there were quality upgrades across the range in 1976. It does seem very odd that there were no similar reports in Europe, so some of these troubles could be put down to unfamiliarity with what were completely new models.

Santana, the Passat saloon that no one wanted, in the UK anyway.

Volkswagen's only problem on their home continent was that the new VWs weren't Beetles, or a little later on, Golfs. I remember clearly someone bringing a Volkswagen Santana to the showroom as a part exchange. This model had nothing to do with the Hispanic guitarist called Carlos, and everything to do with being a booted version of a Passat. It was white and just months old and the owner now realised he would far rather have a 3 Series. Unfortunately no car trader would touch it and only made insultingly low offers leaving the owner out of pocket and in no position to fill my pockets with commission. Here was a car that made no sense in the UK as anyone who wanted a saloon bought a Ford Sierra. Well actually that is another story as buying public adjusted to the radical jelly mould shape. No one was going to give a Santana any time, just as a Golf with a boot, the Jetta, and a Polo with a boot, the Derby, struggled in the increasingly hatchback obsessed UK.

There has been no mention of the Mighty Mercedes, but then apart from the taxi specification diesels, they still have a place of honour in their profitable model line up. So were there really any really grim Mercs? Well not really, especially as most Mercedes have a purpose, even the Mercedes Gelandewagen, or G-Wagen,

Germans, are good at coming second. Fortunately they did so in the last couple of world wars and in 1966. Then when it came to upmarket off roaders, Mercedes for a time in the early '80s were also a distant second to the legendary Range Rover. After that they were runners up to the new order of upmarket Japanese 4 x 4s as represented by the Toyota Landcruiser, Mitsubishi Shogun and Nissan Patrol. Mercedes though could live with that. These were Japanese and were deeply capable, reliable and great value. What Mercedes wanted was to be taken as seriously, if not more so, than the off road royalty as represented by Range Rover. Here was a vehicle that could not be faulted when it came to messing around in the mud, but was shoddily built and likely to gently disintegrate pretty rapidly. All Mercedes had to do was build a classy 4 x 4 and surely they would clean up.

G-Wagen. Definitely not a Range Rover.

Unfortunately the big G looked like an army surplus vehicle that has been retrofitted for civilian duty by someone who wanted to use it for minicabbing, which wasn't far from the truth. Not everyone liked the spartan trim, particularly the earlier models, but there is no denying the rugged appeal of these slab sided and uncompromising vehicles. Where it matters, off road, the G-Wagen was one of the most accomplished if expensive 4 x 4s you could buy.

The functionally ugly Gelandewagen was built by Steyr Puch in Austria from 1979 and came onto the UK market in October 1981. Available as a long wheelbase five door or shorter three door with a choice of two engines. The 280GE had a 2746cc six-cylinder petrol engine that produced 150 bhp. Alternatively there was a five-cylinder 2998cc diesel producing 100 bhp, which was fitted to the 300GD. The gearbox was a four speed with the option of a four-speed automatic. The equipment list was hardly overgenerous although power steering was standard. Headlamps had wash, but no wipe; the tailgate window had a wash and wipe. Also at the back was a tow bar and extra fuel tank. Inside the front seats had head restraints, central locking, childproof locks on the long wheelbase and a first aid kit. Far more important was the three diff locks to get drivers out of trouble off road. However, in normal road use it all started to become clear as to why any sensible person would run a perky V8 Range Rover rather than the hefty truck that was a G-Wagen.

Yes the G-Wagen was a commercial vehicle whereas the Range Rover was the earliest manifestation of a lifestyle vehicle. Elegantly styled, with a good characterful engine it was the only way to arrive at a function either in the West End or Western Highlands. Sure the Wagen could tow and the three-pointed star was a guarantee of quality but it was something that the estate manager might be forced to drive, while the Lord of the Manor had a Rangie. That would clearly have upset and probably baffled Mercedes in their failure to crack the nascent luxury 4 x 4 market. It was a good 4 x 4 and a reliable car, just not a fashionable or very pretty one, so hardly a disaster or even a rubbish German car for that matter. So it is time then to pick a much easier target and remember that there were in fact two distinct German car industries and one company summed that situation perfectly, Trabant.

Zwickau had been the place where the legendary, high technology and exquisitely engineered Auto Union racers had been built and also the elegant and finely finished Horch limousines. After the Second World War of course that all changed as the factory was located far enough east to be overrun by the Red Army and be trapped for a generation behind the Iron Curtain. East Germany therefore owed the Soviet Union and had to pay back war reparations. Under the terms of the payback this new country was forbidden from making four stroke engines, which would prove to be important, as would the rationing of all fuel.

Smelly and slow, it must be the Trabant.

A nationalised consortium called IFA brought together all the car plants in the East which went on to build rehashed versions of the pre-war DKW Meisterklasse. An all-new car though arrived in 1957 and was called Trabant, which meant satellite. That's because the Soviets had just launched the first satellite in the shape of Sputnik, a name that on reflection might have had even more comedy value.

The Trabant had a steel chassis and frame that was made on huge presses which stamped out the basic shapes in a poisonous and deafening environment. The bodywork was made from Duroplast which sounded good, but the ingredients were shredded plastic, brown paper and cotton waste, all soaked in resin. Overall these were not ideal working conditions and if the workers themselves survived all that, they would then have to wait up 14 years to get to the front of the queue. So was the Trabant worth waiting for? After all they made 3 million of them so they must have been good.

Powered by a small 499cc, which grew five years later to a massive 594cc, it could not operate as a normal four-cycle engine thanks to the Soviet restrictions. So just like a noisy, smelly, old motorbike it ran on a combination of petrol and lubricating oil. Despite that the Trabant could reach a top speed of 62 mph although it took all day to get there. The Trabbie could not really be described as styled and to me it resembled a late model Morris Oxford, with just two doors that had been shrunk in the wash and powered by a motor from a strimmer. Its specification was equally bad for all citizens. No one got a fuel gauge or an interior light. For most of its existence it made do with 6-volt electrics, although a decadent, capitalist automatic gearbox was eventually added to the otherwise non-existent options list.

First came the 600, then the 601 in 1964. Without a hint of irony the saloon was called the Limousine and an estate version the Universal. There was even a military version which must have had some unspecified role that could have involved poisoning NATO troops who were not used to a vehicle producing more than ten times the hydrocarbons of a Western vehicle.

Clearly the Trabant was not a very good car and came to symbolise all that was wrong with the communist way of doing things. A committee can design a car but an ideological dictatorship can't. It is significant that the Trabant owners who left the Communist regimes in East Germany, Czechoslovakia and Hungary immediately abandoned them as soon as they got over the border. Nothing showed the contrast between the two peoples and just how their industries had fared over the last 28 years with the Wessis in their Volkswagen Golfs and the Ossis in their Trabbies. Without competition and without a true marketplace the Trabant was the undeveloped and unsatisfactory result. A late engine transplant from a Wessi Polo failed to save it. The Trabant died in April 1991 and no one mourned.

Wartburg Knight (impossible in an egalitarian Communist state) and the Tourist (not an option for residents of a Communist state).

So what did those in East Germany who were more equal than the Trabant owners (party members, union officials and diplomats) drive? A Wartburg of course. Another product of IFA, these were manufactured in the former BMW plant in Eisenach. On the face of it these Wartburgs from 1956 looked quite good with nicely designed bodies, lots of chrome and two-tone paintwork. There were even coupé, cabriolet and roadster versions. Unfortunately these handsome creatures were powered by nasty, smelly three-cylinder, two-stroke engines. Also the build quality was far from competent.

For 1966 those dated though elegant bodies were replaced by a single fairly brutal design of saloon and Tourist estate car, which was officially sold on the UK market as the Knight, both fairly ironic model names in the circumstances. Despite the two-stroke engine and the indifferent build quality the bolt on body panels made replacement easier and there was even a degree of crash protection with a collapsible steering column. Despite the incongruity of LED instrumentation by 1984, the model had long disappeared from overseas markets due to the amount of pollution it belched into the atmosphere. By 1988 it had expired, outlived even by the inadequate and wholly unappealing Trabant.

DDR, the German Democratic Republic, was not really Germany, just a very bad experiment in social engineering that didn't turn out very well and had to be conducted behind a great big wall. The real German car industry had a post-war shakeout, but the Ro80 apart they put their faith in well-researched high technology and a commitment to proper build quality. That's why selling German cars in the 1980s was relatively easy. At least you weren't going to have to placate disappointed customers. Yes they may have paid more than if they'd bought a Rover or a Fiat, and perhaps a radio and speakers was extra, but that was a small price to pay for cars which wouldn't break down.

So German cars weren't rubbish. However, the price of making all German cars equally good cost a large fortune and during the 1990s led to a noticeable dip in quality. But this is another story and possibly another book, which may or may not be called, The Japanese Car Industry, its Part in my Downfall.

The German Car Industry vs The British Car Industry

There was no competition was there? Essentially the British Car Industry was winding down. The grim full details can be found in *The British Car Industry Our Part in its Downfall*. Renaming BMC as British Leyland, then Austin Rover followed by the Rover Group didn't exactly work out although close co-operation with the Japanese car industry certainly did. Rover saved itself by working with Honda. The Triumph Acclaim and the Rover 200 may not have looked it, but they were the transplanted future. Yes, the British Car Industry was turning Japanese.

The German Car Industry vs The French Car Industry

Peugeot continued to make fairly tough but dull cars, although the 205 managed to be stylish and fun and in GTi trim a real rival to the hot Golf. They built the 309 at the former Chrysler plant in Coventry, but it was no more exciting than the 605, which also failed to have an impact in the executive market. Only the 406 managed to take on the Ford Sierra, but the lack of a hatchback was a big mistake.

Although Citroen had lost much of its creative eccentricity when bought by Peugeot in 1975, some individuality had returned by the '80s with the BX. It may have had a Peugeot engine but it also had the self-levelling hydropneumatic with fashionably right-angled styling. At the end of the decade the XM also proved that the Citroen had not lost their talent to amuse and entertain. It never troubled the BMW 5 Series in the executive car sales league. Saddest of all the 2CV passed away and was never properly replaced.

Renault incredibly won Car of the Year in 1982 with the dull and forgettable 9. But at least the 5 guaranteed supermini sales. The Espace championed a completely new type of vehicle, the People Carrier. So at least they were thinking ahead. Overall, apart from some Golf and Polo alternatives not much to worry Germany. But at least they still had an industry.

The German Car Industry vs The Italian Car Industry

It all boils down to one question, just how were Fiat doing? They were the Italian car industry and they continued to do small, very well. The Fiat Uno deservedly became Car of the Year for 1984 and then there was the Tipo in 1989, basically a bigger Uno. Galvanizing the body and a plastic boot lid meant that rust finally wasn't an issue. Fiat's upmarket Lancia brand though still had a reputation for turning to red powder overnight and apart from the rally winning Integrale there was nothing to get excited about.

Ferrari though were ramping up production and beginning to understand that their customers would pay handsomely for racing technology and exclusivity. Buyers would also tolerate sky high prices and servicing, and a certain amount of unreliability, in return for the kudos of owning and running a car with a prancing dobbin badge on the bonnet.

The German Car Industry vs The Swedish Car Industry

Saab's car division always struggled whilst the planes and trucks did really well. General Motors invested heavily in the cars hoping that the prestigious badge could take on BMW and Mercedes. All Saab really had was some quirky sporty alternatives like the 900 Turbo and the popular convertible, whilst the 9000 was never truly special enough to worry the Germans. At least Volvo kept on making those big square estate cars, otherwise nothing very exciting happened in the 1980s in Scandinavia apart from the demise of ABBA and the rise of Aha.

The German Car Industry vs The American Car Industry

Ford didn't look too clever in the early 1980s after the oil crisis and the early stages of the recession. However, designing a middle market, middle-sized car called the Taurus to take on the Japanese seemed to work. Ford made big profits again while General Motors were seriously struggling. Chrysler were even further behind and could only rely on Jeep as a consistent seller. Ford would eventually have the cash though to buy prestigious brands like Jaguar, Aston Martin and Volvo so that they could take on the Germans.

The German Car Industry vs The Japanese Car Industry

Steadily the Japanese were catching the Germans with a broad range of products in just about every possibly niche from supermini to sporting to off road. Toyota started with the Starlet, then the small family Corolla, bigger Carina and into the sporting MR-2, Celica and Supra, finishing off with the legendary 4 x 4 Landcruiser. Volkswagen struggled to match that breadth of models. Honda were more upmarket and lower volume and were working closely with Rover at the time, which seemed to help the UK company make more credible vehicles that now competed predominantly at the Golf end of things. It was hard to go wrong with any sort of Civic. Nissan pointed the way to the manufacturing future for

Japan by establishing a factory in Sunderland in 1984. Not only that, they would follow that up with plants in Holland, Belgium and Germany.

In the Cassette Deck ...

 Bronski Beat – The Age of Consent Odd falsetto based electro pop, comprising covers and originals, but strangely hypnotic. Handy guide in the cassette to the age of homosexual consent throughout Europe, so a good thing to keep in your glove box (in 1984) and that's not a euphemism. Very good on those longer journeys where the eurobeat keeps you focused even though the temptation to play with the Golf's MFA computer is overwhelming.

14 Outroduction – Life in the Bus Lane

All those models you never thought were German, plus why all cars should have been made in Germany anyway.

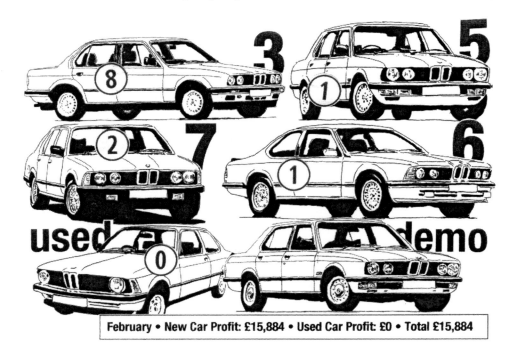

February • New Car Profit: £15,884 • Used Car Profit: £0 • Total £15,884

I think its pretty clear by now that if all car development had stopped in 1990, we'd have been pretty happy to drive German cars in perpetuity. But before I expand on that, it is worth remembering just which other cars we knew and loved in the '80s were also built in Germany.

The Ford Granada had been a very successful middle to upper management company car especially in full on Ghia trim. It was also heavily used as a pool car by big companies and driven by chauffeurs. I knew this because my Uncle Joe had several generations of Grannies whilst driving for the Port of London Authority and then News International. The Granada never looked better than when it was being driven with some vengeance through cardboard boxes in the highly popular TV series *The Sweeney*. Dennis Waterman (Detective Sergeant George Carter) and John Thaw (Detective Inspector Jack Regan) were never behind the wheel, they had a chauffeur, or rather driver (Bill) for that. Crucially though they had the shooters and the catch phrase 'You're nicked.' It was brilliant and the Granny was a big working class saloon chasing down the crims in MOT expired Jags. Except that it wasn't a Granada, because in the first series it was a Ford Consul 3000GT. It certainly looked very similar to a Granada so it really doesn't matter, unless you want to win a pub quiz. Then something happened in 1977 when all the big Fords became Granadas.

A very clever re-skin of the original Granada by designer Uwe Bahnsen instantly updated the model to the right angled '70s and thereafter it was built exclusively in Germany. The estate version was especially successful with a large load bay and clean purposeful lines. 'The Sweeney' got one and it carved an even more impressive dash through the cardboard boxes. Few other manufacturers could offer the same levels of equipment, refinement, space and low running costs. A mild facelift in 1981 only enhanced the model's appeal and popularity. A British built icon lost to the Germans, but at least it was better built.

Ford Granada. Made in Germany, don't you know.

The same fate befell 'The car you always promised yourself' in the distinctive shape of the Capri. In many ways this was the European version of the phenomenally successful Ford Mustang. That meant the car looked great, was fun to drive yet was still very affordable. Designed at Ford's research centre in Dunton, Essex and codenamed Colt, this just about four seat coupé with a long bonnet pretty much replicated the success of its American cousin. That was back in 1969.

'Project Diana' was the codename for the new generation of Capri that was launched in 1974. Sales had been falling away in Europe and the Capri II was meant to be a more practical car with a more convenient hatchback boot. It was larger, heavier, and much less exciting than the old car. However, this model seemed to strike a chord when more than 183,000 were sold in its first year. Sales in Europe though were soon on the decline again. Strangely, production in the UK, the Capri's biggest market, stopped in 1976 and was transferred to Cologne in Germany.

'Carla' was the next project name for the final generation of Capri. In many ways the car looked better than it had done since the 1960s. Four round headlamps, reprofiled bonnet, larger tail lamps, black wraparound bumpers and a revised interior all helped give the car a more purposeful look. There was a familiar line up of engines that included the 1.3, 1.6, 2.0 and 3.0 litre. The only really sporting model remained the S although this was essentially a cosmetic package which amounted to a sidewinder stripe, alloy wheels, rear spoiler and overriders. Inside was a smaller 14-inch steering wheel and optional Recaro seats. A sunroof, 5-speed gearbox and sports seats were not fitted until 1983.

'Bodie' (Lewis Collins) in *The Professionals*, yet another British TV show with unconventional policemen, this time working for the mythical C15, had a 3.0S which was enthusiastically handbrake turned at regular intervals. Another brilliant piece of product placement that undoubtedly helped the sales of this German built, American owned car.

Although there was no return to the glorious old RS models, arguably the best version of the standard Capri was the 2.8i, which was launched in 1981. The fuel injected 2.8 litre V6 produced 160 bhp and came with a sunroof, pepperpot design alloy wheels, sports steering wheel and Recaro seats, although a 5-speed gearbox was only standardised in 1983. A year later it was rebadged as the 'Special' with spoke alloys, colour coded grille and from 1985 a limited slip differential. The final run of 1038 Capris in 1987 exclusively for the UK were called the Capri 280. Finished in Brooklands Green with 15-inch RS alloys, 'Raven' leather trim with burgundy piping, it was a fitting end to a great car.

Ford Capri 2.8i, loved in the UK, built by GER.

Meanwhile the Escort which had been built both in England and Germany, was poised to take on the Volkswagen Golf GTI. Ford had been past masters at adding a bit more power and some natty stripes and charging more for it. However, the GTI was something else altogether and simply having a brand new

Escort that was front-wheel drive was hardly enough to make the XR3 very special as it struggled to cope on a bumpy road. The British end of Ford at SVE – Special Vehicle Engineering operations in Dunton, Essex – worked their magic by revamping the suspension for a far superior ride and handling result to sort out the fuel injected XR3i for the better. Trouble was, the quicker Escort was now built in Saalouis just inside the German/French border.

Then there was the Cabriolet. Whilst Volkswagen stuck to the Mark 1 bodyshell for their open topped Golf, Ford changed the body shape along with any tin top improvements. Both models were built at the same place, Karmann the coachbuilders in Germany. Oh yes, and as well as the legendary XR3i, the RS1600i was also built in Saarlouis along with a turbo assisted XR3i, rebadged as the RS1600Turbo. So when production of all these models finished in 1990 few realised or actually cared that what had been regarded as a British car by the majority of the public came from abroad. At least a lot of the engineering had been Essex based.

Rear-wheel drive, six-cylinder, well-built saloon, it must be German. It's actually a Vauxhall Senator.

Another company that was American owned but with a long established British badge was also transferring production to Germany – Vauxhall, owned by General Motors. The era of designing and building cars specifically for the UK market was well and truly over by the 1980s. This meant that a European design office would come up with a car which would be identified as an Opel first and then a Vauxhall as almost an afterthought.

Yes it is that concept called 'badge engineering' which may bother engineers and journalists, but if the customers get what they want, then it doesn't really matter. Although some of these designs such as the Cavalier and Chevette were made in Britain, the bigger, posher ones were simply rebadged from Opel Senators into Vauxhall Royales and the Opel Rekord into the Vauxhall Carlton.

Germany was the home of build quality and innovation and represented the best that anyone could buy in any class of vehicle. So if you wanted a solidly built little shopping car a Polo was the answer. A small family car needed nothing more than a Golf. For sporty types, it was a GTI and all manner of 3 Series.

Solid family saloon or estate? Then the W123/W124 would be perfect. Quality saloons for the executive? 5 Series and E Class, whilst those who wanted to be different would be tempted by the Audi 100. When it came to upmarket luxury saloons, coupé and convertibles Mercedes had a model for absolutely every occasion. Supercar anyone? Well the M1 was underrated and the 959 never bettered.

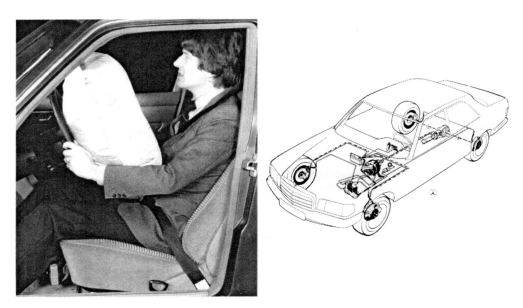

Just a couple of good things about Mercedes in particular and German cars in general and that's air bags and ABS brakes.

If all car development had ended in 1990, you'd have ASC traction control, ABS brakes and airbags thank you Mr Benz. Four wheel drive, well it's been around for ever in an agricultural form, but Audi tamed it and made it suitable for your average family saloon. BMW made racing cars for the road and for the masses. Those Motorsport models were unbeatable then and are untouchable now. From a standing start in the rubble of 1945, it took just 35 years to get back to the point where the cars manufactured in Germany were regarded as the very best in the world.

And finally, what about my early retirement from the BMW selling business? You may not care by this point, but surely it is obvious that I played a hugely signif- icant part in a small Bavarian company becoming the toast of the West End Yuppie. Not really. Victory for them was inevitable and I was just a car salesman who was passing through. I didn't see a future in management. There weren't too many retirement parties in this business, you moved on to somewhere else for more pay, or when you'd been blamed for failing to reach an impossible sales target. So what did I have to show for being a BMW Sales Executive? Two pewter tankards. One was engraved with 'Bronze Award'. I qualified for it under a system that attributed a certain number of points to a particular model, and the number I hit meant I got bronze. Fairly unimportant in the scheme of things because at Park Lane it was always about profit not unit sales, this was just something to put pens in. The other tankard had 'Top Salesman' on it, which meant a whole lot more. Within five months I'd hit the top spot, which I was told was a record. Even more important than a couple of old mugs was one thing that made my own ugly mug beam from ear to ear, I had an awful lot of money saved in the bank.

Park Lane had also provided me with a fund of memories. There was the car seat cover which was actually a dog, which bit me. Another car that smelt so comprehensively of dog that I had to drive along with my head out of the window, like a dog. And of course there were several quite frightening test drives, but then I've told you the one about The Mall, 100 mph and a 635CSi.

I was cheerful, positive and open minded about what I should do next and really thought I would have a month to think about it. Management had other ideas and as I made clear at the beginning of Chapter 1, I really would be walking home that night. They didn't believe that I was leaving to pursue a more creative career. A new BMW showroom a mile away in Holland Park was just about to open and they thought I was off there. Now, apart from going to an interview at Jack Barclay in Berkeley Square out of curiosity, I didn't see a future in selling cars.

Oh and how did the interview go? Quite well until I asked what the company car was and instead of a Silver Spirit, the wonderfully turned out sales manager said Golf GTI. I think my face probably said it all, but I may also have blurted out, "Well I could go and buy one of those myself." Which is what I did. I either had BMWs or Volkswagen GTIs for the next 20 years, but always ones designed or built in the '80s.

There was also the possibility of full time car trading. I could have filled many pages about the strange, exotic creatures who came and bought the part exchanges. Some were wide-boy stereotypes with leather jackets and Arthur Daley demeanours whilst others could only be described as rather posh. Some were straight, at least one was gay, and another had a yacht in Monaco. Yes it was a meritocracy and well paid and didn't strike me as that difficult. Valuing a car incorrectly was a sackable offence and I seemed to get it right, but you needed a larger than average pile of money to do it properly and I had other ideas.

For a job that lasted less than 18 months I was poised to ruthlessly turn that minimal amount of motor trade experience into a career. In short order, I wrote a book called Dealing with Car Dealers, did some articles on the back of that including bizarrely Woman's Own and Tatler. *I sent the book proof to Steve Cropley, editor of Car Magazine and he was interested enough in my writing and ideas to give me a go. Indeed, I am still wringing the last few words out of every last reminiscence and I won't stop, even if I'm asked nicely. And anyway if it all goes wrong at some point at least I will have a mint and boxed Chitty Chitty Bang Bang to fall back on.*

So I didn't walk all the way home that night, but I did amble to the top of Park Lane and down into Hyde Park Corner tube. I may not have left in a car, but I did leave with something far more important than that: the clever, funny, cheeky and really pretty girl who worked in the export department and the future Mrs Ruppert.

In the Cassette Deck ...

Tina Turner – Private Dancer Adult themes on this one, combined a soulful Ike free voice with light rock accompaniment, which was so utterly irresistible at the time. Play this whilst behind the wheel of a 928 and you really believed that you were slap bang in an episode of *Miami Vice*. Just so you know, 'What's Love Got to do with it?' was our tune.

Also by James Ruppert
The British Car Industry Our Part in its Downfall

The true story of what happened to the British Car Industry from 1945 until it effectively ended with the implosion of MG Rover in 2005. It occurred to me that my Dad's car owning, driving and buying history (from a Triumph Mayflower to a VW Golf) was a great way of injecting some social history into it all. I also wondered whether his decision in the 1970s to buy an Audi triggered the downfall, or was it the inept motor industry management, stupid unions or meddling governments. I think we know the answer, but it is fun finding out and there are some good stories along the way. There are also tons of small black and white pictures of cars and people from the era, plus all the cars that my Dad bought. Essentially you do not need to be a petrol-head to enjoy it. Also reviewers have said very nice things.

Beautifully written with considerable wit. Honest John – **Daily Telegraph**

We're big fans of Ruppert's writing … it's a great read. Highly Recommended – **Dep-O Magazine**

A light emotive and charming view of a difficult period for British pride – **Classic and Sports Car**

A mixture of social history and personal insight – **Classics Monthly**

A funny and informative account of the industry – **Autocar**

Writing a readable motoring book is difficult enough, but writing something brilliant which gives a totally different outlook on a well covered subject is a true achievement … it's the warmth of the family story that really makes this book something special – *Nick Larkin,* **Classic Car Weekly**

From start to finish it is a thumping good read… personal, honest and deadly accurate. The notion of using his family as a microcosm for the country at large is very, very clever – *Keith Adams,* **Austin Rover Online**

It's informative, well written and extremely funny – anyone who bemoans the demise of the British Car industry should make a beeline for this fantastic book – *Nat Barnes,* **Daily Express**

Also by James Ruppert – Bangernomics Bible

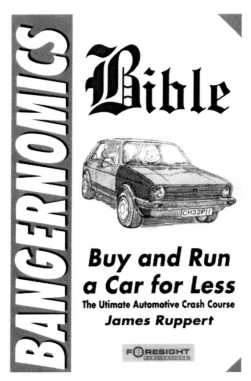

BANGERNOMICS

Bible

Buy and Run a Car for Less
The Utimate Automotive Crash Course
James Ruppert

F⊙RESIGHT

Save money buy a banger – Bangernomics Bible: Buy and Run a Car for Less which sets out the case for why we should all be driving old rather than new.
The Independent on Sunday

What it does do, though, in great clarity (and rather amusingly) is guide you through the processes step-by-step in such a way that buying that banger becomes a clear process indeed.
Keith Adams Austin Rover Online

It's been a long time since we've read something so unpretentious – there's no doubting that James Ruppert is a master at teaching people to buy, run and sell cars cost effectively.
Car Mechanics

Witty book full of sound advice about buying a cheap safe and reliable runabout.
Classics Monthly

Bangernomics could save you a small fortune
Irish Independent

In his book he outlines how anyone can buy reliable cars – like old Golfs – for next to nothing and run them for a couple of trouble-free years.
Used Car Expert

I was hugely inspired by reading a book called The Bangernomics Bible; a superb, no-nonsense guide to buying a 'good' banger. **John Cradden – Irish Independent**

Lightning Source UK Ltd.
Milton Keynes UK
171023UK00001B/3/P

9 780955 952937